G000272426

Hidden Kerala
The Travel Guide

Phil Frampton

Published November 1997
ISBN 1 902167 00 7

MH*i***
Publications

Published by MHi Publications

PO Box 17284, London SW16 5ZP

Photographs: front and back covers, Fred Anderson; inside by Fred Anderson, Monica Forti, Phil Frampton, Steffanie Kalt, Siobhan Kearney, Deborah Tilly and Horst Vogt.

Sketches by Jennifer Orpin.

Book and cover design by Ben Eastop.

Researchers: Monica Forti, Steffanie Kalt, Chetan Patel and Claudia Stenzel.

With special thanks to the Kerala Tourist Development Corporation (KTDC), Indian Tourist Office plus: Rajan, Vijay, Ashish, Perminder, Nina, Kath, Julie, Maureen, Gail, Ellie, Sidonie and the people of Kerala for their help and inspiration.

Printed by Whitstable Litho, Kent.

British Library Cataloguing in Publication Data. This publication is being catalogued and will be available at the British Library.

The publishers and authors have made every effort to ensure the accuracy of the information in this book but they cannot accept responsibility for any form of inconvenience arising from using this book.

✖ Contents

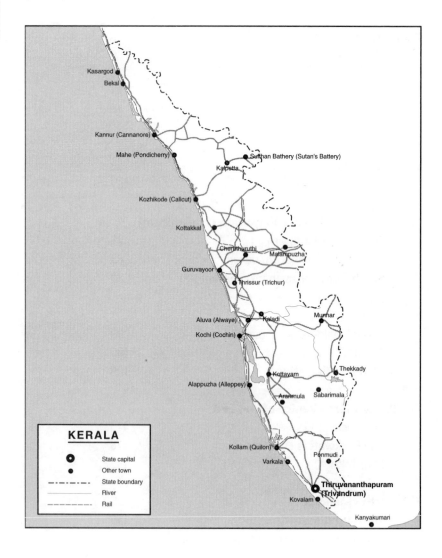

KERALA

- ◉ State capital
- ● Other town
- —··—··— State boundary
- ——— River
- ——— Rail

Kasargod
Bekal
Kannur (Cannanore)
Mahe (Pondicherry)
Sulthan Bathery (Sutan's Battery)
Kalpetta
Kozhikode (Calicut)
Kottakkal
Cheruthuruthi
Malampuzha
Guruvayoor
Thrissur (Trichur)
Aluva (Alwaye)
Kaladi
Munnar
Kochi (Cochin)
Kottayam
Thekkady
Alappuzha (Alleppey)
Aranmula
Sabarimala
Kollam (Quilon)
Ponmudi
Varkala
Thiruvananthapuram
(Trivandrum)
Kovalam
Kanyakumari

Introduction **Kerala - Jewel of India**

Clinging to the south western tip of India, just eight degrees from the equator, is the magical, luxuriant strip of land known as Kerala, "Land of the Coconuts". I first stumbled across its beauty after taking the two and a half day train ride down from Delhi. What a contrast this verdant tropical state made to the harsh, rugged plains and clogged up cities of the north of India.

As the train descended from the mountainous Western Ghats of Tamil Nadu, we entered a world of swaying palm trees, sleeping paddy fields and gurgling streams crossed by hordes of school children in brightly coloured school uniforms and men and women making their way to work. Enter India and one enters another world. Entering Kerala, as my friend Steffanie observed, is like entering paradise.

Reach Kerala by plane and before your plane lands at the main airports of Kochi (Cochin) or Thiruvananthapuram (Trivandrum), you will be treated to a fine spectacle. Out of the window you will see an emerald, luxuriant landscape contrasting with the jade blue Arabian Sea and sandwiched between them golden sands stretching the whole length of Kerala's 800 kilometre coastline. Emerald, jade and gold you will find aplenty in this hidden gem of world travel.

Part of the magic of India to western travellers has often been to immerse the visitor in a totally different culture. Kerala boasts the most tolerant and yet vibrant contrasts of religion, peoples and traditions. Over the centuries African, Arab, Jewish, Chinese and European settlers and traders were attracted to this land, once known as the Spice Coast because of its riches of peppers, coffee, tea, ginger, curry leaf, cardamom etc. and left their influence on the state's culture. Now the peoples are cemented by an education system which produces 90 percent literacy and a standard of life which, though not wealthy, provides for the basic needs of all.

And to cater for your needs you can find a beach with restaurants – serving local cuisine and western food – air-conditioned hotels and swimming pools or you can discover those two dozen or more stretches of sand along the coast that are truly hidden places, deserted by all but a few fishermen – your very own tropical paradise.

Add to all this night temperatures which rarely fall below 20C and daytime coastal temperatures between 30C and 36C, wildlife sanctuaries, huge waterfalls, lazy boat trips through semi-jungle, elephant marches, temples, churches, inexpensive accommodation, incredibly cheap but dramatically tasty south Indian vegetarian food and you may understand the curse that struck me when first gazing on India's jewel - I could not rest till I had returned.

INTRODUCTION

⊗ The Making of Kerala

In the Beginning

All over Kerala, brightly painted on trucks and temple walls, is the tale of Kerala's legendary creation. In his anger, Parasurama, sixth incarnation of the great god Vishnu the Preserver, had wielded his axe to slaughter 21 generations of Kshatriyas known as the warrior caste of India. In repentance Parusarama retreated to the Western Ghats mountain range which at that time was on the edge of the ocean.

Pitying Parasurama, the gods prevailed on Varuna, God of the Sea, to give the warrior sage some land whereby Parasurama was promised as much land as he could cover with the throw of his axe. He flung the axe in a monstrous arc and the land emerged from the sea to create a strip of coastal magic now known as Kerala.

Indian myths and legends, as with the tales from the Bible, often have some elements of historic truth and the age-old tale of Parasurama's deed fits well with scientific theories. For scientists believe that the Western Ghats (which form most of Kerala's eastern border), the Eastern Ghats, the Aravallis and the Vindhyas mountains formed a triangular peninsula that once was part of the Earth's first land mass, Gondwanaland. Movements of molten rock beneath the Earth's surface began to break up the first continent. As the tectonic plates on which the land mass sits moved apart, Asia, Australia, Europe and the Americas were created.

Then part of Africa, India set off on its own eventually crashing into Asia, creating the highest mountain range in the world. Geologists believe that, millions of years later, submarine earth movements forced the sea bed to rise. With the aid of silt carried down by the rivers from the Western Ghats, very slowly Kerala emerged.

Perhaps some intuitive understanding of these great geological events has found its way into folklore to be passed down through the ages.

The process of building Kerala's land mass is still going on today as silt being carried to the sea, particularly at the times of the monsoon tides, is forced onto the shallow ocean floor off the coast. The shifting deposits of silt have directed the fortunes of Kerala's great cities and ports allowing Kochi (Cochin) to come into its own in the fourteenth century, putting an end to the ancient port of Muziris. Tripunithira and Kottayam, long ago the capitals of the Maharajas' fiefdoms and Kerala's present capital, Thiruvananthapuram, were all once sea ports. Now all three are stranded inland.

A Natural Paradise

Kerala's geographic positioning on a sun-drenched coastal strip bordered by mountains draining the monsoon rains, created the lushest landscape in India.

Moist, deciduous forests flourished in the hills and tropical evergreen forests in the valleys and lowlands. Numerous species of birds and animal life abounded in the varied terrain. The coconut palm advanced covering the length of the coastline. Cold ocean currents brought fish. The rains poured down on the volcanic rock formed by the lava which crystallised creating the Deccan Peninsula and the Western Ghats. They carried the silt down to the lowlands and deposited what, when compressed, became laterite - lateris is Latin for brick and laterite became the building brick of Dravidian civilisation. Humanity was furnished with all its requisites for development.

An Historic Civilisation

The entry of humankind into Kerala is still debated. The Western Ghats, at an average height of 900 metres, acted as a formidable barrier to entering the coastal strip by land. The earliest evidence of human activity was discovered in the district of Kollam (Quilon) through the dating of charcoal remains left by settlers in 3000BC. In 1991 an archaeological dig discovered a burial site from the same era containing terracotta jars inside which were bones, iron implements and cornelian beads.

These remains from the Megalithic era have led anthropologists to conclude that the first people in Kerala were the Negritoes, a hunter-gatherer population similar to the blacks of Africa. Broad-headed with tight curly hair and dark skins they lived in harmony with nature using herbal medicines. Today their ancestors still inhabit the mountains of southern India.

The Negritoes were followed into Kerala by the Austrics, a people considered to be similar to the Australian Aborigines. The Aborigines in Australia practised snake worship and it is believed that the Austrics introduced the serpent as a deity in Kerala. They also began the growing of crops of rice and vegetables, laying the basis, it is said, for Indian civilisation.

Thereafter came the dark skinned, frizzy haired Dravidians possibly from northern Africa, the Aegean or the Middle East. It is speculated that they headed east in boats travelling along the shorelines and up the rivers and were responsible for the great Indus Valley civilisations which created the cities of Mohenjodaro and Harappa in what is now Pakistan. In the ruins of these two cities one can see extensive rectilinear drainage systems indicating an extremely advanced society using sewage systems to protect against pollution.

At Mohenjodaro bronze weapons were found: coins and ivory and gold jewellery. They worshipped a god similar to the Hindu god Shiva and his wife Durga. Phallic worship similar to that associated with Shiva the Destroyer and Reproducer took place. Forced south by the incoming lighter skinned Aryans from Central Asia, they are thought to have eventually settled across India establishing towns, cash-crops and trade.

Dravidian society had elements of matriarchy and worshipped the Mother Goddess, later to become Kali, in a range of forms. Interestingly, when Muslim Mogul ruler Tipu Sultan entered north Kerala in the late 18th century he was shocked to find the women practising polyandry.

Eventually the Aryan drift from the Middle East and Central Asia overwhelmed northern and central India and the civilisations merged. The Deccan Plateau and the Western Ghats limited the advance into Kerala and Dravidian civilisation hung on. Notably, as with Kanada the language spoken in Karnataka and Tamil, Malayalam, the language of Kerala is Dravidian and totally different to the Sanskrit based languages in the north such as Hindi and Punjabi. Nevertheless today Kerala is principally a mix of Dravidians and Aryans as reflected in the varying straightness of hair, nose shapes and darkness of skin.

The Foundations of Hinduism

The Aryans introduced the principal elements of Hinduism. In the Vedas, religious scripts of 1500/1200BC, they brought a new religion worshipping the elements of nature, the sun, the moon, thunder and rain. Eventually Dravidian and Aryan beliefs merged as the priest caste triumphed. In the great epics of the Mahabharata and Ramayana we see the introduction of the Hindu trinity Brahma the Creator, Vishnu the Preserver and Shiva the Destroyer. Essentially the south remained a predominantly Dravidian stronghold. However, Hinduism developed strong roots in the south, producing some of the finest examples of classical temple architecture in India.

Just after 500BC the Hindu priests produced the Upanishads, further sacred Hindu texts philosophising on the origin of the universe, the nature of the soul and matter and the relationship between matter and spirit.

500BC saw the rise of the Buddhist and Jain religions which, though they swept through vast areas of India, never took substantial root in Kerala. A few Jain temples still exist in the state, for example the Anathanathaswami temple near Kalpetta.

The Caste Society

At some early stage, a Vedic authority known as Agastya converted the Dravidians to Brahminism. Agastya is now part of Kerala's mythology. The Dravidians adopted the Aryan caste system. The Aryan ruling caste was the priesthood of the *Brahmins*. Then came the warrior caste of *Kshatriyas* followed by the *Vaisyas*, traders and cultivators, and the artisans of the *Sudra* caste. The establishment of distinct roles and codes of conduct brought a stability to the social structure. Cruelly left out of this frame were the *Untouchables* now known as Scheduled Castes, namely those who performed the most menial tasks, which in Kerala included the fisherfolk.

In Kerala, the Brahmin priest caste was filled by the Aryans who were able to gain predominance over the warring chieftains. The Priest Caste used the grip of religion and their hold over knowledge and interpretation of the sacred texts. In Kerala they were known as Namboodiris.

The old chieftains displaced by the Aryan shift south were absorbed into the Kshatriyas caste while fierce battles between different fiefdoms created a special warrior caste known as Nairs. The Nairs were so fearsome that some formed suicide squads known as Chavers, said to have terrified the life out of the invading Portuguese. Beneath them the Sudra and Vaisya castes of farmers, peasants and artisans were known as Ezhavas and the Untouchables as Pulayas.

Alongside the caste system, Kerala kept to its Dravidian matriarchal roots, observing a matrilineal system known as *marummakkathayam*. Ultimate power was generally vested in the family's eldest male known as the *karnavar* but the system meant women inherited the family property and gained a certain independence. The warrior Nairs, like Catholic priests, were forbidden to form any attachments, the Nair women forming family associations known as *tharawads*. Nair women married Namboodiri men for only the eldest Namboodiri son was permitted to marry a Namboodiri woman.

Namboodiri women were expected to remain virgins and their children were surrogates. Those who had affairs with Nair men were ostracised and their children brought up as disenfranchised singers, dancers or actors.

The Nair wife dominated the household to the extent that the husband had to keep his slippers at her bedroom door to warn off rivals. When she got bored with him she didn't have to bother with a divorce court. She just threw his slippers out.

As for the untouchable Scheduled Castes, they lived in a state of utter humiliation. Banned from entering the temples and public markets men and women had to be naked above the waist. In the streets they would have to shout, "Po! Po! Po! Get away!" in fear of their lives, for if a Namboodiri saw them within 90 metres the Namboodiri would be polluted. The Nair could withstand 60 metres and the Ezhava 30 metres. The penalty for the unseeable Untouchable Pulaya was a good beating, even death. The consequence for the polluted castes was a time consuming, ritualised wash-down and cleansing.

Neither was the caste system confined to Hindus, for when the Nairs converted to Syrian Orthodox Christianity they still put the Catholic fisherfolk in a lower caste which led to many converting to Islam and eventually Communism. At the bottom of the pile were the indigenous or tribal people, known as adivasi who kept to their own areas in the hills.

Rice and Spice: Kerala Prospers

The fertile lowlands and valleys allowed the peoples of Kerala to prosper, cultivating crops and fishing the seas. Rice furnished the staple diet and spices grew in abundant variety. Possibly as early as 800BC ivory and spices began to attract seafaring merchants from North Africa, the Middle East, Greece, Rome and Indonesia. The region had wealth but the Western Ghats partially cut Kerala off from the great turmoil on the rest of the continent. References to Kerala were made by the Roman scholars Pliny the Elder and Ptolemy.

The ancient Dravidian kingdoms of southern India can be divided into three dynasties; the *Cholas* ruled Chennai (Madras) and below on the east coast. The *Pandyas* ruled over the extreme south from Madurai and the *Keralas* or *Cheras* (coconut people) ruled over Malabar and the west coast. The mid-south also furnished the Pallava dynasty based in Kanchi north of Madurai.

Some authorities suggest that the Cheras were divided into smaller groups of feudal rulers such as the Ay chieftains in the south and the Nannanas in northern Kerala. The capital, said to be the city of Vanji referred to in the Ramayana, has never been located though some claim it was at Vizhinjam close to Kovalam. The Chera's, the smallest state, constantly lost battles to the Pandyas and the Cholas and had to bow to Pallava supremacy from the 4th century to the 8th century.

The Pallavas loved creative architecture, building not only reservoirs and public works but great temples and monasteries. In AD740 the Pallavas were invaded from the north and were defeated. The central region of the south went through a hundred years of turmoil until the Cholas and Pandyas combined to defeat the debilitated Pallava forces as the 9th century closed. It was during this turmoil that the great Malabar born Vedic philosopher Sankaracharya, or Sankara, wrote his commentaries on the Vedas and the Upanishads, rescuing Hinduism from degeneration and decline and once again asserting the Brahman, universal spirit.

In the tenth century the Cholas soon dominated the Pandyas, Chola king Rajaraja capturing Madurai and the great Sree Meenakshi temple. Rajaraja established great power attacking Sri Lanka with his navy and capturing Kollam (Quilon), then an important port and the capital of Kerala. In the 13th century the Chola empire declined and the Cheras regained their independence remaining effectively so until Mogul Tipu Sultan's troops invaded from Mysore.

The Cheras built temples and palaces with exquisite architecture and delicately carved or fired-clay images. Thiruvananthapuram's (Trivandrum) Art Museum contains bronze statues from the eras of Chola, Chera, Pandyan and Pallavas dynasties, demonstrating the cross cultural influences on the artists of the time. The many temples still contain icons and carvings from this period.

With plentiful local supplies of wood, Kerala's peoples built great wooden structures. Curiously today most houses of Kerala are no more than two storeys high, yet ancient Kerala is noted in Indian architectural history for it's many *kantaka*, 12-storey wooden buildings.

Politics and the Decline of Casteism

Throughout the ages Kerala had attracted spice traders, and Arabs and Jews filled the role of traders in the north Kerala ports of Malabar. Chinese merchants visited Kerala and left a deep mark on aspects of Kerala life, in particular the architecture. In turn, Kerala gave China martial arts. Centuries-old paintings in China show dark skinned men training up Chinese combatants in the martial arts known in Kerala as *kalarippayattu*. The Chinese Emperors had no designs to conquer southern India, but the arrival of European adventurers ended Kerala's era of peaceful trade, issuing in a period of diplomacy, plunder and war.

In 1498 the Portuguese adventurer Vasco da Gama became the first European to sail the Cape and land in India. Rich cheap spices attracted the Portuguese, then the Dutch, the British and the French. The Portuguese tried to impose their will, flattening Kochi and insisting on the supremacy of the Pope and Catholicism against the local Christians. They and the Dutch tried to curry favour with the Maharajas of the different states and were successful for two centuries in dominating trade.

An important figure in Kerala's history is Marthanda Varma, Maharaja of Travancore whose Wooden Palace at Padmanabhapuram near Kovalam still stands. In the mid 1700s Marthanda Varma conquered the fiefdoms of Kollam and Kochi unifying southern Kerala under his rule. The great fortifications he built and the fierce unified army were responsible for preventing the advance of Tipu Sultan's Mogul armies further than Malabar. The unification allowed for a more powerful state.

Eventually the British East India Company, from the beginning of the nineteenth century, took over India and Kerala became part of the British Empire. The British ruled through the Maharajas of Travancore and Kochi while Malabar was under the control of the British Governor in Madras. Throughout the 19th century the Travancore Maharajas encouraged land reform and literacy but the brutal caste system remained intact. One reason why the Maharajas set up literacy schools was to combat the church schools which were attracting the low castes away from Hinduism to Christianity.

In 1893 Ayyankali, an Untouchable did the unthinkable and unpardonable by riding in protest on a bullock drawn cart along a public road. A wave of civil disobedience protests followed. The low castes organised themselves into groups, then united to create the Caste Improvement Associations.

As the campaign for independence led by the high caste Brahmins grew, so the low castes demanded their rights. One important protest was staged in 1925 with

Gandhi's sanction. At Vaikom's Shiva temple they demanded that low caste Hindus be allowed into the temples. In 1936 the low castes finally won the right to enter the temples they had built. The Communists won a great influence in this region and played a significant part in many protests against caste subjugation.

When India became independent the low castes put their votes for Communism and in the state elections of 1957 elected a Communist government pledged to land reform. Kerala's land distribution was the third most unequal in India, giving great power to the upper castes. Many peasants' lives were lost in bitter battles with the landowners but the Land Reform Act was passed in 1969 heralding a new era for Kerala.

The 1969 land reform gave peasants the land they had previously tilled. 1.5 million landless labourers were given plots and no-one could now have more than eight hectares. The process revolutionised Kerala society. In this fertile land a jackfruit tree and mango tree are said to be enough to live on. Families were forbidden from selling on the land so poverty did not develop to the extent of yesteryear.

The Communists also accelerated Kerala's education programme providing free compulsory education for children. Kerala's literacy rate rose to an estimated 90% and more. The physical quality of life - health etc. - was put almost on a par with the UK. Now the streets are much cleaner than the rest of India and begging outside of Kochi is minimal and mainly reduced to aggressive selling of shoddy goods or children forever demanding school pens. The Communists tolerated religion, and even the Maharaja. The Maharaja died in 1991 never to be replaced.

The whole process undermined the old casteism. However, Kerala remains a very conservative society. It is an industrial backwater which has its drawbacks but also advantages in that even the big capital city, Thiruvananthapuram, looks like a market town compared to vibrant but choking and violent Mumbai (Bombay).

Work in the oil rich Gulf states props up the economy giving an outlet to some of the state's 4 million unemployed. Migrant workers will commonly go to the Gulf with the aim of saving up enough money in five years to return to Kerala and set up in business.

Casteism remains a factor for Hindus and Christians as mirrored in marital announcements. 87% of women are literate and many go on to university and fill important jobs. Some people say a Malayali woman should be married by the time she is 23, a man by the time he is 27. The process of marriage is generally arranged rather than forced and the man and woman are both given a certain freedom to choose their prospective partner. Frenetic advertising goes on in the press mainly by the bachelors' and spinsters' mothers.

Matrimonials columns

The newspapers' matrimonials columns carry scores of advertisements for potential grooms and bridegrooms. For many, prospects of marriage are in the hands of the gods and the stars.

"42 year old scantily haired, whigged, well-employed Nair spinster seeks alliance with wheatish 30/40 year old unemployed spinster/divorcee/widower."

"Bride 22, 160 MA, slim, Kethu in seventh house, Makam star, well to do and well known tharavad in Ottapalam Taluka, father senior gazetted officer in Government service. Suitable alliance invited with particulars, bio-data, horoscope and photo from Nair/Menon parents with similar status."

"Roman Catholic 25, 150 cm, slight, limped, rich from decent, groom s caste no bar."

 # Kerala Today

Kerala's politics reflect India's great turmoils. The state is home to 30 million of India's 900 million people. Prior to the Second World War, when the Communist Party temporarily abandoned the Quit India movement, the Communists were, if anything, more influential than Mahatma Gandhi. However, it was left to Gandhi's Congress Party to lead the movement and become the dominant force in the country's politics for the rest of the twentieth century. Only in Kerala and Bengal did the Communists remain a major force.

In purely statistical terms of gross domestic product per head Kerala is one of India's poorest states. Two reasons account for this. Primarily, there is a lack of large scale industry mainly because the small state is geographically isolated and starved of electricity which is directed to the large industries of Tamil Nadu.

Secondly, widespread private ownership of small plots of land means much produce is consumed before entering the market and conceals the real levels of production from the statisticians. The result is India's most equitable, most tolerant and least harrowing state.

Since 1997 Kerala's state government has been controlled by the Left Democratic Front which is dominated by the Communist Party of India (CPI), not to be confused with the Communist Party of India Marxist-Leninist (CPM), a 1960s split off. The CPI and CPM are continually feuding, particularly in the north, where sporadic violent clashes break out. Their policies are broadly similar to old-style Labour in Britain. It is the CPI's fourth time in power since 1957.

In the opposition United Democratic Front (UDF) the dominant force is the Congress Party founded by Gandhi's followers. The BJP, a Hindu nationalist party associated with violent clashes against the Muslim community, has a small following in Kerala.

Local councils known as panchayats have limited responsibilities. Elections must take place at least every five years. The state government based at The Secretariat in Thiruvananthapuram has substantial autonomy and parliamentary affairs at state and national level are run cabinet-style. The national flag is orange, white and green with a charka wheel in the middle representing the spindle.

Political life is open and vibrant in "Red Kerala" and from Kovalam to Kasargod you will see plenty of political graffiti, red, white and green flags, demonstrations and rallies. A visit of a key figure in the Lok Sabha (India's national parliament) may halt the traffic with its 14 car cavalcade but at least there are no power cuts for the duration of the visit.

Changing the place names

Across India states are rejecting the old Anglicised names of their towns, cities and districts and reverting to their native form. It is a complex process since the alphabets used on the continent are quiet different to that of English and in the case of the Dravidian south, totally different. The authorities have attempted to come up with spellings in English which come close to the native linguistic pronunciation. In the case of Malayalam it is difficult but fun when you get to know the rules.

For example Calicut has been changed to Kozhikode – but the pronunciation sounds more Kawr-i-kote. So the letters 'zh' approximate to a trilled 'r'. The letter 'd' at the end of a word is pronounced like the French "de", or like the 'd' you were taught when learning to say the alphabet as a child. But if 'd' is followed by an 'e' it is pronounced softly like a 't'.

Here are some place names, gently introduced into this book. The biggest shock to those vaguely aware of Indian geography comes outside Kerala. If you're catching that plane or train you need to know that Madras has gone and is now Chennai and Bombay has fallen to Mumbai.

The world will get used to the changes just as they got used to saying Sri Lanka instead of Ceylon.

I asked how far it was to Kozhikode. He looked at me blank as I repeated the question twice more. I then said the city used to be called Calicut. He laughed and tried to correct my pronunciation.

The problem you'll find in navigating Kerala will be the pronunciation of the old names. Basically the English changed them because they couldn't say words like Thiruvananthapuram very easily. So when stating place names you might be better to stick to the old Anglicised version until you're well versed in the new.

New place names

Old Name	New Name
Alleppey	*Alappuzha*
Alwaye	*Aluva*
Badagara	*Vadakara*
Calicut	*Kozhikode*
Cannanore	*Kannur*
Cape Comorin	*Kanyakumari*
Changanacherry	*Changanaserry*
Cochin	*Kochi*
Quilon	*Kollam*
Mannarghat	*Mannarkkad*
Ooty	*Udhagamangalam*
Palghat	*Palakkad*
Sultans Battery	*Sulthanbathery*
Tellicherry	*Thalaserry*
Trivandrum	*Thiruvananthapuram*
Trichur	*Thrissur*

also in India

Bombay	*Mumbai*
Madras	*Chennai*

The Districts of Kerala

Kerala is made up of 14 administrative districts all, except Wynad, named after their administrative centre. The coastal districts in the south, Thiruvananthapuram, Kollam and Alappuzha, were all part of the old state of Travancore as was inland Kottayam and upland Pathanamthitta. In the middle of Kerala the coastal districts of Ernakulam and Thrissur were controlled by the Cochin Maharaja as was upland Uddiki. The north was known as Malabar and the coastal districts include Mallapuram, Kozhikode, Kannur and furthest north is Kasargod. Palakkad and Wynad are two upland districts on the edge of the Western Ghats. The Kozhikode Zamorins were the region's principal rulers.

The capital, Thiruvananthapuram (Trivandrum), is the main administrative centre, the principal education, health and research centre, the main airport and has a thriving cultural scene. Kochi is the main port and India's 4th largest. The third city is Kozhikode, the main city of Malabar and a timber exporter. The other important towns, but much smaller, are Kollam, Alappuzha and Kottayam in the Backwaters districts, the northern temple cities of Thrissur and Guruvayoor and the northern textile town of Kannur.

Kanyakumari, Madurai and Kodaikanal are Tamil Nadu towns close to Kerala's eastern border.

What about the weather?

Kerala has a tropical climate. Temperatures in Thiruvananthapuram on the coastal lowlands have average minimum levels of 21-23C and maximum levels of 31-35C. On the other hand, the hill station of Munnar, 1600 metres above sea-level, has minimum winter temperatures of 0C and a maximum summer temperature of 30C.

In the lowlands, temperatures vary little between the seasons but rainfall and humidity increase with the onset of the monsoons. The south-west monsoon and north-east monsoon are winds that bring buckets of the rain so crucial to Kerala's luxuriant flora.

On the coast, the winter months of December to March are virtually dry. Visitors can sit in Kovalam and not see a speck of rain in January/February. The light sea breeze in Kovalam keeps humidity down and, despite temperatures of 33-35C, makes for a very pleasant climate. Blue skies, sunshine, brilliant sunsets and starlit nights – a paradise for sun worshippers.

As March ends the humidity tends to rise very slowly and with it comes the occasional shower. The mosquitoes start buzzing around the residual ponds. By mid April, the days are getting muggy and wetter. April/May is called the warm season and children have two months off school. Finally at the end of May the south-west monsoon arrives bringing strong winds and the heavy rains.

For three and a half months Kerala gets the full brunt of the life-giving monsoon which then makes its way over the rest of India. The sea swells and Kovalam's beaches retire to become seabed. The raging sea sometimes reaches into the beach restaurants causing havoc. Winds can snap trees and rip down coconuts. Swimming becomes very dangerous in the rough waters which swallow up to 100 fishing boats each summer. Be careful where you sit. 500 people are killed each year in India by coconuts landing on their heads.

But for the most parts Kerala's people will tell you they love the rains. The little children watch enthralled, then laugh and dance with excitement. Now the trees blossom and arid plots burst into verdant display. It means food on the table, summer festivals, plentiful water. One only has to make a trip through the semi-arid plains of Tamil Nadu on the other side of the Western and Southern Ghats mountain ranges to see what the rains mean to lush Kerala.

June and July are the months of the heaviest rain. Kovalam can be quite pleasant in August. This is the time when the annual Onam harvest festivities begin through-out Kerala. The weaker north-east monsoon then adds further rain through the autumn, particularly in October before fading out in December.

The climate is fairly uniform as one travels up the coast. If anything Kochi (Cochin) is wetter and slightly hotter than the Thiruvananthapuram (Trivandrum).

Average Temperatures and Rainfall in Thiruvananthapuram (Trivandrum)

	Jan	Feb	Mar	April	May	June	July	Aug	Sep	Oct	Nov	Dec
Min C	22	23	24	25	25	24	23	23	23	23	23	22
Max C	31	32	33	32	32	29	29	29	30	30	30	31
Rainfall mm	20	20	44	122	249	331	215	164	123	271	207	73

Up in the Hill Stations

Climatic conditions up in the hills and mountains of Kerala are somewhat different. The monsoons arrive and the rainfall is heavier filling out the rivers, lakes and reservoirs. But many of these areas, like Periyar, receive some rain all year round as the hot, moist, lowland air sheds its load to climb over the mountain ranges. Temperatures are also much cooler.

In Periyar, daytime winter temperatures can fall to 15C and generally temperatures do not rise above 30C. In Munnar hill station temperatures can fall to freezing point. The temperate climate of the highlands tends to attract Indian tourists, particularly in April/May when the lowland becomes hot and very humid. By this time many international visitors and the backpackers have headed up north to the much more temperate mountains of Nepal.

Religion

Kerala's non-proselytising Hindus have accepted the oncoming of Christianity, Islam, Jainism and Buddhism with remarkable tolerance. In the fifty years since India's Independence the state has remained free of the major pogroms that have so tragically hit other states. Battles occasionally break out between fishing villages of different religions over fishing territories but tolerance is to the fore.

Kerala is 60 per cent Hindu, 20 per cent Muslim and 20 per cent Christian. It once had a thriving Jewish community but inter-marriage and emigration has reduced the Jewish population to literally a handful in Kochi. The degree of tolerance is shown in many towns where mosques, temples and churches of different denominations nestle up against each other.

Muslims tend to predominate in the fishing villages and in the north which came under Mogul domination for a short spell in the 18th century. Gaily painted Christian churches abound in Thiruvananthapuram and in the foothills beneath Periyar. Close to Thiruvananthapuram Airport in Sanghumugham are a pleasant cluster of churches flooded by devotees on Friday nights and Sundays.

Hindu temples in Kerala are spectacularly simple outside and very ornate inside. The older mosques built in traditional Kerala style mirror the Hindu temples while the modern mosques in the large towns and cities tend to be more grandiose. In the poorest villages the mosque may just be a space surrounded by a low wall. Architecturally the religious shrines are quite fascinating, telling many stories. Unfortunately non-Hindus are barred from most temples but entry is permitted at Sabarimala, Lokanarkavu, Parassinakadavu, Kalady and a few others. Entry is generally permitted in nearby Tamil Nadu towns such as Nagercoil, Kanyakumari and Madurai.

Hinduism here goes back possibly 4000 years in Kerala, Christianity and Judaism almost 2000 years. Even the Romans had temples here. Islam arrived some 1300 years ago.

The Hindu religion is founded around worship of three main gods. Brahma the Creator, Vishnu the Preserver and Shiva the Destroyer and Reproducer. Each god, the manifestation of the one supreme being, also has many manifestations of their own. Shiva has 1006. Parvathi (Bhagvathi) may appear as Durga the terrible or Kali who wears a garland of skulls. They have avatars (forms of incarnation) such as the popular Lord Krishna, Rama and Sita. The situation is further confused by the fact that each has a vehicle: Vishnu has Garuda, half-man half-eagle; Shiva's son, the elephant-headed Ganesha, has rats and Brahma's wife; Saraswathy, has swans. All these may inspire worship or a temple.

The *gopurams* at Sree Padmanabhaswamy Temple in Thiruvananthapuram tell a tale of the rich complexity of Hinduism. The key thing to remember is the Brahmin belief that each god merely represents a different aspect of the one soul and as such rests quite soundly on our inner conflicts.

Shiva, who may appear white, dark-skinned or blue, and his wife Parvathi are very popular in Kerala. With Shiva's role in reproduction, shivalingam (phallic symbol) worship is common. Ghee is donated to the shivalingam. In one ancient temple the shivalingam has been totally obscured by hardened ghee said to be 1,000 years old.

The flute-playing Lord Krishna often appears blue-skinned. He is a Vishnu incarnation and the story of how he stole the clothes of the *gopi* cow girls while they were bathing in the river brings merriment.

Hinduism has male temple priests and a temple priestess seen as the guardian of the temple. *Sadhus* are self-appointed holy men dedicated to spiritual enquiry and *gurus* are spiritual guides.

Ettumanur Shiva temple

A twice-daily manifestation of Hinduism is the pooja cleansing exercise and you will see this performed in some of the Kovalam restaurants. The ground is swept and sprinkled with water. The air is scented with incense and garlands of fresh flowers such as jasmine.

Christianity was most likely introduced by the Christian disciple, Saint Thomas, believed to have landed in Kerala 20 years after the death of Christ. The Portuguese arrived in 1498 surprised to find someone had got there before the Pope. They caused deep divisions in the Christian Church, now mainly split into Syrian (St Thomas), Orthodox (Maronite and Jacobite) and Catholic (Roman and Latin).

Islam was introduced by Arab traders and particularly caught hold amongst the poor, outsider Scheduled Castes. The further north one goes towards Kozhikode and beyond the veil is worn but 'fundamentalism' has little hold. Muslims believe that "there is no god but Allah and Mohammed is his prophet". Other basic tenets include saying prayers five times a day, abstinence from wine and pork, observing the fast in the month of Ramadan, being charitable and making a Haj trip to Mecca once in their lifetime.

The Koran, composed of Gabriel's revelations to Mohammed during Ramadan, is the sacred text. Friday is the holy day but is also important for Christians so on that day mosque and church alike are inundated with devotees.

Near Kodungallor, just north of Kochi, India's first-ever mosque still stands in its quiet Kerala style. It was built in AD629, seven years after the founding prophet Mohammed was driven out of Mecca and one year before Mecca was captured and declared the holy city. The pilgrimage to Mecca is an important part of a Muslim's life and every spring during Haj thousands of Malayali make the trip. The airport gets chock-a-block – flights via the Gulf states are often over-booked and it's best to get out before or after.

The Festivals of Kerala

Whether the occasion is harvest time, an elephant march or a religious day, Kerala's people certainly enjoy and make the most out of their many colourful, vibrant festivals. It's worth looking out for the festivals and going along. Many of the festivals are religious and, if they are Hindu, then entry to most temples is barred. Most temple festivals however do take to the streets accompanied by their caparison-tuskered elephants in noisy, joyous parades.

Kerala's religious diversity puts many festivals on the calendar. Hindu, Muslim, Christian and non-religious fetes fill the year and account for 24 public holidays when banks and government premises, including post offices, museums and zoos, are shut.

The Kerala Calendar

The dating of the festivals using the Gregorian western calendar can be confusing because Kerala, like the rest of India, traditionally operated on a lunar calendar. The twelve months only approximate to those used in the Gregorian calendar which predominates in administrative circles today. Nevertheless, below is a rough approximation between the traditional Kerala calendar and the Gregorian.

Chingam	*Aug/September*
Kanni	*Sep/October*
Thulam	*Oct/November*
Virchikam	*Nov/December*
Dhanu	*Dec/January*
Makaram	*Jan/February*
Kumbam	*Feb/March*
Meenam	*Mar/April*
Medam	*Apr/May*
Idavam	*May/June*
Midhunam	*Jun/July*
Karkidakam	*Jul/August*

January

The **New Year** begins with a public holiday and seen in by noisy celebrations, particularly on Kovalam beach. The **Great Elephant March** takes place annually from January 9 to January 12 beginning in Thrissur with dozens of tuskered elephants and ending in Thiruvananthapuram. The elephants don't march all that way. It's actually a special event for tourists combining replicas of Kerala's great festivals - the Thrissur Pooram, Snake Boat Races etc. **Republic Day** on January 26 is a national holiday marking the day when in 1950 India became a republic. January 14 to 23 is the time of the **Gramam-Kovalam Village** Fair when a 1940s Kerala hamlet is recreated displaying past cuisine, crafts etc.

February

Ramadan or Ramzan is the Muslim day for beginning the annual fasting. It is an annual public holiday with the date varying according to the lunar calendar. Kerala's government put on the extraordinary **Nishagandhi Dance Festival** annually from February 21 to 27. The venue is the open air amphitheatre of Nishagandhi Stadium in Thiruvananthapuram where India's best exponents of Indian and Malayali classical dance perform free of charge. Its nightly shows are a must for dance and cultural enthusiasts.

Late February to early March, depending on the new moon, a public holiday is given over to **Shivaratri**, the Hindu celebration of Shiva's wedding to Parvathi (sometimes known in Kerala as Bhagvathi). The day is taken up by mantra chanting and anointing oil-lamps. The night, Shiva's wedding night, is accompanied by dancing, festivities and the setting off of incredibly loud firecrackers through till dawn. Aluva (Alwaye) near Kochi has a great festival when everybody yells and leaps off the sandbanks into the Pamba River. Kovalam has an excellent evening Shivaratri party.

March

Holi is mainly a north Indian festival celebrating the end of winter but with no real "winter" in Kerala festivities are less intense. The evening before Holi, bonfires are set alight to observe the destruction of Holika, the evil demon. Holi is celebrated by the throwing of coloured water and dye across anyone in the temple or on the streets – so look out!

March/April

Maundy Thursday, Good Friday and **Easter Sunday** bring an effective four day public holiday celebrated by Kerala's many Christians. Mid-April brings a public holiday for the celebration of **Vishu**, generally followed by **Bakri-Id**, a public holiday which marks the end of the Muslim Ramadan fast and brings great parties in the Muslim areas. The Thiruvananthapuram **Flavour-Food Festival** takes place annually from April 5-11 when India's ethnic and exotic cuisine goes on display for consumption. The capital's **Arat Festival** involves ten days of festivities at Sree Padmanabhaswamy Temple culminating with a procession to Shankumukham Beach near the airport to ritually immerse the image of temple deity Padmanabhaswamy in the sea. The march, with five caparisoned elephants accompanied by flute and drum players, is begun and ended by a 21-gun salute.

March/April is also the time for many temple festivals or *pooram*, the greatest and most colourful of which take place in the temple towns such as Thrissur and Guruvayoor. Festivals in honour of the temple gods take to the streets led by the gaily decorated temple elephants and accompanied by idols of the gods. The Thrissur festival takes place towards the end of April.

May

May 1, **May Day**, international workers day, is a public holiday and you may see parades by Kerala's many trade unionists and Communist supporters. Mid-May brings **Muharram**, a public holiday in honour of the Muslim prophet Mohammed's grandson Hussain who was martyred in a fight against tyrannical rule.

June/July

Rath Yatra is the Hindu Car Festival popular in south India marking Lord Krishna's trips in his temple chariot(car). In Nagercoil (close to Kerala but now in Tamil Nadu) 1,000 devotees are required to drag the temple's giant metal chariot once around the temple walls. Mid-July also brings a public holiday for the Muslim festival of **Milad-un-Nabi**.

August

The public holiday on August 15 brings major military parades in the capital, Thiruvananthapuram in commemoration of India's **Independence Day**. It is now half a century since British troops finally left India. The end of August is Lord Krishna's birthday **Sri Krishna Jayanthi** which is cause for another public holiday during which devotees fast all day then party all night.

August marks the end of the monsoon onslaught and the coming of harvest time in Kerala. Snakes are said to have power over the monsoon rains and to protect homes from evil. It is time for the great Snake Boat Races in which the villages' 103-metre long boats manned by up to 150 crew race each other across the Backwaters. The greatest of these races, the **Nehru Trophy Boat Race**, takes place annually in Alappuzha on the second Saturday in August. The last Saturday in August brings the annual **Rajiv Gandhi Boat Race**.

September

September brings **Onam**, the climax of Kerala's great harvest celebrations to which four consecutive public holidays are devoted. In 1998 this will also mark a special **Tourism Week Celebration** to draw tourists attention to the state's blaze of Onam festivities - elephant processions, dances, music, sumptuous feasts and fireworks displays. This is the time for the girls and women to show their ability in performing the kaitokkali hand-clapping folk dance.

Thiruvananthapuram, where the main roads are closed to traffic and hundreds of thousands of people pack the streets, is the best place to be for this magnificent mediaeval pageant. Onam is also said to celebrate the annual return of Mahabali, a legendary former good but demon king of Kerala who features in the Ramayana Indian epic. The story of his banishment from Earth is played out in frenetic traditional dances.

Onam: the Return of King Mahabali

While Vishnu the Preserver was sat on a mountain in meditation, King Mahabali, ruler of Kerala, seized the whole world, heaven and Earth. The distraught gods were all invited by Mahabali to his yagna celebration. Vishnu, determined to regain his power, incarnated himself as Vamana, a Brahmin dwarf, and attended the party. King Mahabali was impressed by Vamana. In his vanity to impress the dwarf he granted Vamana one wish. Vamana asked for a piece of land, no more than three strides of his short legs. King Mahabali was pleased to grant such a small gift. In vain Mahabali's guru Sukracharya warned the king of impending deception then tried to block Vamana who promptly blinded the guru in one eye with a blade of dharba grass.

Dwarf though he may be, Vamana was still Vishnu and he used all his concentrated power so that within two strides he had covered the earth and the heavens. Mahabali was suitably cowed. He knelt and offered his head for Vishnu's last stride. Vishnu placed his foot firmly on the king's head and pushed him down to the netherworld, ordering Mahabali to remain there for ever. Recognising that previously Mahabali had been a good king, the gods allowed him to make an annual return to Kerala.

October

October 2 is a public holiday marking Mahatma Gandhi's birthday, **Gandhi Jayanthi.** Some of Gandhi's ashes are kept in the Memorial Centre at Kanyakumari and the building is so designed that on this day, at exactly the time of Gandhi's birth, the sun's rays fall on the black marble slab dedicated to him.

Mahanavami and **Vijayadasami** are two consecutive public holidays for the three-day Navarathri festival dedicated to celebrating the "Divine Mother". The Hindu people of Kerala perform Saraswathy Pooja. Saraswathy is the Goddess of Learning and fountain-head of all knowledge.

The day prior to Mahanavami is called **Durgashtami** when the festival opens up with the Poojavaipu ceremony. In temples, houses and schools a room is set aside and decorated. Books, pens and other articles connected with education alongside fruits, beaten rice, jaggery etc. are placed before an image of Saraswathy.

On Mahanavami more pooja take place until Vijayadasami when the books etc. are removed in the Poojayeduppu ceremony. For the highly educated Malayali this day is auspicious for new beginnings and children are first initiated into the written word. A major festival takes place at Sree Padmanabhaswamy temple in Thiruvanathapuram.

A special Kerala festival is the Muslim **Chandanakkudham Mahotsavam** commemorating the death of Bheema Beevi, a devout pilgrim who arrived in Kerala from Mecca. The ten-day festival is held at Bheemapally near Thiruvananthapuram. Thousands of Muslims and non-Muslims go in procession around the mosque carrying earthenware pots with a jasmine garland and hand them, and the money placed inside, as an offering at her tomb.

October/November

The greatest Indian festival is the Hindu autumnal festival of **Diwali.** marking the start of the new year. It is the happiest in the annual calendar, though surpassed in Kerala by Onam. It takes place over five days when oil-lamps are lit, firecrackers set off and sweets handed out to welcome Vishnu incarnation, Rama, home from his 14-year exile by one of his father's greedy wives. It is called the "Festival of Light" because when Rama returned in the evening the people were curious to see his face and lit lamps.

On the second day, celebrations are dedicated to Krishna's victory over the tyrant Narakasura. The third is set aside for Lakshmi (incarnated as Rama's wife Sita), goddess of money and good fortune and the fourth to the arrival of the friendly subdued demon Bali. On the last day, men visit their sisters who put *tika* on their foreheads. One of the days is designated as a public holiday.

Around this time Thiruvananthapuram's Sree Padmanabhaswamy Temple commemorates **Navarathri**, the Goddess of knowledge and music, with a nine day festival of musical concerts.

December

Christmas Day is a public holiday celebrated by Kerala's many Christians who adorn the facades of their houses with illuminated stars and their shops with streamers and colourful bunting. In Kochi (Cochin) it is the start of the week long **Cochin Carnival**.

⊗ Being There

What to wear?

Cotton casuals are ideal for Kerala. However, if you are going for a stay in the hills, then a sweater and a cagoule are advisable extras. A sun hat of some description is a must except for those who want to go Indian style and wear a handkerchief on their head or carry a brolly.

The traditional Kerala dresswear for men is a *lunghi* or *mundu* and short sleeved shirt. The lunghi is a brightly patterned, wrap-around worn like a skirt and tucked in at the waist. It is a very cool, convenient and cheap form of clothing. The mundu is a smart, white equivalent worn when dressing up is felt necessary.

> *"I was stood with my friend in the middle of the town when his lunghi fell to the floor."*

Take care to learn the technique of how to tuck the lunghi in securely. Lunghis can be bought in the towns or in Kovalam for as little as Rs30 (50p) but the touts may try to sell them for much more.

Women in Kerala tend to wear *saris, shalwar khameez* or dresses. Apart from some of the tribal women in the hills, women here wear a bra and cover their shoulders and most of their legs. Doing otherwise off the beach can be very provocative so merging in with the cultural norm can avoid causing offence. Bikinis are acceptable in Kovalam. Topless bathing is not.

> *"I spent all that time packing and I have hardly worn any of the clothes I brought with me. I just went to the tailors and had him make what I needed."*

Kerala has plenty of good cheap tailors. You'll find some in Kovalam. It means that you don't really have to bring any clothes, save what you stand up in, as everything can be bought tailor-made or ready-made in Kovalam or in other towns. A good cotton shirt can be bought tailor-made for Rs125 in the town or bought ready-made for Rs300. At the tailor's a deposit is normally required and it does mean haggling a price and carefully checking on the quality before handing over your rupees.

Footwear

For the cities and towns, sandals (called *chappals*) or flip-flops are commonly worn. On the beach they are also quite useful for protecting your feet from the sun-scorched sand. In the hills a sturdier pair of shoes is necessary and boots if you're trekking. Good Bata leather sandals can be picked up in the town shoe shops for Rs300.

What to say?

Over 200 languages are spoken in the different parts of India. Kerala's official language is Malayalam. Mahatma Gandhi's mission to make the northern language of Hindi the common language of India failed, particularly in the Dravidian south where the Malayalam and Tamil alphabets are very different to that of the northern Sanskrit languages such as Hindi. Some of the restaurant staff originate from Tamil Nadu and consequently speak Tamil.

Resistance was strong to Hindi's imposition, felt unnecessary since the British had already imposed English as a universal means of communication. Many of Kerala's highly literate people can speak English. So today, when visiting Delhi officials arrive in Kerala they speak English rather than Hindi.

Visitors can normally get by speaking English in the southern towns. There will virtually always be someone around who speaks English. However in the north and the hills English is less often used and communication becomes more difficult.

> *I was in my hotel and the room was very plush but white paint was flaking off the ceiling onto my bed. After two mornings waking up to find myself covered in tiny white specks I rang room service to see what they could do about it. I said, "There are little white flakes falling off the ceiling on to me. Can you do something?"*
>
> *Reply: "You want corn flake?."*
> *I laughed and tried again. "No, no. There are little specks, like white dust, covering the room."*
> *Reply. "You want white toast?"*

A little knowledge can be a dangerous thing, especially with language. You think someone has understood you. They think they have understood you too. But because of differences between Ind-glish and English (both equally viable languages), you have actually communicated something entirely different to that which you intended.

Most amusing or frustrating is trying to cope with the very South Indian and Sri Lankan custom of wiggling or twitching the head to indicate assent, uncertainty or a negative. Stay a while and you'll be back in the west doing it yourself and leaving your friends perplexed. It's not so funny when it's a reply from a taxi driver who you have asked if he knows where he is going and he replies with a silent wiggle and you don't know what he means. No answers. Just patience and good humour.

Some useful Ind-glish phrases

chai shop - cafe or tea shop
bus stand - bus station
milk tea - tea brewed in the milk
bed tea - morning tea served in the room
Where are you coming from? - Which country are you from?
Let me tell you one thing - Let me explain everything
a lakh - 100,000
a crore - 10 million
wallah - worker
dacoit - bandit
tiffin - lunch
dhoti - loin cloth

Malayalam

The Malayalam alphabet is so unlike English and the words so difficult to pronounce that many Malayalam to English dictionaries are misleading. Here are some useful phrases you might win some friends with, or at least humour your audience trying to use. We have written them phonetically for ease of pronunciation. One further complication - pronunciation in the north and south of Kerala is somewhat different.

Some Useful Words

Malayalam	Engish	Tamil
Adeh	*Yes*	*Aamam*
Eella	*No*	*Illai*
Sogamarno	*Hello*	*Vanakkam*
Peenneh karnnam	*Goodbye*	*Senru varugiren*
Narla karnnam	*See you tomorrow*	*Nallekku parkisam*
Dyewhy	*Please*	*Dhayavu seidhu*
Nanny	*Thankyou*	*Nanndry*
Sogamarno? or *Sogamdehneh?*	*How are you?*	*Neengal soukyama?*
Sogam	*...Well*	*Nandraga irukkindren*
Parama sogam	*...Very well*	*Nalla Irukkisen*
Seri	*Agreed, OK*	*Surry*
Vellam	*Water*	*Thanner*
Parleh	*Milk*	*Paal*
Panjasara	*Sugar*	*Sarkarai*
Venam	*I want*	*Venam*
Etra ar ee?	*How much?*	*Yevvalvu?*
Sammaiyam etra?	*What s the time?*	*Ippoludhu mani yevalavu?*

Counting 1 to 10
Malayalam:

Wonnoo, Renndeh, Moonneh, Narlla, Annjeh, Aarreh, Airreh, Etteh, Ambpatteh, Patteh.

Tamil:

Onru, Irandu, Moonru, Naangu, Ainthu, Aaru, Ezhu, Ettu, Onpathu, Pathu.

What's to do?

Sports

Physical fitness is a must in a region that still makes its living primarily from the land and sea. No better reflection of that urge for a healthy agile body is the ancient Kerala martial art, acknowledged by many as the mother of martial arts, *kalarippayattu*. Thiruvanathapuram, Kochi and Kozhikode all have training centres and many hotels put on displays of this vibrant, now ritual, combat.

Kerala has the normal Indian obsession with **cricket** but on the beaches you'll probably see more football played than cricket. Kerala is one of India's principal **soccer** states boasting one of the best teams. Kochi and Thiruvananthapuram both have large stadiums. Kochi has hosted international matches and tournaments. Football matches are shown on satellite television. Indian soccer is pretty weak at the moment but the advent of major sponsorship for a national club league should see major improvements.

Volleyball is also popular and Kovalam has a permanent net on the beach if you want a game. Just watch you don't snarl yourself on the net walking home at night. **Golf** is popular amongst the state's higher echelons and golf clubs exist in Munnar, Thiruvananthapuram and elsewhere including the scenic settings of Kodaikanal just across the border in Tamil Nadu.

With 575km of coastline, Kerala has plenty of beaches providing good **swimming** - save in the swollen monsoon tides. Kovalam, Bekal and Muzhappilangad are just about the best for a dip. Swimming in the rivers in the countryside can be dangerous and regularly results in casualties. **Snorkelling** and **scuba diving** facilities are available in Kovalam. Mariners will readily take visitors out to sea for a small payment.

With the ocean and so many rivers and lakes, **boating** is a popular pastime. Available for hire are anything from ferries to speed boats, row boats and pedal boats to dug out canoes. **Rowing** enthusiasts will take a delight in the splendid pageant of the snake boat races. Anglers looking for saltwater **fishing** can take to sea in boats or go line fishing off the many rocky promontories. For freshwater fishing, Kottayam is recommended and further up in the hills for Travancore trout and the elusive monstrous *mahseer* fish.

Trekking routes of magnificent splendour are there to be discovered in the Western Ghats and Southern Ghats mountain ranges. Alternatively try an exciting trek through the jungle - with a guide. **Rock climbing** is not common here but the buttresses and shear faces of the Ghats offer plenty of chances for immortality to those climbers ready to set up and claim new routes.

Other Outdoor Pursuits

Nature lovers are offered at least a dozen **wildlife sanctuaries** and several **bird sanctuaries** and protected areas where man has hardly set foot. Tigers, elephants, macaque and nilgiri langur monkeys, king cobra and pythons, eagles and parrots are common to Kerala plus many, many rare species of plant, animal and bird life.

Horse riding is popular in the hill districts of Munnar, Periyar and Kodaikanal where horses are available for hire. Of course if you want a bareback ride on an elephant you can get one, whether it be in Kovalam or in Periyar. The people of Kerala will perform whatever service they can for visitors including, as happened recently, taking a group of elephants on an 80km hike so that some wealthy Americans in a remote exclusive resort could see the beast of all beasts.

Literature, drama, dance and film

Kerala's high rate of literacy is reflected in its highly developed cultural aspirations. The state has over 100 daily Malayalam newspapers which you can see being avidly read in the streets and cafes. The major English language dailies available are The *Indian Express* and *The Hindu* both containing lively comment on Indian politics, crime, culture, sport etc.

As for **books**, India has plenty of inexpensive literature. Works by Indian novelists such as RK Narayan, Vikram Seth, Kushwant Singh, Kamala Markandaya and Rohinton Mistry are all available for a fraction of the price paid in Europe, even if the quality of production is not as good. Go 500 yards in Thiruvananthapuram and you'll be hard pushed not to find a book shop or certainly an outdoor stall laid out on the pavement and offering extremely cheap second hand books and magazines.

In Kovalam tiny kiosks on Lighthouse Beach rent out novels for next to nothing and you can sell your unwanted reads to them for others' pleasure.

Arundhati Roy's recently acclaimed *The God of Small Things* published by Flamingo gives a picture of Kerala life through the eyes of an Anglophile family. *OM* by Geoffrey Moorhouse gives an interesting insight into Kerala's recent history. RK Narayan's novels may be about Mysore just north east of Kerala but they offer a vivid account of southern Indian life, customs and outlook. RK Narayan has written three good English translations of Indian legendary epics, the *Ramayana*, the *Mahabharata* and *Gods, Demons and Others* – all pretty useful for unravelling Indian culture. Kerala has plenty of museums and temples displaying traditional arts and crafts.

Just outside Kerala at Padmanabhapuram, the Wooden Palace of Travancore's Maharaja Marthanda Varma constructed in the mid eighteenth century contains excellent examples of Kerala **wood craftsmanship** and fine examples of Kerala *fresco-secco* art in its dramatic murals. The murals to be seen in many of the region's palaces were painted using special vegetable and mineral-based colours and protected by pine resin and oil.

Kerala's native **film** producers and thespians have won international acclaim and in drama the state has developed rich traditional dance forms such as kathakali. One unusual variation is the Christian Chavittu Natakam (Stamping Dance) dance drama in which one might recognise some of the elements of the foot stamping in Flamenco. The dance was developed by the Portuguese Christians as an alternative to the Hindu Kathakali dramas. So Charlemagne is fighting Saladdin etc.

A trip to the **cinema** will normally mean watching one of the many popular Hindi movies - a riotous flare of song and dance - and will put you in touch with the origins of the latest popular **Indian pop** songs. Many cinemas are air conditioned and the best seats will put you back Rs15. Cassettes of Indian and western music are available at very cheap prices in music shops in the towns. The quality of reproduction varies and it's wise to request a listen to your purchase before handing over cash.

Over 80 per cent of Kerala's population have access to **television**. Those with satellite dishes have access to the musical channel MTV, sometimes BBC, CNN and Star Sports which covers cricket and from time to time world soccer. The brilliant natural colours of Kerala mirrored in the clothes of its people make excellent **photography** but it is advisable to purchase camera film before leaving home and wait till you return for developing film.

Kerala spy stories often make the front page of the region's newspapers. Remember that taking photographs of airports, railway stations, bridges and military installations is prohibited. Museums and zoos usually charge Rs5/10 for taking photos, if allowed at all. Video cameras and camcorders cost slightly more.

What's to eat?

An area so naturally bountiful in fruit, vegetables, cereals, fish, herbs and spices as Kerala could not fail to put on a very fine cuisine. In addition Indian chefs are very versatile and visitors can also find restaurants serving European (Continental) dishes, Chinese food, Tibetan, Mogul, Iranian and North Indian dishes. But for this you'll really have to get off Kovalam's beaches. Kovalam is probably one of the best places in India for fresh sea food - from prawns and lobster to barracuda and shark – but a trip to an Indian restaurant frequented by Indians is the only way to taste it's rich cuisine and anything like a "curry".

The diet in southern India and Tamil Nadu in particular, is overwhelmingly vegetarian but Kerala's large Muslim and Christian population do eat fish, lamb, chicken and beef (buffalo). Restaurants will often have a sign outside, "Veg" or "Veg and Non-Veg" indicating whether meat meals are available.

No use ordering a Vindaloo or a Madras curry here. Curry is a term used in Kovalam but in most parts curry simply refers to the Curry leaf used as a vitamin giving herb to add to the 'gravy' (sauce). The British may be buying a million curry meals each week from Indian restaurants in the UK but the fayre in India is very much more varied and generally so much better. Neither it is all produced to scorch the palate. Sri Lanka and Tamil Nadu do produce some very hot food but generally speaking spices are used for flavour in India and the meals contain less chillies than are piled on in the UK. Most of the spices used such as cloves, garlic, cardamom, cinnamon, coriander and cumin do not scald and generally the food is quite mildly flavoured.

Indian people are very conscious of the dietary effects of their food and Kerala, which gave India Ayurveda herbal medicine, is to the fore. Sit down at a restaurant and a waiter will often explain the food in terms of its dietary benefits.

If you want to try Mulligatawny Soup please do but remember that Mulligatawny might sound like a friendly Gaelic town but the name was created in the days of Raj by the British who took it from the indigenous phrase for "chilli soup". Be certain. It's like drinking hot chillies!

Breakfast in Kerala often starts with *iddlis*, fluffy steamed rice cakes or *dosas*, pancakes made from rice and lentils and deliciously served up with a tiny metal dish containing a spiced sauce. *Masala dosas* are stuffed with potato and vegetables and served up with a spiced *sambaar* sauce and a small pot of coconut chutney. Dosas originated from Tamil Nadu but are very popular in Kerala. Puri mixes of onions and potatoes are an alternative dish.

For a refreshing light breakfast one favourite is to order half a *papaya* fruit and sprinkle it with juice from a lime. Apart from being vitamin rich, it tastes delicious. If you want an omelette for breakfast in a restaurant take precautions and indicate whether you wish it to be spicy or not. Generally Indian omelettes do include chopped chillies. In Kovalam, apart from bacon most British and continental breakfasts are available. Steamed banana is a Keralan speciality.

Many visitors take advantage of Kerala's ample supply of fresh fruit and have the muesli with fresh chopped bananas, pineapple, papaya, orange etc. and oatflakes all sprinkled with grated coconut. It's so juicy it's about the only muesli that doesn't need milk added.

Thalis, often called *meals*, are a very popular and cheap lunchtime meal in Kerala. Most of them are vegetarian. The *thali* is a metal/aluminium dish containing indentations for up to eight separate portions of spices, chutney etc. and a large space for rice and the mixing. Six separate pots are also served with it containing a variety of dishes, often *sambaar, olen, thoran, avial, kaallen* and *pachadi*. A crispy piece of lentil-flour *papadam* is thrown in and *paayasam* for one's sweet. Save from being offered extra helpings the diner is then left alone to prepare and mix the food as he or she sees fit.

The idea is to pour the pots onto a section of rice and eat it. Generally no cutlery is provided. It's a time for experiencing the delights of tactile eating - eating with one's fingers. The people of South India are vary dextrous and roll and mix, separate and organise the food until it's ready in a podgy ball of rice and all to be popped into the mouth. Normally costing Rs20 for as much as one can eat, the thali is very tasty and good fun. Just remember to wash those hands first. Use your right hand to eat. The left in India is traditionally reserved for use in the loo and in Tamil is even known as the "hand of filth". Left handers may find it difficult but will get used to it.

Traditionally, lunch and dinner are not served on a thali but a banana leaf cut to the size of a plate. True it's very awkward for a running buffet but it's very eco-friendly. With the banana leaf boiled rice would be served along with some *thorans*, gravy-less dishes of lightly-fried coconut, spiced with mustard seed and accompanied sometimes by chopped seafood or meat.

Alongside the *thorans* appear *olens*, ash gourds and dry beans flavoured with coconut milk to produce a nice gravy. *Avials* are a vegetable gravy dish made from coconut and yoghurt to which mango and the green drum stick are often added. Another dish which might appear is the *kaallen*, banana cooked in a thick yoghurt and spiced with chilly, curry leaf, turmeric and cumin seed. If it's all a little too spicy, *pachadi* is on hand, a sour coconut yoghurt with curry leaf, excellent for calming the intestines.

Kerala fish is a must to try. That's fish spiced up in the way of Kerala, often tuna but *karimeen* if one can get it. It's quite exquisite and a meal worth searching for. The other non-vegetarian favourite is chicken cooked like stew in a coconut milk. The chicken or mutton is served up with *appams* – crisp, fluffy white pancakes made from rice flour leavened by fermented palm sap.

Kerala fish should not be confused with 'red fish and tapioca' which is a hot, spicy dish. It's on the menu at Santana restaurant in Kovalam. Best to remember to say how hot or mild you would like it. Any dish which comes too spicy can always be soothed down by ordering a portion of curd (yoghurt).

The *appam* can also be served as a sweet by soaking it in cream and sugar or butter. *Paayasam* made from vermicelli or rice and sugar is often served hot with a thali as a tasty sweet.

Restaurants commonly have more standard Indian vegetarian food on the menu, for example, *masala* dishes which come in a tasty gravy. *Aloo* (potato), *gobi* (cauliflower), *baigan* (aubergine), *muttar* (peas), *palak* or *saag* (spinach) and *paneer* (soft cheese) are offered in various combinations with gravy e.g. *aloo baigan, muttar paneer* etc. These dishes are often eaten with rice. Another popular and very safe local dish is *dhal* or *daal* (fried lentils) with rice. Two tasty varieties are *tarka dhal* and *dhal makhani*.

Local *rotis* (*chapati*) tend to be pretty heavy. *Tandoori* cooking is a style from northern India and the south's naan breads, though passable, are not the best. The *tandoori* (a clay brick oven) is popular in Kovalam for baking the great varieties of delectable sea food on offer.

Kerala local snacks include banana cake, *wada cake* and *dosas*. In Kovalam, a healthy vegetable or fruit *chapati* appears on the menu. It's actually a pastie but a good mix of starch, vitamins and fibre. Less wholesome but pretty enticing are the varieties of pancakes available on the beach. For the best cooking it's best to try and eat the indigenous cuisine. Home cooking is tremendous here and if you get an invite you'll be able to savour the subtle delicacies of Kerala's traditional cuisine

The most common traditional dessert is *paayasam*, the vermicelli dish served sweet with meals. However India has some excellent sweets (often cakes). *Ras gullas*, sweet little balls of cream cheese served in cream, are a tasty dessert. In the sweet shops of Kerala you'll find very tasty *barfi* cakes made from khoya. Chocolate *barfi*, pistachio *barfi* and almond *barfi* are common. Kozhikode's SM Road claims to contain the best *halvah* in India and it is pretty good.

All over India there is plenty of ice cream about. It's pretty good in the cities but new arrivals are advised to wait at least a week while their constitution gets used to India.

Finally *paan* is sometimes served as an after meal snack. A betel leaf is smeared with lime paste, tannin-rich *catechu* powder and fragrant essences all wrapped around shredded *betel* nut, cardamom and aniseed then secured with a clove pierced though the folded leaf. Said to be an aphrodisiac, it is commonly chewed though the day and the residue spat out, staining the ground and the mouth a hideous blood red.

Kerala cuisine

*There are a number of restaurants in London serving Kerala cuisine, including **Malabar Junction** in Great Russell Street, **Shirefs** near Oxford Circus, and **Rasa** in Stoke Newington Church Street.*

What's to drink?

Coffee and **tea** are grown in the hills of Kerala and the coffee can be very good. Coffee is generally cooked in the milk and known as milk coffee. If you want black coffee with milk added at the end, take a precaution and ask. A request for tea usually brings a cup or pot of *chai* to the table. *Chai* involves boiling up milk, water, tea and often sugar all together. If this is not what you want request black tea with milk. As the spice capital Kerala's kitchens can put on some excellent herbal teas. Ginger tea is very refreshing as is cardamom tea.

Tap water in Thiruvananthapuram and Kochi is safe to drink. Elsewhere and including on Lighthouse Beach in Kovalam it's best to avoid it unless it has been boiled. New arrivals should again wait at least a week before trying it. Precautions on health will protect your adventure. For the same reason it means avoiding salads, iced drinks and ice cream while you're body acclimatises. You will need lots of water so go for the mineral water.

Mineral Water is cheap and plentiful. Some of it is boiled tap water. Check the top is sealed otherwise your mineral water might simply be a tap refill. The mineral water comes in various names and quantities e.g. Golden Valley, Pondicherry, Bisleri etc. If you find one you like it's worth sticking to it.

Water purifying tablets are available in the West (but most don't remove the possibility of hepatitis and dysentery). They will make tap water safe but caution is the operative word. Most people do not get "Delhi Belly" in India if they are cautious.

Fruit Juices are plentiful in Kerala. The most environmentally friendly is the juice of the coconut and the green coconut - pierce a hole and drink. Alternatively use a straw. Pineapple, orange and papaya juice are all available fresh. Very popular and refreshing, providing they have been refrigerated, are the cartons of Mango Fruitti which retail at Rs7. Airports and some hotels charge Rs30.

Soft drinks tend to be more sugary than the western varieties, for example Pepsi is available and less sickly than the local variant Thums Up (Famsap). Limca and Citra are two local brands of lemonade. The yoghurt based lassi drink can be served mixed with fruit juice and ordered sweet or with added salt. It's a cool refreshing healthy alternative but often served with ice and hence to be avoided for the first week. The variant bang lassi used to be served in Kovalam. It contains marijuana which is now a banned substance save for temple priests and the gods.

Beer available in Kerala is almost exclusively brewed in India. It is normally served in the bottle but bars often have the cheaper more variable draught beer served in a glass or tankard. India is hot and lager beer needs to be very cold to be the least bit refreshing. That means checking that the bottle is cold before the waiter or bar hand tips off the bottle top. It also means checking the date of the beer. Indian beer including the very popular Kingfisher brand contains a gelatine-like preservative to prevent it from deteriorating too rapidly in the heat. Nevertheless it's not like an old whisky, it goes off. So "baby beer" – ie. less than one month old – is better. If the beer's a year old then best not to touch it.

> Sometimes in Kovalam or Varkala you'll see visitors sat in a restaurant holding their bottle of beer upside down with its head immersed in a glass of water. For three minutes they sit patiently occasionally glancing at the glass. This is not a party trick. They are allowing the sickly tasting gelatine preservative that is in most of the beers to drain into the glass, whose water turns a sickly yellow.

The price of a bottle of beer in a shop in Thiruvananthapuram and Kochi is around

Rs40. In Kovalam it is probably the most expensive in India at Rs60 in a normal restaurant and Rs125 in the expensive hotels. Prices were kept artificially high in Kovalam but should now fall slightly due to a change in licensing administration. Cheapest beer at Rs45 is available at the Raja Hotel on the hillside going down to the north end of the beach. Beer is half the price in the town of Mahe in the north but it's a long way to go for a pint.

Wines and **spirits** are of low quality in India despite the efforts of the brewers and the Goa vineyards. Some of the best quality – three-star rum, brandy and whisky – is passable but Johnny Walker isn't losing any sleep. Those partial to a drop and wanting the best quality should bring their own from the duty-free or get someone whose taking a short trip across the strait to Sri Lanka. Save up that free bottle of wine from the flight, put it in your restaurant's fridge and keep it for a special night.

Women drinking alcohol or smoking is an extremely rare sight off the most popular tourist tracks so sensitivity is required and curiosity expected.

"We were just over the border in Tirumangalam close to Madurai. Our friend knew a cheap, illegal bar and we were thirsty. It was a ramshackle shack with a corrugated iron roof. I went to go to the bar. They told my friend that I wasn't allowed in. Women shouldn't drink beer. There were men in the bar and they would be upset. We argued. Eventually the bar hand said that I could have a beer but would have to drink it out of view. He pointed to a door. I went inside. It was a closet with standing room for just two people and they brought me some beer in small metal cups. I half closed the door and my friends sat round me so we could talk." – Dorte Jensen.

Local spirits include *toddy, feni* and *arak*. They are brewed from fermented coconut milk and taste like a poor man's gin. *Toddy* shops were banned by the outgoing Kerala government but have been restored by the Communists who have also substantially lowered taxes and hence prices of all spirits. *Toddy* is very popular with the fishermen but not so popular with their long-suffering wives and anti-alcohol agitation is strong particularly in the north.

Where to Stay?

Kerala has a vast range of accommodation up to tourist standard. The hotel industry has a grading similar to that in the UK, one star to five star. But outside Kovalam, Thiruvananthapuram and Kochi most towns are generally limited to one luxury hotel. Kerala has a significant Indian tourist trade with slightly different expectations with regard to service etc. That means that hotels off the normal tourist route tend to be different to those en-route. Therefore Kovalam, Periyar and the big towns have hotels used to accommodating international visitors. Elsewhere is more of an adventure.

Prices of accommodation are generally quoted for double rooms with attached bathrooms and AC (air conditioned) or non-AC (fan only). Prices in the international tourist areas tend to be much higher than off the beaten track and are higher in the winter tourist season. Prices in this guide are for 1997 and are only given as a rough idea of what prices you might expect to pay. Prices are usually quoted exclusive of state's expenditure tax and luxury tax.

Travelling in season or out it is quite easy to get somewhere to stay in a town but **prior booking**, even for the first night of a stay, will mean you're more likely to get the type of accommodation you want and saves the hassle of traipsing round searching for a room after a long journey.

"We arrived in Kochi quite late at night and our taxi driver took us on a tour looking for a hotel. Everywhere seemed to be full and if it wasn t they wouldn't take us because we didn't have our passports. We ended up with me and my sister sleeping in the back of the car and our husbands on the pavement."

Every hotel and guest house is required by law to keep a record of who is on their premises. This means you need your **passport** handy when booking in.

Kerala's power needs are currently beyond its capacity to generate or purchase in electricity from other states. This means power rationed by the use of daily, sometimes twice or thrice-daily, power cuts. Power cuts may last from half an hour to four or five hours. Unless the hotel has an alternative source of power, a power cut means no fan, no air conditioning, no lights, no refrigerator...

"We paid more for the air conditioned hotel but when the power went off we had nothing."

The **luxury hotels** tend to be centrally air-conditioned. Many middle range and some basic hotels claim to have **air-conditioning** but spending money on these rooms can be a waste if the hotel does not have its own electricity generator.

Some luxury hotels have excellent rooftop or garden swimming pools. They also take most credit cards and have facilities to exchange currencies. Some do a pick up service from the airport/rail station which is very handy. Taj group runs a few "international standard" hotels including Taj Garden Retreat in Varkala and Taj Residency and the Malabar in Kochi. The Casino Group have a similar slightly cheaper range of hotels including Spice Village in Periyar and Casino Hotel in Kochi. The Indian government (Indian Tourist Development Corporation) runs the Kovalam Ashok Beach Resort but the nearby KTDC (Kerala Tourist Development Corporation)

Hotel Samudra is cheaper, and offers a better stay.

The most **basic accommodation** is in dormitories which are by nature not very secure for property, nor very clean. In the sections on accommodation rooms referred to as basic generally have a single, twin or double bed, a table, a chair, a fan and if they are with attached bathroom, a toilet and shower. The toilet may be Indian (a whole in the ground) or European-style. Basic rooms tend to be very drab but can be relieved by a balcony. They are also very cheap (Rs30-100) and hence very popular with budget long stay backpackers.

For **security** it's wise to take a strong padlock which prevents anyone else from entering your room. Petty crime is not a massive problem for tourists but India is a poor country and there's no need to put temptation in the way.

An international survey on honesty placed wallets containing cash and an address on the streets of various cities across the five continents. The people of Kerala were found to be more honest than those of Europe.

Some hotels, even guest houses, have nice gardens which can provide a relief from sitting in one's room. Many have attached restaurants and provide room service. It is common for budget travellers to take a cheap room for example in Kovalam and then use the other facilities provided by the more expensive hotels - swimming pools, restaurants, bars etc.

Very cheap accommodation is available in Youth Hostels and you're not normally expected to be a member of the Youth Hostel Association (YHA) but members get cheaper rates. The government-run Rest Houses, (PWD) Rest Houses and Bungalows and the Tourist Bungalows are generally cheap and available through KTDC. Sometimes they are reserved for government officials so it is worth booking in advance. The government also run Tourist Bungalows which are generally good value.

Fascinating Stays

A few top-of-the-range hotel complexes have taken to recreating old traditional wooden Kerala houses as accommodation units. Four sided houses are known as *nallukettu* and eight-sided houses as *ettukettu*. Each is built around a central courtyard allowing for modular expansion outwards. The houses made from rosewood and teak are very cool and superbly crafted. The bathroom is open air with modern toilet and shower facilities and surrounded by a high wall.

These places include: **Surya Samudra Beach Garden** and **Somatheeram Beach Resort** near Kovalam, **Spice Village** in Periyar and **Coconut Lagoon** near Kottayam. A basic, much cheaper version of the same are the Wild Huts at the **Coffee Inn** in Periyar.

The 250-year-old Dutch built **Bolgatty Palace** on Bolgatty Island, in Kochi, oozes history and is beautifully located at the water's edge away from the bustle of the city. For a taste of the old days of the British Raj the very cheap **Tourist Bungalow** set in spacious gardens by the water's side in Kollam is quite splendid. A more expensive and luxurious option is to take the boat to the KTDC's lake palace **Aranya Nivas**. This grandiose former hunting lodge of the Maharajas is by Periyar Lake in the middle of the Wildlife Sanctuary.

The two-room government **Traveller's Bungalow** sat on the cliff's edge in the middle of the secluded, vast grounds of the centuries-old Bekal Fort offers you a peaceful sanctuary in a glorious setting. **Kappad Beach Resort**, near Kozhikode at £13 a night is 20 times more expensive but every room's balcony overlooks a palm-fringed, long, quiet beach where it is the only hotel.

Visitors in search of inner peace and philosophical contemplation might head to the *ashrams* - centres for mediation and contemplation. **Shivananda ashram** near Neyyar Dam is quite popular with foreign visitors as is **Mata Amritanandamayi Mission** run by The Mother near Alappuzha. Kalady, north of Kottayam is a virtual shrine to Advaita Hindu philosopher Sankara and has two ashrams.

What about Money?

Indian currency is based on the Rupee and the Paise (pronounced "puy - sa"). 100 paise (p) are equivalent to 1 rupee (Rs). There are 5, 10, 25 and 50 paise coins. Rupees can appear as 1, 2 and 5 rupee coins or as 1, 2, 5, 10, 20, 50, 100 and 500 rupee notes. The notes can be in bad condition as they are often stapled together creating holes in the note which enlarge over time. With the worst cases, they are difficult to get rid of so don't accept them.

Exchanging Money

The current rates of exchange as of October 1997 are:

Britain	1 pound sterling	Rs59
USA	1 US dollar	Rs36
Germany	1 deutschmark	Rs20
France	1 French franc	Rs6
Italy	1000 lire	Rs21
Australia	1 Australian dollar	Rs26

INTRODUCTION

When you purchase rupees in India you must be given an **Encashment Certificate**. This is proof of the legitimate purchase of your rupees and should be kept. Indian currency cannot be taken out of the country and any amount more than Rs1000 cannot be exchanged back for foreign currency unless accompanied by an Encashment Certificate.

Travellers' Cheques in the major currencies are widely accepted. Thomas Cook have an office in Kochi. **Credit Cards** are also widely accepted in the more expensive hotels and the more sophisticated travel agents. The major credit cards (American Express, Visa, Mastercard, Access) can secure money at most banks which exchange money. The agent may well charge a fee, on top of which the credit company will do the same. Changing any money is a laborious, bureaucratic affair and is best done in the cities.

Credit cards are a handy back-up in case you are financially stuck but if you are making a purchase in a shop with your card, don't let it out of your sight. If you hand over advance cash for some product you have bought, check that the company is reputable or you may end up with a big whole in your pocket and nothing else.

Tipping

Tipping is very common in India and generally a must if you want to get anything moving. There are no hard and fast rules but lower tips are expected in the areas off the international tourist circuit and in *chai* shops. Remember that the average Indian worker is paid just over Rs2000 per month or Rs80 per day so work out what is reasonable. *Baksheesh* is the Indian term for oiling the wheels of transactions and *baksheesh* may be required to get whatever you are trying to achieve. Give something and then you can tell whether it's considered enough.

What to take?

Here's a check list of some of the things you might need in Kerala. Many of the clothes items can be bought cheaply on arrival so don't over-pack especially if you're planning to stay 90 per cent of the time on the beach: clothes: underwear, swimming costume, shorts, T-shirts, short sleeved shirts, cotton trousers, shoes, socks, sandals, lightweight jacket/cagoule.

Other useful things: washing gear, sewing kit, shaving gear, medical kit, padlocks, a watch/alarm clock, clothes line, clothes pegs, a brolly, one sheet or sheet sleeping bag, passport, credit card, key home addresses/phone numbers, mosquito net, toilet roll, a knife, insect repellent, bite soother, spare specs/lenses, sun-block cream.

For those take electronic gadgets India operates on a voltage of 220v. Back up batteries are handy because of regular power cuts.

Stanfords in Long Acre, Covent Garden, London, have maps of Kerala.

What about health?

The key to health in India is taking care of yourself properly. Kerala is India's healthiest region with an average life expectancy of 70 years. Nevertheless standards of tap water are very poor and precautions must be taken. When taking out travel insurance make sure it provides comprehensive medical cover.

The **sun** is the biggest day-to-day threat to health. In temperatures of 30C, with a blazing sun, body dehydration is rapid and takes place without the tell-tale sign of being thirsty. Many people suffer from upset stomachs and loose motions not because of what they have eaten but because of what they've not drunk. They are dehydrated and the loose motions add to this.

Try and drink at least two litres of mineral water a day especially if you're drinking beers or spirits. Have some rehydrating medication with you if you do succumb and drink as much water as you can.

The sun is deceptive especially with the freshening coastal breezes. Take it gently on arrival. Take your sun-block and don't stay out too long with your head uncovered. Sunburn and sun stroke can ruin your trip. Calamine lotion helps with slight sunburn.

Just the **change of climate, water and diet** can bring on diarrhoea which can be tackled by lots of water and Imodium. One useful tip is to use the body-strengthening powers of garlic and take garlic pearls for 30 days before arriving in India. It's never failed me.

Taking care of what you **eat** and **drink** is important. It's best to avoid tap water and stick to bottled mineral water. When eating out there are basic signs of a clean restaurant but also those most frequented by customers will be more likely to be hygienic. Salads should be avoided for the first week unless you have washed them down with mineral water.

Meat can easily go off and get infected in the heat. The safest bet in this land of rich vegetarian diets is to avoid it altogether. The other option is to order a whole fish or chicken – they're bantam-sized – as it's pretty well guaranteed to have been freshly cooked.

Immunisation against cholera, typhoid, malaria, hepatitis-A and tetanus are generally advised for India. Outbreaks of cholera and malaria are very rare in Kerala. No immunisations are compulsory for India unless you have come from an area infected by yellow fever such as parts of Africa. There is much debate about the effectiveness of the immunisation medicines. Ask your doctor and make up your mind but whatever you do plan well in advance because some immunisation processes must begin well before you enter India.

Bites. Insect repellent will help keep mosquitoes away. Kovalam in the dry season has very few but a bit of rain and they're back. In Kochi and other areas you'll find more. At night the most effective method is to switch on or light a mosquito coil in your room. Mosquito nets are extra bulk but they'll probably give you a more peaceful sleep. Creams and gels are available for when outdoors and also if you get stung.

Dog bites are more serious. Indian dogs are usually very friendly even if stray but they and many monkeys can carry rabies and are best avoided. The danger of snake bites when walking through undergrowth can be limited by wearing shoes, socks and long trousers – not a major problem on the tourist route.

Hospitals in Kerala can be quite good. The problem is getting into a good one in an emergency. Visitors may find themselves rejected even in emergencies and sent to the "poor" hospital which is very poor. In the case of serious illness contact your country's embassy or consulate for aid and if you think someone needs flying home and it's on your insurance policy don't take no for an answer from your insurance company.

Ayurvedic medicine

Ayurveda is the centuries old Vedic herbal medical approach used in many parts of India. Kerala is the home of ayurveda and Kottakal has the famous Aryavaidya Sala college and hospital.

The approach is holistic and bent on overcoming imbalances in body and spirit. It is based on diagnosing the "humours" of the body (wind, mucus, gall and sometimes blood) to achieve a balance. It makes use of 107 extremely sensitive areas (marma) of the body. Ayurveda has classified substances and chemical compounds based on panchabutas, the theory of five key elements. The trick as anywhere is to find genuinely capable doctors and hygienic clinics.

Treatments are available for many medical disorders and for toning and rejuvenating the body. Courses of sustained treatment are offered for periods of up to and sometimes more than a month involving massages with herbal oils and powders, administering of internal medicines, special diets, steam baths, yoga and even dripping oils onto one's forehead. Below is an ayurvedic doctor's description of some of the available treatments.

In pizhichil, lukewarm herbal oils are applied all over the body by two or four trained masseurs in a special rhythmic way continuously for 60 to 90 minutes daily for a period of seven to 21 days. Pizhichil is very useful for Rheumatic diseases like arthritis, paralysis, sexual and nervous weakness and nervous disorders.

In kizhi, herbal leaves and herbs or herbal powders are applied to the whole body in boluses with hot medicated oils for 45 minutes daily for seven to 14 days. This treatment is for osteoarthritis, sports injuries and spondilosis.

Navarakizhi *is a process by which the whole body, or any specific part thereof, is made to perspire by the application of certain medical puddings, applied externally in the form of boluses tied up in a muslin bag. This is applied by two to four masseurs for about 60 to 90 minutes per day for a period of 14 days. This treatment is for all types of rheumatism, pain in the joints, emaciation of limbs, blood pressure, cholesterol and some skin diseases.*

Dhara *involves herbal oils, medicated milk and butter milk etc. being poured on the forehead in a special method for 45 minutes in a day for seven to 21 days. This treatment is mainly for insomnia, mental tension and certain skin diseases.*

In vasthi *certain herbal oils herbal extracts etc. are applied through the rectum daily for five to 21 days. Vasthi is for arthritis, paralysis, numbness, gastric complaints, rheumatism and constant constipation.*

Nasyam *applies herbal juices, medicated oils etc. through the nose for seven to 14 days. It is highly effective for certain kinds of headaches, mental disorders, paralysis and some skin diseases.*

Shnehapanam *administers medicated ghee internally in a proportionately increased quantity for seven to 14 days and is used to combat osteoarthritis, leukaemia etc.*

Rasayana *is a very special Ayurvedic vegetarian diet. A course normally involves a combination of treatments. For example kayakalpa chikilsa is offered as a 28-day body immunisation and longevity programme including pizhichil, nasyam, shnehapanam, rasayana, body massage, medicated steam bath, yoga, medication and several other treatments*

Some of the big hotels offering courses costing up to $1200 include Hotel Samudra *in Kovalam and nearby* Somatheeram Beach Resort *and* Surya Samudra, Taj Garden Retreats *in Varkala and Kottayam. Also in Kottayam, Coconut Lagoon and close to Kozhikode the* Kappad Beach Resort.

Many ayurvedic massage parlours squat in Kovalam where herbal oils are used by masseurs and masseuses. Short courses in massage are given in Kovalam and Varkala. Thiruvananthapuram also has Ayurveda College Hospital (0471-74823) *on MG Road.*

Communication in India and abroad

Time differences

Up till less than a century ago, Kerala kept a different time to all India and most of the world. Now like the rest of India it depends on Greenwich Mean Time (GMT) plus 5.5 hours (BST plus 4.5 hours).

Telephone/fax

Phone calls in India are relatively expensive. **Telephoning abroad** is pretty simple as most areas are now on the ISD/STD network. Outside the towns in rural regions phoning can be more perilous with problems getting through and frequent cut-offs.

The telephone code for India is (00) 91. All towns have ISD/STD booths often in abundance and charging much cheaper rates than the exorbitant rates of the top hotels. The booths are clearly marked with ISD/STD signboards and reveal how much you are being charged as you make the call. Most budget hotels have telephones and many middle range and upwards have telephones in the rooms.

Many ISD/STD booths have **fax** equipment, although the fax signal is not always reliable in confirming that the fax has got through. A follow-up phone call will be useful to confirm your fax has been received. India has a thriving computer industry centred in the "silicon city" of Bangalore, close to Kerala. One in 1,000 Indian homes now have a computer but bad telephone lines limit use of the **Internet**.

Posting

Sending a **postcard** abroad means attaching stamps for Rs6 for an **airmail** letter Rs11. These stamps will buy a meal in India and they and their letter may disappear, so pre-stamped airmail letters are more likely to get through. Posting from rural regions can be haphazard sometimes taking much longer but considering the size of the country India has a very good postal system.

Recently a television programme revealed that a government centre in Delhi processes all incoming mail for sensitive material which may explain some unusual delays. Postcards sent within India require a Rs1 stamp. Minimum charge for a letter is Rs6.

Parcels go by **parcel post** unless they are books or printed matter which go at a cheaper rate by book post. Most parcels must be wrapped and stitched up in cotton cloth and sealed with a non-duplicable wax. The stitching can be done cheaply at a tailors. If they cannot do the waxing, a service is often available outside the post office where the parcel should be taken. At the post office two forms must be filled in and one attached to the parcel. Leave enough time for this long-winded but secure process. Parcels marked gift are charged less. Taking antiques over 100 years old out of India is forbidden.

 **Travel Options**

Though people have been known to scan the teletext on the Thursday and opt for a charter flight leaving the following Sunday, travelling to India fully prepared normally takes more thought.

Visas

The first thing you will need is permission to enter the country. Unless you have an Indian passport that means getting a visa stamped in your passport by officials at an Indian Embassy, High Commission or Consulate. Visas are generally issued without a problem. Tourist visas are available for periods of three months and six months and business visas for one year and up to 5 years.

Visas allow residence in India for a set period from the date of issue of the visa – so be careful of applying too long before your trip. Requesting a multiple entry visa saves hassle if you want to pop over to Sri Lanka or a nearby country and return to India.

Short stays will require a six month tourist visa costing £19. One year visas cost £32 and five year visas, £64. Acquiring a visa requires presenting the Indian visa office with a passport application form, three photos, your passport and cash or a postal order. Application forms are available from the visa issuing offices or from local travel agents.

Postal applications with a crossed postal order should be sent recorded delivery with a stamped, addressed, recorded-delivery envelope for the applicant's returned passport. Things can go missing and don't expect the officials to contact you in the event of a problem. Visas are normally returned by post within five working days. If your passport has not been received within a week it may be that it's been divorced from the recorded envelope, as happened once to me, and is then left to fester.

The quicker, surer but more expensive option is to make a visit to the Embassy, High Commission or Consulate and queue up. The Indian High Commission in London is very quick. You can have your visa back the same day if you wait around. The Birmingham and Glasgow Consulates are slower but you can still collect your visa the following day.

I'd been to India every year for four years and it was expensive, annually taking time off work and travelling to Birmingham. I requested a five-year visa for the future. I was told, no five year visa until I had had a one-year visa. So he gave me a one year visa and said try next year.

Five-year visas are available but more expensive and more discretionary for those with business dealings with India.

Useful Addresses

High Commission of India
India House
Aldwych,
London WC2B 4NA

(Tel. 0171 834 8484)

Consulate General of India
19 Augusta House
Jewellery Quarter
Birmingham B18 6DS

(Tel. 0121 212 2782)

Consulate General of India
6th floor, Flemming House
134 Renfrew Street
Glasgow G3 7ST
(Tel. 0141 331 0666)

Embassy of India
6 Lesson Park, Dublin 6
(Tel. [00] 3531 497 0843)

All offices are open for visa applications
Monday to Friday 9.30am to 12 pm.

Visa Extensions

Visitors who want to stay on in India after their visa has expired must secure an extension. However these are rarely given. They are available from the Office of the Commissioner of Police in Kerala's main towns and may take ten days to return. The other more successful way of staying on is to take out a new three or six month visa by going to the Indian Embassy/Consulate in Sri Lanka. The Colombo embassy may take ten days to process your application but a pleasant rail trip to the Buddhist temple city of Kandy will secure a visa from the consulate within 24 hours.

Flying to Kerala

That Kerala attracts less than 10 per cent of the international tourist trade arriving in Goa has partly been due to the difficult, often expensive ways of getting there by air. Whereas Goa is close to the key international airport at Mumbai (Bombay), with its plentiful relatively cheap flights, getting to Thiruvanathapuram Airport has required a long stopover waiting for an ongoing flight.

British charter companies *Manos*, *Somak* and *Inspirations* now offer a direct flight every Sunday between November and May. The flight takes 11 hours with a stop at Bahrain's duty free. Travellers to date have reported that the plane is very cramped but it's the quickest option around. Last minute offers in newspapers and on teletext can be as low as £199. However for stays longer than four weeks, the flight only (dormitory) option may prove more expensive than taking a scheduled airline.

Scheduled flights tend to be more expensive but are more flexible than the charters for extending or cutting short one's stay. Gulf Air currently run five weekly flights, all involving a change of planes in the Gulf. They have only one weekly flight (via **Doha** and **Muscat**) back to London/Europe. Kuwait Air has four flights (change in Kuwait) arriving and departing weekly from Heathrow. Kuwait Air does not serve alcohol on its planes but permits alcohol to be taken aboard. Smoking is permitted on all current international airlines flying to Kerala.

Gulf Air and Kuwait Air run other regular services to **London** and **Europe** through their respective bases in **Abu Dhabi** and **Kuwait**. Passengers required to stay for sometime at an airport en-route can request free accommodation and a meals voucher. The transit hotels are of a good standard.

Air India put on flights daily from London and twice-weekly from **Manchester** "direct" to **Mumbai/Bombay** (picking up in **Rome** and **Delhi**). They also fly to Mumbai from **Paris, Frankfurt, Geneva** and **Zurich**. The beauty of travelling with them is that the onward domestic flight to **Thiruvanathapuram** is thrown in with no extra charge. The problem is the onward connections from Mumbai may not be for 16 hours so a trip into Mumbai is an option. Flights from Manchester to Mumbai and Delhi leave on Monday and Friday afternoons. Mumbai to Manchester flights leave at noon on Mondays and on Thursday mornings.

Accommodation in Mumbai is expensive by any standards. Air India sometimes put passengers up at their plush transit $180/night Hotel Centaur by Juhu Beach. If you can't afford that much take the free Hotel Centaur bus to the hotel. Two minutes to the hotel's right is the Rs1100 Juhu Hotel which has the bonus of its swinging Bollywood late night Rhinoceros Bar where, residents apart, men unaccompanied by women are barred. Next morning wake up and take breakfast and a dip in the Hotel Centaur's pool.

Air India and Indian Airlines have daily planes from Mumbai to Thiruvananthapuram and Indian Airlines a daily flight from Delhi to Thiruvananthapuram.

Another more expensive option is to fly in via **Colombo Airport**, just a $60 ride away in Sri Lanka. Entry into Sri Lanka does not ordinarily require a visa and many visitors combine a trip to the island with their Kerala holiday. British Airways and Air Lanka operate frequent services to Colombo where Air Lanka and Indian Airlines have daily flights to Thiruvananthapuram. British Airways also have regular flights to **Chennai/Madras** in Tamil Nadu from whence daily flights operate to Thiruvananthapuram.

For those wishing to link a trip to Kerala with visiting **Thailand**, Air India now operates a twice weekly direct flight from Thiruvananthapuram to **Bangkok**. Air India also operates flights direct to **Singapore, Tokyo** and **Riyadh** and have routes linking Kerala with **Melbourne, Sydney** and **Cairo**.

Air India have offices in London (0171 491 7979), Manchester (0161 236 3958) and Birmingham (0121 643 7421).

Trains and Buses from other parts of India

Many people arrive in Kerala after a trip to "hard India". Getting to India's southern tip is easy by plane with Air India, Indian Airlines and Jet Airways having daily flights from the main cities. However domestic flights are relatively expensive (Mumbai-Thiruvananthapuram one way around Rs5000). Taking the train is a much cheaper and more pleasant option for those who have time.

Express trains from Mumbai (45 hours) via Bangalore (18 hours) to Thiruvananthapuram include the Trivandrum Express and Kanyakumari Express. The Kerala Express train runs daily from Delhi (52 hours) via Agra, Bhopal and Nagpur. The Himasagar Express train travels weekly from Jammu Tawi in Kashmir (three days). A weekly train goes to Kochi from Varanasi (Benares) and a thrice-weekly train from Hyderabad to Kochi and regular trains arrive in Kochi and Thiruvananthapuram from Madras.

An air-conditioned sleeper (AC SL) is probably the most comfortable way to travel. Prices of AC SL tickets are Mumbai Rs1458, New Delhi Rs1920, Madras Rs791, Varanasi Rs1920 and Bangalore Rs759.

Travelling by Train

Travelling on India's vast rail network is one of the best ways of getting a glimpse of the huge variety and richness of this country's life. The 52 hour journey from Delhi was for me a voyage of gentle introduction to a vast sub-continent of palaces and sprawling slums, industry and pastures, desert and jungle, mountain and swamp and the *chai-wallah*!

Arriving in the stations the trains are beset by chai-wallahs selling tea from urns for a handful of rupees. They do good welcome business during the day but when the train pulls in at 3 am and the passengers are fast asleep, they put out an eerie forlorn cry for business, "Chaieee! Chaieee!". Waking up, it's almost like you've arrived to cross Hades.

Crossing the rugged Western Ghats into Kerala is a magnificent experience. Throughout central India, dust and semi-aridity throw up pastel shades in the fierce sun but once that train hits the Ghats at dawn and rushes down to Kochi the environment undergoes a magical metamorphosis; bright colours uncowed by the sun, scarlet reds, emerald greens, regal blues, yellows, olivine's all splendidly clashing and embracing. For two days you've been studying India, patiently observing the fields and apprehensively watching the train cross monstrous rivers using thin string line bridges. Suddenly studying is over and wonder is all – and shock – that a land could be so blissfully exotic.

Leaving India

Leaving India from an airport requires paying a Departure Tax currently set at

Rs750. If you're flying out of Kerala remember to confirm your flight at least 72 hours beforehand.

> *I had confirmed my flight one week before. It was a domestic flight connecting with a flight to Manchester. I got to the airport 70 minutes before the departure time only to be told the plane had left half an hour previously.*
>
> *"You should read the papers. It was announced on Thursday!!"*

If confirming much before that, phone again 24 hours before departure time just to check your flight has not been changed. Normal international duty-free allowances apply. If you have any rupees left remember you need your Encashment Certificates to exchange them for foreign currency.

How to get around Kerala

Taxis and auto-rickshaws

The attractive 1950s Austin Cambridge type Ambassador taxis are the most convenient way of getting around and quite cheap if there are four passengers in the car. Rates in Kochi are Rs3.75 per km. Kovalam rates are higher. Taxis are usually fixed with a fan or air conditioning and will take you wherever you request. The key is to be exact about where you want to be, check the likely fare and if you don't trust the meter or the driver won't use it, negotiate a prior price.

The taxis offer an excellent and very flexible method for touring around. However, if heading for the Malabar coast it's pleasanter to take the train up then taxi round.

Auto-rickshaws are generally referred to as rickshaws in Kerala because hand and cycle rickshaws are thankfully not in use. Travelling in an auto-rickshaw, a diesel-powered three-wheeled scooter carrying a flimsy covered seat for two, can be fun and very cheap. Three can squeeze in and they're handy to nip in and out of when shopping in town. With no doors, they guarantee plenty of fresh air unless you're stuck in traffic when fumes abound.

Tower Hamlets council in London have considered introducing the "tuk-tuk" to London. In summer they'd be popular for nipping in and out of the traffic. In winter their drivers would be too cold to kick start the engine. The rickshaw cannot travel very fast on the open road but their manoeuvrability can make them quicker than taxis in the city. London drivers aren't as philosophical as the wacky Indian rickshaw drivers who while bobbing in and out of the traffic experience at least a dozen near misses every day without ever raising their voice or showing alarm.

Kovalam rickshaw prices are the highest in India but the drivers argue they only have November to May to make their living from the foreign visitors. Prices elsewhere are Rs3 per kilometre.

Buses

Buses are the cheapest way of being ferried around. They're often very packed and the long distance drivers career around like maniacs. Getting a seat can be the biggest problem so one of you might have to guard your luggage while the other joins the charge for a seat. It's not unknown for people to dive in through the windows to secure their place. Watch your pockets for light fingers.

A bus from Thiruvananthapuram to Kollam costs just Rs21 and a bus for the 18km to Kovalam less than Rs4 (eight pence).

The main long-distance bus company is the Kerala State Road Transport Corporation (KSRTC), who have booking facilities at their stations (stands). Private buses also operate and it's a case of booking for long journeys and just turning up. for shorter journeys. The Karnataka and Tamil Nadu State Corporations also run buses in and out of Kerala from Bangalore, Mysore, Mangalore, Kanyakumari, Madurai, Madras and Coimbatore.

Car, Motorbike, Scooter and Bicycle Hire

Motor bikes and scooters are available for hire here and the former English, now Indian-made, Enfield motor bike is a favourite with biker visitors. Cars are only available for self-drive from Hertz cars. Whether driving a car or riding a bike it should remembered that India's roads witness 1,000 deaths each week. Many of those killed are in two- or three-wheeled vehicles. An International Driving Licence (IDL) is not compulsory but without one the police may get heavy demanding *baksheesh* before allowing you to continue your onward journey.

Trains

Trains offer a slower but more comfortable means of travelling around the state. An indication of the length of journeys involved can be taken from the fact that Kerala's northern border is a 14-hour rail journey away from Thiruvananthapuram in the south. That's pretty short by Indian standards but a rush if you've only got a week in the area.

Trains run all the way up the coast from Kanyakumari to the northern border. In the north they run from Kochi, north-east through Thrissur, to Palakkad on the edge of the Western Ghats. In the south, trains run eastwards up to Punalor beneath the Southern Ghats.

Getting a train ticket requires a trip well in advance (though not more than a month) before travelling. Trains are often packed and you may end up on the Waiting List, which means an anxious wait to see if you're name is on the list to travel. If you're less than 20th on the Waiting List you're almost certain to be on and the booking office can tell you.

The alternative is to apply for being put on the "Tourist Quota" of seats specially set aside for international visitors. At Thiruvananthapuram tourists applying must go to a special desk in the booking office. If all else fails go to the manager, explain your story of the importance of your journey politely and he will do his best to find you a seat.

When booking you will need your passport. Pay in rupees. If you pay in traveller's cheques it can take forever as a man sits and writes out forms in triplicate! If you're travelling a short distance during the day you can turn up, and chance your arm to get a seat or place on the train. For Rs20 a porter will virtually assure you of one. One way of avoiding all the booking hassle is to pay a travel agent Rs50 or so for the pleasure of them taking the matter out of your hands. Of course you may not get exactly what you want but it saves time.

There are several classes of ticket. Air-conditioned sleeper (AC SL) is more expensive than first class (often not available) and both entitle the ticket holder to a sleeping birth to stretch out on. The usual arrangement is two ground and two upper berths. Those with physical disabilities should make sure they specify what level berth they require, otherwise the upper berth is handy because it means you can have sleep and relative privacy when required.

Second-class sleeper should also get you a berth but is likely to be fuller. It's probably OK for travelling within Kerala. Train travellers here are a pretty affable bunch and you may end up with someone sharing their lunch with you, playing cards or telling you about their family.

Where possible take a mail or express train. They are slow but the other trains are even slower with interminable, seemingly inexplicable stops. You won't need a blanket in Kerala but taking a book, mineral water and toilet roll is a good idea. If you're taking luggage, lock it up and padlock it firmly to something in the compartment – it will reduce the temptation to lift your property.

Tour Itineraries

If you don't want to laze by the beach and opt to see Kerala, there are several different routes one can take. KTDC (reservations 0471-330031) run day-tours very cheaply by bus. They also do tours involving overnight stays from **Kochi/Thiruvananthapuram** to **Periyar Wildlife Sanctuary** (one night, Rs300).

Other KTDC tours (prices exclusive of food and accommodation) from Thiruvananthapuram include;

Kodaikanal Tour (two nights, Rs500) via Periyar and Madurai;

Rameswaram (holy city) **Tour** (three nights, Rs500) via Kanyakumari and Madurai;

Mookambika Tour (four nights, Rs1500) via Kodungallor and Guruvayoo;

Bangalore Tour (Six nights and Rs1500) via Mallampuzha, Ooty/Udhagamandalam, Mysore and Madurai.

The British package tour companies Manos, Somak and Inspirations also do more expensive, slightly more comfortable, accommodation-inclusive tours to *Bangalore, Madurai*, and *Backwaters*. The problem with the KTDC and package tours is being shunted on and not having time to explore. Travel by bus is also not very comfortable. Alternatively one can organise one's own itinerary, hire a taxi or go by public transport.

A popular route from Kovalam is **Wooden Palace - Nagergercoil - Kanyakumari - Madurai - Kodaikanal - Periyar - Backwaters - Kovalam** (Rs5000 for five day's taxi). Best to leave six days to enjoy Periyar.

Kovalam - Periyar - Backwaters/Kochi - Kozhikode - Guruvayoor temples - Thrissur will take at least six days for a sampler of Malabar.

Better to take a train/bus up to Kozhikode then travel **Kappad Beach - Thalassery - Muzhappilangad - Kannur - Bekal Beach- Wynad Forest - Kozhikode** taking at least five days.

Kochi - Backwaters - Munnar - Kodaikanal - Periyar offers a cool hill station alternative taking at least five days.

More adventurous visitors might look at going from Kochi through Cheruthuruthi (Kathakali School) up to Malampuzha before going on to Silent Valley Sanctuary returning to Kochi via Guruvayoor's temples and its nearby Ponnani beaches.

Kerala Tourist Development Corporation (KTDC)

Kerala Tourist Development Corporation (KTDC) is a government overseen company in operation for over 35 years which has principal responsibility for attracting and aiding the 100,000 international visitors who annually arrive in Kerala. KTDC has the state's largest hotel and tourist network. KTDC's operations include running its many basic to luxury hotels, motels, resorts, Backwater cruises, coach tours, tourist information offices and the promotion of Kerala as a holiday destination.

In the 250-year-old Bolgatty Palace and the Maharaja's former Periyar hunting lodge, Aranya Nivas, KTDC own two of Kerala's most exotic residences. KTDC has tourist information and reception centres in the main cities and they are ready to advise on most tourists' needs. Without their aid this guide would not have been possible.

KTDC Tourist Reception Centres are at:

Hotel Chaitram (0471-330031) close to the central bus station on Station Road.

TRC (0484-353234) Shanmugham Road, Ernakulam/Kochi near the main boat jetty.

Malabar Mansions (0495-65391), SM Street, Kozhikode

KTDC Tourist Information Centres are at;

Thiruvananthapuram Domestic and International Airports (0471-451085).

KSRTC Bus Stand, Thiruvananthapuram (0471-67224).

New Delhi (011-3316541).

Chennai (Madras) (044-8279862).

The KTDC central office is based behind its Hotel Mascot in Mascot Square, Thiruvananthapuram (0471-438976, fax 0471-434406). Central Reservations (KTDC Ltd, Mascot Square, Thiruvananthapuram 695 033) can be written to or faxed and phoned on the above numbers for help in booking accommodation and tours.

KTDC should not be confused with the Indian Tourist Development Corporation which has an office in Kochi close to the Malabar Hotel on Willingdon Island (0484-668352).

For Further Tourist Information Contact:

Government of India Tourist Office, 7 Cork Street, London W1X 2AB
(Tel. 0171 437 3677)

For further aid in India contact:

British High Commission, Shanti Path, Chanakyapuri, New Delhi,
India 110 021
(Tel. 690371)

British Deputy High Commissions are also in Mumbai (Bombay), Chennai (Madras) and Calcutta.

House boat on the Backwaters

Starting Out **Kovalam**

Whether arriving on the train from the north of India or jetting into the state capital's airport in **Thiruvananthapuram** (Trivandrum), a good bet is to take a cab or auto-rickshaw to Kovalam, 60 km from India's southernmost tip.

Both the domestic and international airports are small and easy to exit. Each has an official taxi kiosk inside the airport close to the exit where one can order a taxi (Rs150/175 for the 18km, 10 mile journey). It saves the hassle of haggling with the hordes of drivers waiting outside who in any case will rarely give you a cheaper price. Alternatively take a bus into Thiruvananthapuram to **East Fort** then another to Kovalam and you will be set back Rs6.

Kovalam with its bountiful facilities built up over the last 25 years, mainly to cater for western backpackers, is often called 'light India'. It's a beach resort until recently frequented by backpackers travelling throughout the subcontinent who found in Kovalam a place to rest from some of the stresses of their travels. Today Kovalam is a useful base camp for those travelling into India.

Many people find that Kovalam provides all they need for a relaxing warm, sunny holiday. Others who wish to sample India's rich cultures and exotic landscapes find it an ideal location from which to assimilate the climate and culture then step out into the rest of Kerala, especially after a long intercontinental flight or the cross-continental train journey. The lapping waves, gold/black sands and light sea breeze which wafts the palm trees, form a cradle of sublime relaxation. It's a good idea to book at least your first night in Kerala here if you are new to India.

Kovalam's Beaches

When I first sat down at a table by the beach, with the sun blazing down on the coconut trees and jade blue sea, I smiled, shook my head and murmured, "Paradise, paradise".

Kovalam has been variously described as one of India's finest beaches, India's best beach, tropical heaven and, yes, paradise. Kovalam is actually not one but a series of beaches each with different ranges of facilities and privacy. Those

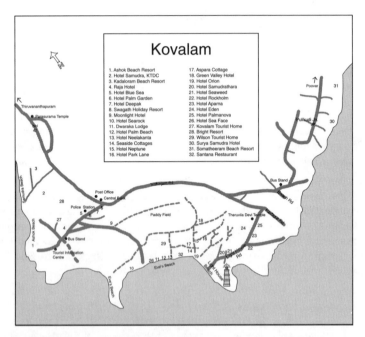

Kovalam

1. Ashok Beach Resort
2. Hotel Samudra, KTDC
3. Kadaloram Beach Resort
4. Raja Hotel
5. Hotel Blue Sea
6. Hotel Palm Garden
7. Hotel Deepak
8. Swagath Holiday Resort
9. Moonlight Hotel
10. Hotel Searock
11. Dwaraka Lodge
12. Hotel Palm Beach
13. Hotel Neelakanta
14. Seaside Cottages
15. Hotel Neptune
16. Hotel Park Lane

17. Aspara Cottage
18. Green Valley Hotel
19. Hotel Orion
20. Hotel Samudrathara
21. Hotel Seaweed
22. Hotel Rockholm
23. Hotel Aparna
24. Hotel Eden
25. Hotel Palmanova
26. Hotel Sea Face
27. Kovalam Tourist Home
28. Bright Resort
29. Wilson Tourist Home
30. Surya Samudra Hotel
31. Somatheeram Beach Resort
32. Santana Restaurant

visitors who find they need more privacy than on the busy Lighthouse beach can find their own beach 15-minutes walk away which they can share with the fishermen and their attendant cawing crows.

Kerala boasts many even finer beaches but if one is to discover them Kovalam is a good place to begin. Travellers beware! In Kovalam, they say: "Your feet grow roots in the sand."

Lighthouse Beach

Of course, it wasn't the backpackers who first discovered Kovalam. Long ago Kerala's Maharajahs would use Kovalam for bathing and as a summer retreat, particularly at what is now known as Lighthouse Beach. Strip away in your mind's eye the modern additions to the shoreline and you can understand why.

Lighthouse Beach is beautifully set with palm trees dotted on the headlands to the south, which hosts the lighthouse, and north where a 20 to 40 metre stretch of fine gold and black sand arches around the bay, only interspersed by a rocky promontory which offers a smaller stretch of beach at the north end. Behind the shoreline a thick carpet of green is woven by the coconut palms beneath which nestle the ramshackle array of restaurants, hotels, guest houses, massage parlours and shops catering for visitors.

Here one can sit from dawn till dusk contemplating the eternal onrush of waves crashing then lapping the shore as the Arabian Sea dumps its loads carried over thousands of miles. At first light a few fishing boats are still out rowing their way home after a night's fishing trip. Others are moored in the bay as divers dressed only in their loin cloths breach the waters in search of prawns and mussels. Stood on the rocks that jut into the middle of the bay are the silhouettes of two men linefishing with long rods made from bamboo cane.

Lighthouse Beach may be a resort attracting international tourists but the trades carried out here for a thousand years go on in the fashion of old. Fishing boats are often dugout canoes or a simple assortment of four bits of wood, lashed together with coir rope and pushed out to sea.

On the beach half a dozen lean looking men, bearded or at the minimum moustached, stand around in traditional Kerala working clothes - the *lunghi* (worn as a wrap-around like a skirt), a shirt and large sheets of cloth tied around their heads as sweat bands. One has updated – he wears a baseball cap. They are watching a man who is holding a taut coir rope which disappears into the sea.

Soon more men will come and each takes his post grasping the rope ready to begin hauling in the nets which have been in the sea overnight. With much chanting and singing they will start the long heaves to bring in the catch. They are quite happy for you to join in but be careful. If they are using nylon ropes your soft unweathered hands can get cut if they are not protected.

Now five young men are splashing the waters and making deep whooping sounds that seem like they've come from beneath the sea itself. This is no strange exotic ritual. They will swim out there in the waters for 30 minutes and more, driving fish into the nets. Now another ten or so men haul in the rope connected to the other end of the net and soon the two groups are converging until, with a rush of interest, the catch of mainly tuna fish comes ashore to be distributed amongst the toilers or sold off to the local restaurateurs who might venture to make an offer and add their purchase to the night's menu.

Some locals are not rushing to get involved in the action. Their silhouettes can be seen on the headlands or rocks gazing out across the mesmerising blue ocean, no doubt meditating on life's conundrums. From behind the beach comes the constant "caws" of the cheeky crows. Listen carefully and you will hear one of these birds break off imitating its friends and begin whooping or singing. It is the even cheekier Mynah bird. A cock struts about having announced the dawn and rarely, but very rarely, you'll see a bright green cane snake slithering its way home after a night's work.

More noise on the beach. The lifeguards have arrived to carry out their morning exercises. Centuries ago a British traveller through India saw a group of inhabitants on a beach waving their arms about, leaping and squatting. He concluded that he had seen some strange mumbo jumbo worship. In fact, he had seen an Indian keep-fit course which, had their been videos around, would have ensured Jane Fonda never got a look in.

Swimming

The waters are generally clean and warm in the season, a friend's thermometer showed the temperature to be 24C. No dangerous fish lurk except a spherical small spiky fish which is poisonous and should be avoided. **Surfing** is possible, though the waves break a little too early for really good surfing. I have seen a man ride the waves standing on board for ten seconds but most swimmers content themselves with body surfing or hire small surfboards from the local shops. **Boats** of many shapes and sizes are also available for hire. **Snorkelling** is possible and equipment is available. Prices are negotiable.

The sea may look calm and be generally safe to swim in but occasionally a 12 foot high wave can catch bathers unaware and turn them right over dumping them on the beach. Those who prefer calmer waters might try the northern end of the beach where the smaller bay restricts the size of the waves. The other peril is a dangerous rip-tide which lurks further out and which the lifeguards are trained to spot. Caught in it, all but the very strongest of swimmers can be dragged out to sea.

The lifeguards are there to ensure that sea bathers can enjoy the water whilst being protected from its menaces. When they post out red flags on a section of the beach it is to warn that swimming is too dangerous in that area. When they blow their whistles it is to direct sea bathers to a safer stretch of water. They do not think highly of those who ignore them – after all it is the lifeguards who will have to risk their lives to rescue those who get into trouble. They are called into action twice a week.

Three or four times a year the lifeguards are unsuccessful. It is important to note that in the monsoon season, generally late May to early August, the sea covers the whole beach and swimming is not possible. August is the time when the keen surfers arrive. If you decide on a more relaxed swim you can always pay the Rs120 charge to use the swimming pool on the beach at Hotel Sea Face or pay more at the hotels on other beaches.

Sun Bathing

By 8am any morning mist has cleared. If you have accommodation on the beach you can virtually roll out of bed and start sunbathing as the sun is beaming down and has already hoisted the temperature to 25C. A man is putting up parasols along the beach. You might be prepared to pay the Rs50/100 day charge when the sun rises higher in the sky. Alternatively you can take a 15 second stroll to the shade provided by any of the two-dozen restaurants that sit immediately adjacent to the beach.

Do beware of the sun when you first arrive. The light sea breeze which cools the air fools many people as to the intensity of the sun and by the end of the day they look like sore, red lobsters. Topless and nude bathing is frowned upon and too-liberal displays of flesh will invite groups of strolling Indian tourists to gaze at the semi-naked white flesh that would never be allowed to grace their village. Neither should there be surprise should a restaurateur request scantily dressed bathers wishing to sit in his restaurant to cover themselves up. Apart from being polite, it saves any discomfort for Indian visitors, male or female.

All day long during the season a parade of beach sellers trudge the beach hawking their wares – cigarettes, gaudy speckled cotton and silk *lunghis*, beach mats, blankets, trinkets, ornaments, wood carvings, buffalo hide drums, rosewood chess sets, delicate leaf paintings and most famously the fruit ladies smiling and shouting: "Mango? Pineapple? Banana? Papaya?" Do be careful at first. One English woman was asked to pay Rs400 for a slice of papaya. She wasn't hungry and eventually the asking price fell to Rs10. A less fortunate lady paid out Rs150 for two mangoes and a pineapple which she could have picked up for less than Rs20.

Haggling with a smile saves money and irritation. And, if you don't want anything just follow the rule: No Eye Contact, and generally they will leave you alone. Sometimes you might find the attention annoying but I always remember those days when I was lying on the beach dying for someone to come along with some fruit or cigarettes or a cheap *lunghi* I could use to lay on the beach and protect me from the scorching sand.

"It's not like Spine (Spain)," commented an apparently disappointed middle-aged woman from London. I thankfully had to agree, observing that Spain's overcrowded and expensive beaches were over 4,000 miles away. Kerala is another culture which the Spanish hardly touched and the international tourist industry is in its infancy, conveying a freshness, even primitiveness, that Spain has long since lost. India remains a very poor country. International visitors gain from the cheapness of its wares and the glory of its ancient cultures so it is worth respecting the people and its cultures and tolerating some of the deficiencies.

Daytime Entertainment

No one-arm bandits and casinos here. Nevertheless one can hear western rock or pop music being played in some of the restaurants throughout the day. If you have a favourite cassette and take it along, you are pretty sure to get it played whether it is classical music or hip hop.

Signs advertising saunas, steam baths and massage parlours abound. A one-hour massage can cost as little as Rs150. The massage method here utilises ayurvedic (herbal) oils rubbing their soothing powers into the skin. Masseurs and masseuses are available. Ask around and you'll soon latch on to somebody else's favourite. It all depends on what you like. Above the exchange centre at **Wilson Tourist Home** is a clean almost professional set up with hot water available to wash off that clinging oil at the end of that hour of bodily indulgence.

KOVALAM

The friendly Mr Prabhu and Dr Santosh run **Amritha Health Resort** behind Seaside Cottages. A massage at Amritha's can be taken for as little as Rs150 as part of a medical or relaxation course but unless your hotel is nearby you will need to take a steam bath at the end as the massage parlour, constructed with thatched palm leaves, has no shower. Yoga classes are also well advertised. Again the best advice is to ask and shop around for your own taste and budget.

Shopping

There are also a good variety of shops on the beach. Here you can browse round shops selling blankets, goods, jewellery and ornaments mainly from Kashmir, Rajasthan or Nepal. Most popular and useful are the **tailors** producing handmade cotton and silk clothes to your instruction or design. A good haggle and shopping around will give you a price you would never dream of in Europe. Some of the stitching can be poor so check your purchases fully before you hand over the cash. Otherwise you can sort it out when you get home. Mr. Nagendran's **King Tailoring Shop** by the rickshaw stand behind Sea Rock Hotel is one of the best on the beach. For Rs1000 he will make a gown out of pure silk that in England you would be ready to pay Rs9000.

Shops also sell bags of spices one might wish to take home. There are little shacks selling the day to day things one might need – in general way over the prices charged outside Kovalam. But is it really worth going all that way into the city to buy tooth-paste, toilet roll, batteries, razors, pens, soap etc.?

From time to time itinerant entertainers pass along the beach. King of them all is a sunglasses seller with black swept-back hair and sunglasses shielding his eyes, an array of sunglasses also hang down from his khaki suit.

Every day 'Sunglass Man', who hails from the next village traipses the beach. For years he has turned, with a pleasant smile and his sunglasses in hand, to face his potential customers and chime in a high pitched squeaky voice: "Me sunglasses! Me sun coconut oil! Many, many colours, cheap price!" And if no sale is forthcoming to bid adieu with an "OK see you later, byeee!" Without doubt he is the most photographed man in Kovalam even gracing the brochures of two British package tour operators. Nowadays it seems he makes more money from donations for his act than from the sale of his sunglasses. Then there are the palm and tarot readers – harmless enough. Just make sure you negotiate a price beforehand.

Beach Entertainers

"Look!", cried one first time visitor to India as she sat in a restaurant observing the beach, "there's one of them cow things!" She had seen the top of an elephant brought along by its *mahout* carer for the amusement of the tourists. A placid female "cow" elephant, she will kneel and give a ride to any taker and at Rs100 a ride on her coarse bare hide, it's good value for an unforgettable experience on the world's finest mammal.

Fire swallowers and young circus performers occasionally arrive. Kerala's nimble people provide most of the acrobats for India's circuses and just now and then on the beach you will see a quite amazing display of balance and daring.

Kovalam Village Fair

January 14 to January 23 each year brings on the Kovalam Village Fair when an entire traditional Kerala village from centuries ago is recreated in a hamlet near Kovalam. Period dress, cuisine, arts and crafts are displayed.

Near-Empty Beaches

Beyond Lighthouse beach there are plenty of near-empty beaches to explore. Take a walk behind the line of hotels into the paddy fields and among the banana plants or branch off to the north of the road to the Samudra and you will pass through semi-jungle to the beautiful peace of the **Blue Lagoon** with its exotic bird and plant life. Alternatively there are plenty of places of interest to visit (see Around Kovalam, page 67) by taxi, rickshaw or bus. The state capital, **Thiruvananthapuram** (Trivandrum), is just a 20-minute, Rs3 bus ride away.

Kovalam is not just Lighthouse Beach. There are five good beaches nearby where one can swap the extensive facilities of Lighthouse Beach for peace and quiet interrupted only by the crashing waves and the chatter of the crows.

Ashok Beach is a private beach run by the ITDC for guests at the *Ashoka Hotel.* It is quiet and secluded and just a five-minute walk from the hotel. Most people prefer to use the excellent swimming pool in the hotel grounds.

Samudra Beach is so called because it is dominated by the KTDC's excellent *Hotel Samudra.* This beach is not private but, a fifteen minute walk or Rs50 ride northwards from Lighthouse Beach, it is virtually free of pestering beach sellers. The first little bay is edged by small rocky promontories. The same warning about swimming applies. Then past the Hotel Samudra is a long narrow stretch of palm fringed beach which, even though it extends as far as the eye can see, sports a solitary *chai* shop and the occasional fisherman.

Rockholm Beach is accessible either via a track leading down from the Rockholm Hotel (and Palmshore Hotel), or alternatively by walking southwards from Lighthouse Beach over the headland on which the lighthouse stands. Swimming is possible and once again bathers are left virtually in peace. There is a similar bay slightly further south.

Cafe life

But for many people the time spent out of the sun is spent chatting away over a coffee, a beer or a pineapple juice in one of the restaurants. Kerala people are friendly as are most of the visitors and Kovalam generates its own little cafe society where politics, philosophy, sport and global travel experiences get chewed over in an incessant wheel of multilingual tongue-wagging and hand-waving till dusk draws near and it is time for *pooja*.

> **Pooja** *is the twice daily ritual that takes place all over India which is essentially a cleansing and refreshening exercise. Floors are swept and cleaned and water sprinkled around which helps settle the dust. Incense is burnt and jasmine is strung up giving the air a sweet-perfumed scent and offerings are made to particular gods.*

KOVALAM

Evenings

After 6pm many visitors take their places on the rocks, on the beach or in the open air restaurants to watch the evening spectacle, the Kovalam sunset, a breathtaking kaleidoscope that in 45 minutes turns the sky from blue through every imaginable array of colours finally to a star-studded black.

Eating Out

Dining out is the principal evening activity and Kovalam is a must for those enjoying fresh fish. The early morning's catch is displayed on tables at each restaurant allowing diners to select which fish or portion of it they would like to eat. **Santana** restaurant generally mounts the biggest display: shark, swordfish, barracuda, sear fish, butter fish, king fish, white snapper, red snapper, pomfret, squid, prawns, tiger prawns and sea salmon line up a gourmet's delight. Fish is most commonly prepared in the tandoori oven here but you can request the way you wish your meal to be prepared and frying helps the fish to arrive in its full succulence.

The fare provided on Lighthouse Beach has undoubtedly been shaped by two to three decades of catering for backpackers using the beach as a resting hole on their travels round India. Most of the food provided is designed to be amenable to the western pallet. Many of the items appearing on the menu were actually created by intrepid travellers invading the kitchens and demonstrating how their favourite dish could be made. Spaghetti Napolitaine, pizzas, tagliatelle, rosti, egg chips and baked beans, porridge, apple strudel and pancakes all appear somewhere on a menu. In Kovalam you can find food cooked to most styles you might wish - South Indian, Moghul, Chinese, European, Vegetarian. The quality might vary but here are some tips.

Try different styles and remember, generally the chef will cook to your specific wishes. It is in your hands how well-cooked you want your fish, how spicy, what sauce etc. If the chef can do it he will. Try different restaurants.

For **breakfast** the **German Bakery** is popular for those who would like something akin to German bread or a breakfast of egg, baked beans and toast and

European-style coffee. It is also popular for those who love its cakes – apple strudel, chocolate cake, banana cake etc. The rooftop restaurant on the second floor is wafted by a cool breeze and gives a panoramic view of the beach. Prices are slightly more expensive than other restaurants but they are not German prices and unfortunately the restaurant doesn't live up to reputed German efficiency and cleanliness. The *Hotel Samudra* puts on a good *masala dosa* for those who want to try Indian cuisine but you may have to combine a visit with your early morning stroll.

For **lunch** and **dinner** vegetarians enjoying Indian cuisine often make their way to the *Lonely Planet* restaurant (no link to the guide book). Situated behind the Surya and close to the paddy fields, the restaurant's surroundings – sometimes snakes are visible sliding through the paddy – give a healthy ambiance for some good cheap Indian food with *thalis*, *masala dosas*, spinach and *paneer* dishes for less than Rs50 a time.

But for Indian food the best value for money on Lighthouse Beach has to be the tiny **Sudhi House** above Green Valley. All the cooking is done by the lady of the house, Shanta. Orders for breakfast (Rs10) and dinner (Rs25) have to be given the day before so that the food can be bought in. Dinner is always at 7pm, just after sunset. The menu is on request but Rs25 for large helpings of rice, *dhal*, carefully spiced vegetables, chutney and curd washed down by ginger tea is good value when it is Indian home cooking.

For Rs50, Shantha will buy in some tuna and put sumptuous Kerala-style fish on the table such as you will never find anywhere else. The house only has three chairs, one table and four spoons. Most people eat with their hands and sit on steps, the wall or mats laid out on the ground on the secluded hillside spot which catches the breeze and offers a good view of the beach.

Santana Restaurant is the most popular on the beach. It is the cleanest and most efficient and has the best sound system for those who like music to interrupt the sounds of the crashing waves. The variety of fresh fish is the biggest attraction. While it has to be said that tourists often automatically assume that the busier the restaurant the better, it must be said that here this general rule works well.

The Santana is one of the few restaurants that never closes – even in the monsoon season. Try Santana's fried sear fish, spiced up or otherwise (Rs100) with salad and chips or *naan* bread. It's a treat. So too is the *pomfret*. Often one helping is more than enough for two people. The vegetable *pakora* (Rs20), vegetable *chapatis* and pancakes are popular snacks.

Seashore Restaurant is smaller than the Santana but its varied menus and pleasant staff give it a homely, pleasant atmosphere. *Leores* also has a good reputation. It is a tiny restaurant near to the Santana and puts its fish on the plate for Rs80/90.

Garzia Restaurant's signboard declaring 'fresh pasta' attracts many Italians – and most of them are pleased with the quality. Tagliatelle with a cheese tomato, mushroom sauce costs just Rs75 and you can sit at a table on the shore itself if the mood takes you. **Coral Reef Restaurant** is also popular putting on a wide variety of fish.

A ten minute hike up from Eve's Beach will take you to the **Kovalam Ashok Beach Resort** where for Rs300 a good plate of steak is available.

Drinking

Up till now drinking has been a haphazard experience in Kovalam. Water from the local wells should be avoided. Stick to mineral water. **Coffee** and **tea** are best prepared in the more expensive hotels unless you like coffee and tea Indian style. Freshly made orange, pineapple or papaya juice is a treat but the tendency to add tap water to the drink means these should be avoided by those having their first week in Asia. Little reasonable **wine** is available. But if you have brought some in the duty free you can get a restaurant to keep it in their chiller for you.

Beer, all Indian-made, tends to vary from restaurant to restaurant depending on the stock they carry. Here the Raja Hotel has usually won out. Because they have been licensed to sell, they can put fresher beer on at cheaper prices, Rs45 a bottle compared to Rs60 at the other restaurants and Rs120 plus at the Kovalam Ashok and the Samudra. An annual 'pub-crawl' along the beach has left my companions opting for the Santana as the restaurant most likely to serve up a good, cold beer with a clean glass. But the Raja Hotel draws those, especially Aussies, Brits and Germans, who want to drink inexpensive beer through the day.

Spirits are not available for sale on the beach except at the Raja Hotel. If you can't be bothered to hike up there ask around in your hotel or restaurant and someone will fetch it for a Rs20 tip. Make sure you say exactly what you want and that you get a receipt. That way there is no misunderstanding. Alternatively, when you take a visit to Thiruvananthapuram (Trivandrum), stop at the **government alcohol shop** and you can get whatever Indian alcohol you desire at the cheapest price. Obviously, if you are to take your own alcohol into a restaurant you will be expected to eat a little something there unless that is you have become a regular feature.

One tip for keeping drinks cool in your room. In 1996 when there was a temporary ban on serving beer on the beach, a few British holiday-makers dug into tricks learned by their fathers in the days of the British Empire. Soldiers in the colonies close to the tropics would hang their bottles of beer or water in a wet sock. The process of the sock drying out caused the bottle's contents to cool. Tip 2 – wash the socks first.

Cultural Performances

Some hotels put on performances. Three times a week in the season the Hotel Neptune puts on performances of **kathakali**, a Kerala dance style which like many Indian dances tells a story. This dance is performed specifically by men (see inset). Before the dance performance an hour is taken up by explanations of how the dramatic masks and costumes are made up and why. Then the rooftop dance performance lasts another hour. Also excellent entertainment and culturally enriching is the **Nishagandi Dance Festival** which takes place in Thiruvananthapuram (Trivandrum) during the last week of February. Entrance is free yet you will see some of India's greatest dancers performing in the open-air amphitheatre.

Some hotels also give displays of the ancient Kerala martial arts, *kalaripayettu* (see inset) believed to have been developed centuries ago by the Chinese, after visiting Kerala, into martial arts such as karate.

Cinema

For those who want less weighty entertainment, there are air conditioned cinemas where it costs Rs15 for the best seats to watch the latest Hindi movie in town - no subtitles unless the actors are speaking in English. In Kovalam, videos of popular western movies are shown in the **Flamingo** restaurant and a few others each night often announced for example as: "For Weedings and a Fenural" or "Acopalips Now". The quality of the videos is variable but for those who have been travelling around India for a while or those with children, it can be a welcome light relief. The shows are free but viewers are expected at least to drink or eat something from the premises while they are there.

Late Night Entertainment

This is certainly not Spain. Most restaurants are closed by 11pm and visitors retreat to their rooms to sleep or sit on their balconies and watch the bejewelled night sky. Others who feel the hour is to early for sleep might go to the beach with their musical instruments for little parties. Alternatively there is one all-night bar, the **Surya**, which serves up food, drink and music for night birds from all corners of the globe. On a good night a few musicians will turn up and a crowd will generate their own entertainment till they turn up the music and get up to dance but whatever happens some will still be chatting and laughing away at dawn.

Once a week a restaurant on the beach might have a beach party, light a big fire, slightly raise the price of beer and bring a huge sound system onto the shore. If you like techno and hip-hop you'll be happy jiving away on the sand or in the sea but it's rare that soul and rock lovers get a look in. The latter can take taxis to the **Hotel Lucia's** Friday and Saturday night discos in Thiruvananthapuram (Trivandrum). Beer is expensive and there's a small entrance fee but, lasting till 2am, it's good fun.

Two annual parties worth a note are New Year's Eve which sends the beach wild and in February, Shivaratri, the Hindu celebration of Lord Shiva's wedding night with Parvathi. The latter is a festival attended mainly by people from the local village but takes place one minute from the beach over the road from the Sea Rock Hotel at the north end of the bay. A large stage is constructed for popular Kerala and national musicians to perform. They are followed by an open-air disco which carries on, in between hourly explosions from the nearby Hindu temple until five in the morning.

One last thing. Remember your torch. Kovalam's little tracks are not all straight and clear and covered by street-lighting and they wouldn't have the same charm if they were.

Accommodation

Accommodation in Kovalam is plentiful and though expensive by Indian standards it is still a snip of what you would expect to pay in Europe. The advent of one flight a week of Charter tourists in 1995 initially pushed up prices dramatically but since then prices have tended to stabilise and a surplus of accommodation in 1997 saw some prices go down.

Booking in advance at least one night by phone or fax saves any trouble for those who have just arrived. There are plenty of rickshaw drivers on commission waiting to take new visitors to particular hotels. Follow them and you can end up paying slightly over the odds but booking in for one night will then give you the chance to look around.

Best advice is probably to go for cheap, basic, clean and close to the beach. The last place most people want to stay in this beautiful climate is in their room. For searching around, it is best to park one's luggage first (if it comes to it there will be a restaurant who for a few rupees will watch over it while you are out scouting). Don't worry, Lighthouse Beach is compact and most places are within ten minutes of the beach.

Budget range

Time was when backpackers could simply roll out their sheet sleeping bags on the beach and settle down to be cradled by the musings of the ocean. Now the authorities,

fearing that it would entice criminals, frown on such activities. But if accommodation isn't free it is nearly so. It is still possible to get a room in a family's home for Rs50 a night dropping to Rs25 in the low season. The cheapest accommodation is available on the hill behind the cluster of beach hotels. Very good value for money is **Sudhi House**, Avaduthura, situated on the hill behind Green Valley Hotel. A basic clean room with fan and common bath costs Rs75 a night in the high season (November-February) and Rs50 out of season. It is run by a delightful family. There are only six rooms but it means landlady Shanta can serve up delicious Indian home cooking for breakfast and dinner for a snip of the prices on the beach.

Subesh Bhavan (0471-480140) is a five-room guest house positioned by the rickshaw stand on the road down to the Sea Rock. At Rs200 high season and Rs75 low season for a clean, basic room with fan and separate bath (Indian style), it is just two minutes from the beach. **Santana Restaurant** (0471-480368, fax 471-480055) has clean basic rooms with fan and separate bath (Indian style) which, by February, only cost Rs100 a night and are just 15 seconds walk from the beach. By March many rooms are available across the beach for less than Rs100 but availability is often determined by your willingness to haggle and search.

Slightly more expensive at Rs300 high season and Rs150 low season (February) is the clean and bright **Deepak Hotel**

(0471-480667) on Vizhinjam Road, ten minutes walk up the hill from the beach. Management are friendly and helpful. *Hotel Surya* (0471-481012) a minute's walk from the beach is in a similar price range and clearly very handy for the hotel's 24-hour bar. The rooms are clean and generally sleep is unaffected by the partying. Others in this price range include: *Achutha Lodge* next to Santana restaurant, *Sea Sand Home*, *Hotel Pass International*, *Palm Garden* and *Holiday Home.*

Seaside Cottages (0471-481937), with its rooms directly on the beach and barely obscured by the handful of chairs and tables that make up the restaurant, is probably the best located guest-house of all. The rooms are clean with separate bathroom and constantly refreshed by the light sea breezes. The service had been run down over the last couple of years but they are now under new management. Prices in 1997 were Rs150 to Rs450 (Christmas) for a room.

Medium range

All these hotels have separate bathrooms with European-style toilets and often room service.

Papakutty Beach Resort (0471-480235 fax 471-480234) just behind Santana Restaurant and again only fifteen seconds walk from the beach, has the advantage of being a new building (completed in 1996). Consequently its rooms are light, bright and airy with marble floors, spacious bathrooms and a generator guaranteeing almost permanent electricity to those staying in the more expensive apartment rooms. Cottage rooms cost Rs200/450 and the apartments Rs400/750 rising from the May-Nov low season to the Dec-Jan peak season.

Hotel Blue Diamond has bright clean rooms, the best of which are on the second floor. Room service is available for those who prefer to eat their meals from the adjacent Sea Fish restaurant on their balcony. Others in this range include:

Moonlight Tourist Home (0471-480375) costs Rs600 plus for clean rooms situated three minutes up the road from Sea Rock Hotel but a bit close to the booming sounds from the local Hindu temple.

Royal Retreat Cottages (0471-481010).

Green Valley Hotel is pleasantly situated in the palm trees behind the beach. Quiet and clean, the rooms cost Rs300 plus a night.

Apsara Cottages (0471-480507) are slightly more expensive but much closer to the beach. The rooms are very pleasant and clean if lacking the sea view provided by Seaside Cottages which they lie behind.

Thushara Hotel, next to Royal Retreat and two minutes from the beach have clean pleasant rooms with attached bath for Rs250 (April to October) to Rs1200 over Christmas and New Year.

Jeevan House, just behind Coral Reef, is popular for its basic rooms.

Wilson Tourist Home (0471-480051) has clean rooms ranging from Rs300 to Rs1000 plus. It is just two minutes' walk from the beach and also offers a money exchange and credit card facility, a massage parlour and a tailors.

Like Papakutty, Neptune and many other hotels they offer to arrange tours and transport for guests but if you have the time it's worth checking round to see if cheaper offers are available.

Hotel Raja (0471-480355) over 25 years old is arguably the grandfather of hotels in Kovalam. To date it remains the only hotel on Lighthouse Beach to have a license to purchase and sell beer legally. It is a steep five minute hike from the Sea Rock.

More expensive still is the *Hotel Rockholm* (0471-480406/7 fax 0471-480607) on Lighthouse Road. The hotel has pleasant rooms for Rs900/1000 per night, money change facilities. The linked *Hotel Aparna* below has clean spacious rooms from Rs600 to Rs1500 and automatically change the sheets every day,

KOVALAM

KOVALAM

Top of the Range

Probably the best value for money offered by the top hotels is the Kerala Tourist Development Corporation's *Hotel Samudra* (0471-480089) a statement underlined by the experience of one English family who had tried to book in June 1996 and found that there were no rooms available until March 1997. The cottages are probably the best rooms. They are spacious, equipped with air conditioning, baths, showers and bidets, television and telephone. The balconies look out onto an elegant terrace which gently slopes down to the quiet beach below.

Like many top hotels in Kerala the Samudra offers *ayurvedic* health programmes for those who wish to use their holiday to improve their health through massage and steam-bath treatments. The hotel also has a swimming pool and a small space for a disco which takes place on Saturday nights. There are 50 rooms costing per night from Rs1000 to Rs3,000 depending on the room and the season. They accept most credit cards.

Hotel Palmshore (0471-481481 fax 471-480495) is up the steep hill on Lighthouse Road. It commands a beautiful view of the beach below. Go down the steepish hill below and you are on one of Kovalam's quieter beaches. The hotel has 37 rooms all with balconies facing the sea, a beauty parlour, a beach umbrella service, money changing facilities and, if requested in advance, a pick up service from the airport. They also accept most credit cards. Prices for double rooms range from $20/25 in the off-season to $25/40 in the season. But December 21 to January 20 brings peak-season prices of $52/62.

Hotel Seaface (0471-481591) is the most expensive hotel directly on Lighthouse Beach. Its rooms are slightly cheaper than Palmshore and the balconies are equipped with comfortable cane swing chairs. Each room has television and air-conditioning, as at all the top hotels, is guaranteed by back up

generators. Its location on the shore and its swimming pool are perhaps its best assets.

The Indian government runs *Kovalam Ashok Beach Resort* (0471-480101) on the hill at the north end of Lighthouse Beach. The hotel has a good swimming pool to retreat to as does the nearby newly built *Treasure Cove Hotel.*

Money Changing

If you do not have a money change facility in your hotel then the most convenient place to go to change money is the *Wilson Tourist Home*. The exchange facility is open 9.30am to 5.30pm each day except Sundays when the management will change certain money but at a slightly worse rate. The centre also takes credit cards, sells stamps and posts letters - all with a smile. *Kovalam Ashok Beach Resort* also has an exchange facility but it is further from the beach and the opening hours are less convenient. Otherwise hotels which change money generally only do so for guests.

Communications Abroad

Fax and phone facilities are available at the bigger hotels but they are generally inordinately expensive. Fax/STD booths exist at both ends of Lighthouse Beach. The cheapest 1996 rates for Europe were Rs60/minute for phone calls and Rs100/minute for a fax. Hotel Neptune and Santana Restaurant also have reasonably priced phone/fax facilities. Many hotels will post letters off as part of the service. Letters posted to you should be addressed to your accommodation, otherwise to Vizhinjam Post Office, Vizhinjam Rd, Kovalam, Kerala, India 695-527.

⊗ Around Kovalam

Vizhinjam is a small fishing village a kilometre away from Kovalam where mornings find a vigorous trade in fish. Fishing boats line the beach until nightfall when they set out. Their lights can be seen bobbing on the horizon from Lighthouse Beach like lamplights strung along a distant causeway. Daytime, and the picturesque pink-domed, green **Moyuddin Mosque** can be seen and heard when swimming off Lighthouse Beach. Take the road south through Vizhinjam and come evening you can join in the early evening washes when whole families go to wash at the roadside wells. On a Friday evening it's worth a stop-by or visit to the local churches from which beautifully harmonious strains of unaccompanied singing emerge.

It's hard to find traces now, save for some decaying rock-cut temples and shrines close to the village but Vizhinjam was the capital of the Ay chieftains from AD600 to AD1000. You will not find the villagers as friendly as those in Kovalam but it's worth a visit. In the 1960s, the once utterly impoverished Vizhinjam fisherfolk established a new type of fishing co-operative called *Marianad*.

Instead of selling fish cheap to the powerful fish merchants, the villagers allowed the co-operative to sell their fish at the best possible price. The co-operative also became a source of cheap credit, bypassing the extortionate rates of the moneylenders. Incomes rose and *Marianad* became the model for fishing villages throughout Kerala.

Surya Samudra Beach Garden (0471-480413 fax 471-481124), eight kilometres from Kovalam and off from Pulinkudi Junction, is a private hotel complex with 20 traditional Kerala-style wooden cottages, a swimming pool and restaurant set in 2,600 square metres of fabulously designed, lush, tropical gardens with walkways running down the cliff to two clean picturesque beaches. The houses have fridges, fans and phones but, like a traditional Kerala house, no air conditioning. This is partly compensated by the seaward-facing buildings catching the breeze.

The houses have open-air bathrooms which, though surrounded by high walls, may or may not be to your taste. Overall the architecture is superb, even down to the Rajasthan Tent at Rs1900/5600 a night but you have to want utter seclusion, rest and a sense of exclusivity to stay here. Prices range from Rs1700/7000 in the monsoon to Rs3600/15,000 a night in peak season But between December 16 and January 15 expect to be quoted from Rs4500 to Rs19,000 per night. Breakfast and lunch or dinner is thrown in as are the special open-air displays of traditional **Kerala dance** and martial arts.

Beer is expensive at Rs120 a bottle, so too is the food (but worth a splash-out), the *ayurvedic* treatment and the Rs250 charge for visitors using the ornately-sculpted swimming pool. Unfortunately, the sea here is not recommended for swimming in. Nevertheless for a Rs130 rickshaw ride there and back, it is worth a visit to this adventurous project especially if you ache to escape Kovalam and find a little solitude.

Nine kilometres from Kovalam, **Somatheeram Beach** is a hive of activity for the local fishing village. From afar, the golden beach appears bespattered with boats and people right up to the horizon. If you want to get a picture of life in a Kerala fishing village with its palm-leaf thatched houses hidden amongst the trees adjacent to the beach, then Somatheeram is a place to visit. You might even see a local football or cricket match in the afternoons. Football matches here don't need a stadium to be well attended. Unlike most of India, soccer is one of Kerala's most popular sports.

On a hill looking down on the village is **Somatheeram Ayurvedic Beach Resort** (0471-481600 fax 471-480600) which offers *ayurvedic* treatment and **yoga** courses. 50 non-air conditioned rooms are available in wooden and stone cottages excellently styled in traditional Kerala fashion. The cottages are spread out over 15 acres on a hill that has steep steps down to a beach. Night time offers a splendid vista of a starlit sky beneath which appear such a plethora of lights from the gathering fishing boats that they appear as if from a village – Somatheeram at sea.

Swimming is too difficult here but this secluded part of the beach is a perfect venue for the daily yoga classes. The resort offers full facilities including pick up from arrival, money change and credit card facilities, phones, cultural activities and indoor games to meet most of the guests' needs so that they can partake in the 12 *ayurvedic* and yoga health/relaxation courses. The cottages are perhaps slightly more comfortable than the Surya Samudra but, as with all health centres, you are advised to check out the facilities, hygiene etc. before you sign up for a health course.

Prices in the monsoon range from Rs350/1200 for a double per night rising to Rs1200/4500 for December to February. Luxury tax and expenditure tax are additional. **Massages** cost Rs500, a yoga session Rs300, and health courses lasting 14 days anything from Rs2000 to Rs33,000.

Manaltheeram Beach Resort (0471-481610 fax 481611) is owned by the same company and sits slightly further down the hill on the north side. It offers the same facilities with brick or mud cottages costing anything from Rs700 to Rs2100 plus tax per night for two depending on the season and the type of accommodation. Meals are charged at the same rate as the Somatheeram.

Poowar is the next village going south. The people are impoverished and not particularly friendly. Nor is the sea. A sandbank normally protects the beach from the raging waters but we were standing on the beach when a two-foot wall of water which had surmounted the sand bank rushed around our legs. Not a place for sunbathing! Some tourist accommodation is under construction here. Perhaps it's an area better left alone.

Five kilometres north of Kovalam is the peaceful **Pachalloor** village close to the Blue Lagoon and Pozhikkara Beach. **Lagoona Beach Resort** (0471-480049) has basic rooms without air conditioning for Rs350 a double.

Kovalam Backwaters

Kerala's most renown backwaters are 200 kilometres north of Kovalam but if you are stuck for time then the local backwater trip from Pachalloor village is an enjoyable interesting alternative. The best time to arrive for the two hour, Rs150 trip is 7.30am allowing you to avoid the heat in the shelterless dugout canoes which are punted through the canals which link the villages.

The guides are good, pointing out and explaining the local plant and wildlife. They take the boats close up to a local village offering scenes of village life including **coir-making**, temple activity, washing, cooking etc. Then out to **Pozhikkara Beach** where the backwaters meat the sea. Finally the trip is rounded off by a little local food served on the traditional plate, an eco-friendly banana leaf.

To book a local backwater trip, either take a chance and just turn up or contact **Golden Tours** (0471-481647) who proudly announce that they have been running this tour for 26 years.

Temple Festivals

Around Kovalam are the **Avaduthura Devi, Theruvila Devi** (Lighthouse Road) and **Parasurama** (Trivandrum Road) Hindu temples. While entry is limited, these temples are the central points for the multiplicity of Hindu festivals throughout the year. At Parasurama, the festival atmosphere is often like a garden fete during the day with mainly women and children stood around talking or watching over their clay cooking pots heated by charcoal and covered by piles of banana leaves on which the pot contents will be served. The steaming pots form a border around the festive area, empty during the day save for children at play.

At night when the men and women have returned from their work a drama will be performed and the gaily decorated temple elephant may appear leading a procession and the party will go on till early the next morning. If you hear that a temple festival is on or due to take place don't worry about joining in the fun.

Attukal Pongala is a special Hindu women's festival which takes place every February at Attukal temple on the banks of the River Killiar 2km south-east of East Fort, Thiruvananthapuram (Trivandrum). The nine-day festival culminates on a full moon night and attracts thousands of women from across the state who patiently queue to offer *pongala* food as offerings beseeching Goddess Parvathi to grant them good health, happy marriages, family harmony, jobs etc.

The *pongala* offering is food which must be cooked on the spot at certain times using only dried coconut palm leaves for cooking fuel and any odd number of earthenware pots up to 101. None may start cooking until they have bathed in the river and none may eat of the many offerings until the priest has blessed them with holy water.

Tours and Day Trips

All the places listed in the next section on Thiruvananthapuram are within easy reach of Kovalam. For a day long trip a rickshaw driver may ask anything from Rs200 to Rs400. Rs200 is reasonable but with the monopoly the Kovalam drivers have you will have to bargain hard for that price. Alternatively a Rs3 bus ride into the city and using rickshaws where necessary to get around will be cheaper.

Further afield and comfortable for a very recommended day trip are the Wooden Palace of **Padmanabhapuram** (1 hour), **Nagercoil Temple** (2 hours), **Kanyakumari** and the **Vivekanand** island temple at India's southernmost point (2 hours) dealt with in the section on western Tamil Nadu (page xx).

Peppara Wildlife Santuary

Surprisingly off the main tourist route, Peppara Wildlife Sanctuary, is 50km southeast of Thiruvananthapuram on the road to Ponmudi. By wildlife sanctuary standards Peppara is small covering a rolling 53 sq km of evergreen forest. However those who have been testify that it offers a better chance of seeing its wildlife of elephants, leopards, lion-tailed macaque monkeys and samber deer than some of the more famous sanctuaries.

Ponmudi

Ponmudi is a hill resort 75km from Kovalam and a two and a half hour drive up the winding roads to beautiful panoramic views 1066 metres above sea level in the Cardamom Hills. KTDC organise a day tour for under Rs60 leaving Thiruvananthapuram daily at 7.45am and returning at 7.00pm. But the best time to be in Ponmudi is early in the morning and an overnight stop is preferable for those who wish to trek amongst its hills and valleys.

Here the **KTDC** have a basic but clean **guest house** (0471-89230) with double rooms available in its ten cottages for Rs48 and 24 single rooms in the main building for Rs45. The restaurant is very cheap and the hillside walks promise breathtaking views. "I couldn't believe it, a 150km round trip, all my food and good accommodation for two nights for only 180 rupees", a 46-year-old woman from Bavaria commented.

Neyyar Dam

For a comfortable trip to Neyyar Dam climb into the back of an Ambassador taxi with its luxurious seats and wooden dashboard. The cost for the day out should be no more than Rs500/600. Leave around 9am and you'll have plenty of time to pass through the local villages stop off at a *chai* shop for a Rs5/6 breakfast of *dosas* and chutney, *wadee* or banana cake washed down with tea or coffee. Then the car climbs into the gently rolling foothills of the Southern Ghats or Sahyadri range.

Agasthyakoodam mountain, the most prominent peak in the area, culminates in a sharp conical peak. Good for **trekking** and **climbing** it can be reached by trekking from Neyyar Dam.

If you wish, the driver will take you to the **crocodile sanctuary** where a score of crocodiles lie around in cages, some with their broods. As you might expect there's not much going on with these sleepy beasts. Then on a hill looking over the valley beneath the dam in picturesque settings is **Shivananda Ashram** (otherwise known as Swanada Yoga Vedanta Dhanwantari). This ashram is one of India's leading **yoga centres** teaching *hatha* and *raja* yoga run by Swamy Shivananda, dubbed the "flying guru" for his exploits flying aircraft over war zones to drop leaflets with peace messages. It is a popular peaceful destination for Westerners and Indians alike. Drugs, alcohol, sex, smoking, meat eating and rock music are banned. For booking places there to rest up, learn or practise yoga and meditate in the attractively laid out grounds contact the *Ashram's* branch at: 27/1929 Airport Rd, West Fort, Thiruvananthapuram (0471-450942).

In the valley beneath is **Neyyar Wild Life Sanctuary** which contains elephants, gaur (large oxen) and sloth bears. There is also a lake besides which reside a couple of working elephants. If there *mahout* is around he will oblige for a tip if you want a short ride aboard. Otherwise the lake is a beautiful spot to sit and relax – even if you forgot to pack your picnic lunch.

At Neyyar Dam the waters from the Southern Ghats gush out, generating much-needed electricity for the state. You are still in the sanctuary but don't worry if you here the roar of a big cat – it will be from the lion safari park besides the dam. The local **Forest Department** has an **Inspection Bungalow** for hire in the sanctuary.

Kathakali

Kathakali is a vibrant, colourful traditional Kerala dance form as classical as ballet and opera. Based on stories from the great Indian epics the Ramayana and Mahabharata, it is said to have evolved from competition between two princes one who wrote a story based on the life of Krishna, the Krishnattam and the other around Rama, the Ramattam. It has been evolving since the days of Shakespeare and transformed for popular consumption by a once illiterate people. Huge masks, bright red, green, white and gold costumes, clashing symbols, drum rolls, chanting and dance and martial arts techniques are used by the all male dance team to evoke humour, wonder and tragedy.

Luckily, many performances provide an explanation of the story and some of the hand gestures prior to the show for Kathakali uses 24

K O V A L A M

primary hand and finger gestures giving 404 signs, 44 secondary hand and finger gestures conveying 55 different signs and then a vast number of movements of the eyes, eyebrows, lips, teeth, tongues, head, neck, hands, arms, toes and feet which must be read as correctly punctuated sentences and paragraphs! Long and rigorous training is required to put body and soul together to portray all the requisite nuances. Fortunately a brief explanation and the dramatic body language – watch those flashing eyes behind the masks – gives the audience the gist of a highly entertaining evening.
Traditionally the Kathakali dance performances begin at 8am and go through to 2am the next morning. But tourists are usually proffered a shortened version.

Other dance forms common to Kerala include *koodiyattam, mohiniyattam, theyyam, patayyani* the *thullal* pantomimes and, with glove puppets, the *pavakathakali. Koodiyattam* preceded *kathakali* by 2000 years and is traditionally performed in the temples as an offering to the deity and to educate the audience.

In contrast to *kathakali, mohiniyattam* is danced by women. In fact Mohini, the beautiful dancer, is the female form adopted by the god Vishnu. Her grace so enchants Lord Shiva that he takes her in his arms, symbolising the coming together of Keralan and north Indian religions via the Dravidian (Kerala) god Shiva with the Aryan god Vishnu.

Called the "Dance of the Enchantress" it was originally danced by professional dancing girls and, some say, courtesans before it was refined in the last century by a Travancore Maharaja, Swati Tirunal. *Mohiniyattam* emphasises grace and sensuousness and requires performers to wear gold-edged white cotton *saris*, adorned with jewellery with white jasmine flowers encircling the hair.

In the *theyyam* dance, men get back into the act, glorifying the goddess. They use colourful costumes and make-up to play the female roles in stories which revolve around the victories of the goddess over the demon Daruka and other evil spirits.

Thullal is a satirical slapstick show of ribaldry and rhyme using ancient tales to highlight modern corruption and hypocrisies. You'll only join in the enthusiastic laughing from the audience if you can find a translator - or have learned Malayalam.

Kerala Kalamandalam in Cheruthuruthy, north of Kochi, is the place to go if your passion for dance leads you to want to find out more. The Kalamandalam (see page xx) is the state's flagship training centre for indigenous performing arts. But if you're based in south Kerala and can't get up north you can make an appointment to watch classes in *kathakali* and *koodiyattam* at the **Margi School** in Fort High School, West Fort, Thiruvananthapuram .

Getting to and from Kovalam

Trains and planes

Kovalam's nearest railway station and airport are 18km away in **Thiruvananthapuram** which is dealt with in the next section. There are several generally reliable travel agents on Lighthouse Beach who, for a small add-on fee, will book your ongoing travel arrangements and save you the hassle of a trip into the city and waiting in the queues. However, if you're intent on taking a train journey then you may miss out on getting on the tourist quota which keeps a special number of seats for international tourists.

Buses

Buses go every 15 minutes into **Thiruvananthapuram** from the main bus stand outside the Kovalam Ashok Beach Resort. The fare is Rs3. Buses return from Thiruvananthapuram to Kovalam from stand 19 at East Fort on MG Road. There are also direct buses four times a day from Kovalam for the two hour trip to **Kanyakumari** (Cape Comorin), daily to **Thekkady** (Periyar Wildlife Sanctuary) and also a daily KSRTC service to **Kochi** (Cochin)/Ernakulam via **Alappuzha** (Alleppey) and **Kollam** (Quilon)for **Backwaters trips**.

Taxis and Auto-rickshaws

Taxis and rickshaws will take you anywhere you want in Kerala but it's best to shop around for the best price.

Kovalam Beach

TRIVANDRUM

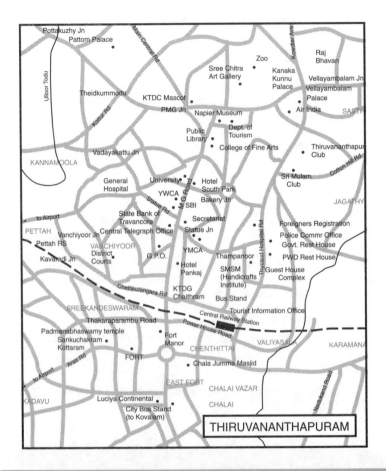

Pottakuzhy Jn
Pattom Palace
Zoo
Raj Bhavan
Sree Chitra Art Gallery
Kanaka Kunnu Palace
Vellayambalam Jn
Vellayambalam Palace
Theidkummodu
KTDC Mascot
PMG Jn
Napier Museum
Air India
SASTH
Public Library
Dept. of Tourism
College of Fine Arts
Thiruvananthapur Club
Vadayakattu Jn
KANNAMOOLA
Sri Mulam Club
General Hospital
University
Hotel South Park
YWCA
Bakery Jn
SBI
JAGATHY
to Airport
State Bank of Travancore
Secretariat
Statue Jn
Foreigners Registration
PETTAH
Vanchiyoor Jn
Central Telegraph Office
Police Commr Office
Pettah RS
VANCHIYOOR
District Courts
G.P.O.
YMCA
Govt. Rest House
Kavaradi Jn
Hotel Pankaj
Thampanoor
SMSM (Handicrafts Institute)
PWD Rest House
Guest House Complex
Chettikulangara Rd
KTDG Chaithram
Bus Stand
Tourist Information Office
SREEKANDESWARAM
Thakaraparambu Road
Central Railway Station
Padmanabhaswamy temple
Sankuchakram
Kottaram
Fort Manor
Powar House Road
CHENTHITTA
VALIYASA
KARAMANA
FORT
Arat Rd
to Airport
Chala Jumma Masjid
EAST FORT
CHALAI VAZAR
KADAVU
Luciya Continental
City Bus Stand (to Kovalam)
CHALAI

THIRUVANANTHAPURAM

A magnificent array of gods, goddesses, nymphs, sprites and demons adorn the seven storey gopuram which forms the Padmanabhaswamy *temple tower. The Dravidian style common to Tamil Hindu temples is not to be found anywhere else in Kerala. While historians are uncertain as to the age of the temple, it is recorded that it was renovated in 1733 by Marthanda Varma, the Maharaja of Travancore, and dedicated to the Maharaja's household deity, Vishnu, Padmanabha being a local form*

THE CAPITAL **Thiruvananthapuram**

Thiruvananthapuram (Trivandrum), Kerala's state capital, may have the appearance of a busy provincial town but three million people live in or around the city. Fortunately, the city, spread across seven hills, is free of the tower blocks of Mumbai (Bombay), Delhi and Bangalore whilst the underdevelopment of manufacturing industries in the state lends to the capital a pleasant, amiable atmosphere. Nevertheless, the diesel and petrol fumes from the choking traffic common to all India's cities pervade the air.

The narrow streets are quite charming. Small ramshackle shops sit alongside traditional Kerala houses with their flowering bushes and red-tiled, gabled roofs cocked up at each end reflecting the centuries-old influence of the trade with China. Ancient architecture is haphazardly mixed with more modern styles like the circular Coffee House and the magnificent, white Secretariat building which houses the state government on MG (Mahatma Gandhi) Road.

While Trichur and Kochi to the north are lauded, Thiruvananthapuram sports some of the most elegant buildings in the state. After all Thiruvananthapuram was the capital of the old kingdom of Travancore and still boasts the Maharaja's palaces, ancient temples and churches and the walls of the old fort.

The streets are generally clean and safe. Widespread literacy, land ownership and welfare programmes have resulted in a limited number of homeless children and beggars. Pleasant cafes are easy to find as are pleasant helpful people and the added bonus, if you are staying in Kovalam or Periyar, is it is relatively cheap. It is an excellent shopping centre for hand-made or ready-to-wear clothes, shoes, books, cassettes, jewellery, portraits, incredible theatrical masks and conch shells and ornaments in sandalwood, brass and rosewood for taking home.

Travelling around Thiruvananthapuram is quite cheap. The rickshaw drivers will even put the meter on and give you the official rate of Rs4 per kilometre. A taxi is more expensive and an air-conditioned cab more again but it might save you from the fumes and suffering in the heat (Thiruvananthapuram is normally one or two degrees hotter than Kovalam and bereft of the refreshing sea breeze). Walking around is easy enough but make sure you take a cap or something to protect your head. Children should also be kept close by to protect them from traffic chaos.

TRIVANDRUM

If Thiruvananthapuram remains one of the easiest cities to get around, travelling still needs patience. A car can easily find itself in a traffic snarl up. On a wide street sometimes there will be six lanes of traffic with each adjacent lane going in the opposite direction! Then a cart drawn by two of those magnificent white oxen with long-curled horns will breakdown at a busy junction and the rickshaws will pour like cement into every nook and cranny of the stalled traffic until nothing at all can move. Pay up, get out and walk, it's quicker.

Places to Visit

For simplicity we will start at the south end of the city at **East Fort** which is on MG Road, the main thoroughfare through the capital and also a major bus terminus from Kovalam, Ponmudi and other areas. The East Fort, naturally on the west side of MG Road and opposite the City bus station, was built for the protection of the Maharaja's city palace. Its cream coloured entrance watched over by two turrets with white colonnades is near a Freedom Gate celebrating the liberation from British rule in 1947.

Sree Padmanabhaswamy Temple

Take the road through the Freedom Gate then past the CVN Kalari, first right down a busy road with Panchalis Restaurant on the left and Hotel Lucia on the right before turning left at the end and you arrive at the city's historic landmark, the Sree Padmanabhaswamy temple. Thiruvananthapuram (the place of the sacred serpent) takes its name from the idol in the temple which has Vishnu sat upon a serpent.

A magnificent array of gods, goddesses, nymphs, sprites and demons adorn the seven storey gopuram which forms the temple tower. The Dravidian style common to Tamil Hindu temples is not to be found anywhere else in Kerala. While historians are uncertain as to the age of the temple, it is recorded that it was renovated in 1733 by Marthanda Varma, the Maharaja of Travancore, and dedicated to the Maharaja's household deity, Vishnu, Padmanabha being a local form.

Sadly the gopuram could do with a good clean and only Hindus are allowed inside the temple. But if you are Hindu the temple contains interesting murals and carvings. In October/November each year the Navarathri Mandapam of the temple holds the nine day **Navarathri Festival** of musical concerts dedicated to the goddess of knowledge and music.

Face away from the temple steps and on the left in front of the temple tank is a tiny shack with sandalwood carvings on sale. The two craftsmen are very friendly and you can watch them working through every stage of the sandalwood carving process right through to the polishing. Prices are more expensive than in Mysore but if you can't afford the time to go the 1,000 kilometres to the 'sandalwood city' then a good haggle can secure you a reasonable price. The left side of the street is a row of souvenir shops with vendors cajoling you to buy. But don't rush off. Behind them is a little gem not mentioned in most guide books, Puthen Malika Palace.

Puthen Malika Palace

Twenty yards away from Sree Padmanabhaswamy temple, sandwiched between the shops of the right hand side of the road, is an innocuous sign announcing the Puthen Malika Palace. The entrance fee is Rs15. Rs10 is charged for taking a camera inside but photographs of the interior of the palace are forbidden.

The palace was built by Maharaja Swati Thirunal in the early nineteenth century. It was owned by the Maharajas until the last one died in 1991. Now the palace is in the hands of his heirs who, not using the palace, opened it up to public viewing in late 1995.

The whole appearance is of a stately home belonging to a family fallen on bad times. Step along the path to the palace entrance and it is splendidly ill-kept. Through the gateway and then behold the classical Kerala architecture – white-washed walls and granite and marble columns supporting the wooden gables, slatted windows beneath the red-tiled roof all protected by 122 wooden horses under the gables. Shoes off and inside. Don't be fooled by first impressions. In the foyer, gold-framed 120 square foot Italian mirrors hang forlornly like salvage from a tip. Persevere and what follows is a fascinating insight into the lives of Travancore's ruling elite.

No explanatory literature is currently available and some of the guides' Indian-English is spoken so rapidly that it is impossible to follow. However, most objects have a little explanation beside them.

Each of the 16 rooms has a different ceiling carved in sandalwood. Upstairs is a dancehall with special lattices allowing the wind to cool down the revellers. Another telling feature is the series of *kilivarthil* or bird windows. The ladies of the dynasty were not allowed to be seen in public or gazed on by lower castes so the palaces had *kilivarthil* to allow the long-suffering women an occasional view of the kingdom their menfolk ruled.

The first room houses 14 life-size figures from *kathakali* and Kerala legend. There are the magnificent ivory cots and thrones used by the dynasty, a bathing pool, a room for the Maharaja to compose his odes, a musical tree producing the eight *saptaswara* chords when tapped, and paintings by Roerich, amongst others, of the dynasty at work and play. One of the portraits of a Maharaja is in that delightful 3D style so that his boots and eyes point at the viewers wherever they might stand.

For the blood thirsty or military historians, the Maharaja has collected a host of historic weaponry including the *kandakodali* used by the Maharajas for beheading errant subjects. There is also a good collection of rifles and cutlasses taken from the defeated Dutch in 1741 after the **Battle of Collachel**. In January/February the palace stage their Carnatic Music Festival in the grounds (further details from KTDC).

TRIVANDRUM

CVN Kalari

Most of the inside of the fort is now turned over to shops and restaurants but on the right of the road leading from the Freedom Gate is an unpresumptuous building, the **CVN Kalari Sanghan** (0471-74182) which is one of the homes for Kerala's great fighting traditions encapsulated in *kalarippayattu* (pronounced, kalaripayat).

Kalarippayattu (see inset) is the ancient form of Kerala martial arts requiring rigorous training to discipline mind and body and worked on day-in day-out for years. Participants learn to use different weapons of combat then the highest art – hand-to-hand fighting.

The Gurukal has taken his trainees on displays and run workshops around the world. Short or longer courses are available for visitors. Onlookers are welcome if they can get out of bed to watch the trainees going through their exercises between 6.30am and 8am.

The Gurukal at the head of CVN Kalari is over 60 years old but is still a capable combatant. It takes years to train up a combatant and during this time the Gurukal is also responsible for his trainees' moral and physical well being. Consequently the Gurukal must also understand medicine. His practice and success with his trainees has resulted in the CVN also being a popular 'doctor's surgery' with queues of patients in his immaculately tidy offices ready to use his *ayurvedic* skills, medicines and ointments.

Kalarippayattu

The two bare-chested men dressed only in loin clothes show total concentration as they watch one another wield the sword and shield they have chosen for potentially deadly combat. Striding and turning this way and that they lunge at each other then turn and spin before launching at their opponent with such a high leap that it seems they could slice the coconuts off the nearby palm trees.

A series of stormy staccato leaps and clashes come to a crescendo of ferocity and agility that enthrals the onlookers. This is kalarippayattu, *the mother of martial arts.*

Kalarippayattu *is a centuries old form of martial arts indigenous to Kerala. This fascinating, rhythmical, disciplined yet fierce style of combat originally developed for the protection of the Brahmin caste to defend their local and caste interests. It covers the use of all hand-held weaponry and unarmed combat and as such is an awesome ancient military drill.*

Legend has it that after the warrior sage Parasurama had claimed Kerala from the sea. He taught the martial art sequence (ppayattu) to

21 Brahmin disciples and created a military training ground (kalari) for each of them. However kalarippayattu is widely believed to have been developed between the ninth and twelfth centuries and visiting Chinese nobles took the ppayattu back to China. Chinese works acknowledge that their martial arts, which gained world renown, had their origins in this little-known part of India.

Each Kerala village would have its own kalari close to the temple pond. The kalari also used for religious worship would be run by a Gurukal responsible for every aspect of his trainee s education and health. The ppayattu produced such fierce effective fighters that under British rule it was banned, almost becoming extinct.

Training traditionally begins at eight years old and continues for eight to ten years during which much concentration is put on long physical warm-up exercises, producing powerful but supple bodies and disciplined minds. Kerala's warm climate helps to produce lissom bodies which make the slow, deliberate warm up contortions a difficult challenge for even the best of Western martial arts enthusiasts.

After several hours of warming up, the Gurukal oversees the trainees practising combat with various weapons such as the kettukara (long stick), cheruvate (short stick) and ottakal (a wooden club with nodules for attacking the body's pressure points). The fiercest looking weapon is the urumio, a two-metre long flexible sword which when flayed can chop a fighter in two. Little wonder it is only taught to the chosen inheritor of the title Gurukal. Maithozhil is the art of combat through kicks.

Only then does combat take place. Nowadays it is only ritualistic. The highest form of Kalarippayattu is verumkai, 'hands only combat requiring a knowledge of the body's central nervous system. Displays are given using all but the urumio in Kovalam, Thiruvananthapuram, Kochi and elsewhere. An interesting difference exists in the development of kalarippayattu between the more stylised and graceful northern version practised at CVN Kalari and the southern version often used in shows around Kovalam. The northern combat form appears to have been developed by the high-caste Brahmins whereas the southern more day to day style is said to have grown from its use in the low-caste villages.

Short training courses are offered to international visitors wishing to learn this magnificent historic art. A video cassette on the art in German, but with interviews in English, is available from: Horst Vogt, Rud-Seeberger-Allee 31, 82407 Wielenbach, Germany (phone 0049881-69246).

TRIVANDRUM

Kalarippayattu Centres

CVN Kalari Sanghan, *East Fort, Thiruvananthapuram (0471-74182);*
Balachandran **Nair Kalari** *martial arts gymnasium, Cotton Hill, Thiruvananthapuram (opens 6am-8am, 6pm-7.30pm, tel: 0471-65140);* **ENS Kalari**, *Nettoor, Ernakulam/Cochin (0484-809810);* **Arjuna Kalari Centre**, *Ernakulam/Cochin (0484-365440).*

I met a young woman with a large growth on the bridge of her nose. Doctors in Germany had advised that it would have to be surgically removed. She had just received some ayurvedic ointment which the Gurukal had instructed her to rub on the growth twice a day. Within a fortnight the growth had gone. I joined the queue at CVN.

Chala Bazaar

Out of East Fort and left down Chala Bazaar Road is Chala Bazaar, a thriving market with shops providing almost everything you could wish to buy – and cheap at that. Vehicles are not allowed to park in the bazaar's narrow streets so visitors will have to park in the square outside and make the short walk.

Further up MG Road to the right is Central Station Road where the interestingly designed main railway station and the circular Indian Coffee House stands. A kilometre or so behind the railway station is the Chachu Nehru Children's Museum at Thycaud. With a collection of 2,000 dolls, masks and stamps, it might amuse the children. Opening hours are daily, 10am to 5pm, except Mondays.

The Secretariat

Two kilometres further up the MG Road is the splendid white Secretariat building where the Communist-led Left Democratic Front currently rules over state affairs. Hardly a day will go by without a demonstration of one character or another being staged in front of its gates. Kerala's people are generally peaceable and friendly, with great traditions of tolerance.

> There is a field in the backwaters near Alappuzha where bullet holes still mark the trees besides which in 1947 troops under British orders massacred 450 unarmed striking farm labourers. The British Resident is said to have gone along specially to watch the events. Yet despite this and numerous other atrocities hardly a word of bitterness against the injustices of Empire lingers in the air.

Only occasionally do the marches become violent. But the colourful protests can be so big or numerous that the MG Road is blocked, requiring a long detour through the narrow back streets.

Jama Masid Mosque in Pallayam is an attractive modern twin-towered mosque, in the pale orange and white colours that adorn other major buildings in the city. It is a kilometre north of the Secretariat by Pallayam market, where MG Road meets Pallayam Road. It's worth a stop. Over the road is a stall selling fresh jasmine you can buy to freshen up your room if you forgot to buy it in Chala Bazaar.

Christian Churches and cathedrals also abound in Pallayam including the Syrian Orthodox *Cathedral of St George*, the Christian denomination which has its roots in times dating back to before Christianity reached the British Isles. On a Friday night mass or on Sundays these churches are packed to overflowing with devout worshippers. Also of interest is the old cemetery at *Christ Church* which has plenty of decaying gravestones testifying to the presence of the English Raj.

The *Science and Technology Museum* is off to the left at the north end of MG Road, near the Mascot Hotel. It opens daily from 10am to 5pm (except Mondays). Inside the grounds is the *Priyadarshini Planetarium*.

Napier Museum

A better bet is too turn left at the end of MG Road and you will soon arrive at the attractive gardens which are home to the *Napier Museum* complex (spot the sweet scented lemon blossoms of the huge frangipani tree and purple-flowered jacaranda trees). The Napier is part of a government owned complex which also includes the Sree Chitra Art Gallery, the Natural History Museum, the KCS Panicker Building and Thiruvananthapuram Zoo.

The design of the Napier Museum is a magnificent example of the early "Indo-Saracenic" style of architecture. Kerala gables, carved and painted wooden beams, Hindu pillars and Muslim arches combine to mesmerise the viewer. Completed in 1880 it bears the name of the then British Governor of Madras.

Kerala with its plentiful and varied tree life, has long been famous for its wood carvings. Some temples dating back to the twelfth century still have their beautifully carved temples intact - including Shiva's temple at Lokannarkavu displaying brightly painted erotic scenes.

The external and internal wooden beams and roof supports of the museum have mythological animals ingenuously carved onto them. Inside the Napier are a wonderful collection of traditional Kerala woodcarvings, the earliest of which date back to the fifteenth century.

The earliest of the bronze castings and stone sculptures in the museum date back to the eighth century. It is a measure of the domination of religion and the role of the temples in preserving historic artefacts that 90 per cent of the items displayed are iconic. In addition there are collections of gold necklaces and belts – intricate ivory carvings and a carved temple chariot. Napier Museum opens daily, except Wednesday mornings and Mondays. Entrance is Rs5.

Sree Chitra Art Gallery

In the same grounds as the Napier is the **Sree Chitra Art Gallery** with its collection of **Raja Ravi Varma**, Svetlova and Nicholas Roerich paintings and exhibits from the Rajput, Moghul and Tanjore schools of art. The most significant paintings are probably those of Raja Ravi Varma, the grandfather of modern Indian art. After the Moghul period, Indian art went into decline for 150 years until the end of the nineteenth century.

Ravi Varma combined the best of occidental and Indian traditions in his portraits covering both traditional and modern Indian themes. Two years after the British Government gave him the title of Kaiser-i-Hind he died of fever aged 58.

The gallery also includes a collection of paintings from China, Tibet, Japan and Bali. If you have a spare half hour, the Sree Chitra enclave hosts a 30-minute video show on the history, lives and times of the Maharaja dynasty up to the last Maharaja's death in 1991. Opening times are 10am-5pm. The gallery is closed on Wednesday mornings and all day Monday.

Art enthusiasts may also be interested in the paintings in the **KCS Panicker Building** opposite the Napier Museum. This musty building houses the works of KCS Panicker (1911-77), another modern Kerala artist working mainly in oils. The collections show his water colours and oil paintings in the Tantric style, particularly around the theme of mathematical order in astrology. Opening times are the same as the Sree Chitra above.

Natural History Museum

Also opposite the Napier is the Natural History Museum, first opened in 1857, with a vast collection of animal skeletons and stuffed animal and birdlife common to Kerala.

Thiruvananthapuram Zoo

Unless you are squeamish, the city's zoo is a better bet than the 'stuffy' Natural History Museum. Close to the Napier Museum, it is recognised as one of the best and least inhumane zoos in India. Open since 1859 it houses a vast number of varied mammals, birds and reptiles, a hippo run, open enclosures for elephants, lions, tigers, giraffes, deer and crocodiles and a snake house. Not everyone approves of keeping animals in zoos. Those who are not too upset will get a good idea of the types of animals and birds they may meet during their stay in southern India.

The zoo opens daily from 9.30am to 5pm but is closed on Mondays. Admission costs Rs2, Rs1 for children aged seven or older. Parking costs Rs3 and cars can enter the zoo for Rs5. There is a charge of Rs2 for taking cameras inside and Rs10 for video cameras/camcorders. By the main gate you'll find a cheap cafe.

Opposite the entrance to the Napier complex is a park in which there is the Thiruvananthapuram Waterworks Swimming Pool, open to the public daily, 8.30am till noon, 2pm to 3.30pm and 6.15pm to 8pm. The pool is closed on Mondays.

International Centre for Cultural Development (ICCD)

Run by a Dutch man and an Indian woman doctor, the ICCD (tel/fax 471-465368) at 31/1719 Anayara Rd, near Pettah Junction puts on displays of Indian dance, theatre and art exhibitions. However its main function is to offer visiting artists opportunities to study south Indian culture and develop their own artistic skills.

Hotel Lucia's Discotheque

Fridays and Saturday nights you can have some fun at Hotel Lucia's discotheque if you remember that you are in India. The lightshow, air conditioning and combination of western rock and popular modern Hindi film songs should get you on your feet. The floor is often occupied by Indian men trying to dance like their favourite Hindi film stars but it's not crowded. It's best not to go on your own. Drinks are expensive but if you join in the fun you should have a hoot.

T R I V A N D R U M

⊗ Around Thiruvananthapuram

Matsya Kanyaka

Matsya Kanyaka is a gigantic 35 metre long, ten metre high sculpture of a reclining voluptuous mermaid, standing on its own on a patch of grass near the airport at Shanghummugham Beach. No explanation is given as to why she is there. Her interesting features include legs which part into two tails instead of uniting to one and gigantic breasts. This enigmatic creature is the creation of local artist Canai Kunuram who lives nearby. Canai also has his work displayed at Medical College and in other parts of the city.

Shanghummugham Beach

Shanghummugham Beach is eight kilometres from Thiruvananthapuram. Its yellow sands and rough seas do not really merit a visit but there are half-a-dozen churches and a mosque in this area where the devout congregate with passion and in incredible numbers on a Friday evening. During the day, Christian devotees finding the church doors locked simply kneel down on the ground and make their appellations to their god.

Veli Tourist Village

Veli is an attractive beach resort on the coast nine kilometres from Thiruvananthapuram City. It has a **boating lake** and a small backwaters with facilities for water ski-ing, diving and boating. Motor boats (Rs100 for 10 minutes), paddle boats, rowing boats and ponies are available for hire. The adjacent grounds are surprisingly green and well laid out with large trees offering good shade for picnicking.

The ornamental park has several modern sculptures and there is also a playground for children. Few western tourists visit what is really a place for Kerala at play, a joyous site that is sure to relax you.

The beach is 200 metres from the park. The sea is too dangerous to swim in but quite fascinating when it turns from blue to red as its waves churn up the laterite-terracotta sands.

Buses go regularly from East Fort to Veli, Veli also has a youth hostel offering dormitory style accommodation. A rickshaw from Kovalam should cost no more than Rs100 for the round trip.

Akkulum Lake

Akkulam Lake, three kilometres from Ullur Junction in the north of Thiruvananthapuram city also has facilities for boating rides. It has a boating club and a **children's park** in picturesque surroundings.

KTDC Day Tours

KTDC conducts daily tours beginning from their reception centre at Hotel Chaitram:

> Around **Thiruvananthapuram**. Starts 8 am, returns 7 pm.
> Cost Rs60.
> **Half-day city** tour. Starts 2 pm, returns 7 pm.
> **Ponmudi Hill Station** and **Neyyar Dam**. Starts 7.45 am, returns 7pm. Cost Rs100.
> **Kanyakumari** and **Padmanabhapuram Palace**. Starts 7.30am, returns 9pm. Cost Rs150.
> **Thekkady** (Periyar). Starts 6.30am Saturday, returns 9 pm Sunday. Cost Rs259

KTDC also run a weekly three-day tour up to Periyar, Madurai and Kodaikanal hill station in Tamil Nadu. The tour starts at 6.30am on Saturdays, returning 9pm on Monday. The fare is Rs420 and is exclusive of accommodation which can be arranged on request by KTDC.

TRIVANDRUM

Accommodation

The city has plenty of accommodation but visitors will most likely find it more relaxing to take themselves off to the cooler, more relaxing shoreline around Kovalam. Thiruvananthapuram can be noisy and humid.

Budget range

The best of the cheapest accommodation is around Manjalikulam Road, almost opposite the main railway station. There is little to choose between most of these very basic guest houses.

The cheapest you're likely to get is the Rs60 a night at **Bhaskarabhavan Tourist Paradise** nearby on Dharmalayam Road. Better to try the clean **Manacaud Tourist Home** at Rs140 for a double.

Others on Manjalikulam Road include **Sundhar Tourist Home**, Rs70; **Pravin Tourist Home**, Rs100: **Bhava Tourist Home**, Rs75; **Sivada Tourist Home** Rs140 (air-conditioned Rs300); and **Hotel Ammu**, Rs165 (air-conditioned Rs275).

Middle Range

In the Manjalikulam Road area there are also a few slightly more expensive hotels offering more facilities.

There is little to choose between them but if you want a bar in your hotel go to the **Hotel Pankaj** (rooms Rs420, air-conditioned Rs850) which has a good rooftop restaurant. **Hotel Regency** (0471-330377) on Manjalikulam Cross Road has rooms for Rs300 (air-conditioned Rs450).

Nearby KTDC's **Hotel Chaitram** (0471-330977) next to the bus and train station in Thampanoor has a nice bar, a coffee shop and book shop though you might eat elsewhere. Rooms cost Rs400 (air-conditioned Rs850).

Paramount Park Hotel (0471-63474)

on Aristo Road has rooms for Rs350 (air-conditioned Rs500). Other hotels include **Hotel Residency Tower** (0471-331661) on Press Road with rooms for Rs325 (air-conditioned Rs750); **Jas Hotel** (0471-64881) in Thycaud with rooms for Rs350 (air-conditioned Rs575).

Top of the Range

All these hotels have en-suite bathrooms, restaurants and air-conditioned rooms. **South Park Hotel** has rooms for Rs1375/1750.

The KTDC-owned **Mascot Hotel** has a swimming pool, friendly staff and is very clean. Doubles cost Rs995/1495. **Hotel Lucia**, as it is known, needs refurbishing but has a bar serving imported spirits and wines and a weekend discotheque. It also has a swimming pool, sauna, beauty parlour and gymnasium, fax and money changing facilities and an airport pick-up service.

There are 100 rooms costing Rs1195 to Rs3000 a night. **Madison Fort Manor** has rooms for Rs1000 at Power House Junction opposite East Fort and has a rooftop restaurant. **Hotel Horizon** (0471-66888) also has rooms for Rs950 (air-conditioned Rs1450).

Eating Out

Everyone who visits Thiruvananthapuram for a while has their own favourite restaurant but for value for money, friendliness and ability to serve up a hot meal quickly my favourite is the vegetarian **Arulukam** on Station Rd opposite the cinema. Always crowded with families and office workers, conditions are cramped. Mornings, and you can get *iddli* or the freshest, hottest (rather than spicy) *masala dosa* in town for Rs10. At lunchtime you can have as much as you want of the delicious vegetarian thali for Rs21. Or try the tasty *gobi masala* for Rs12. Wherever I

TRIVANDRUM

TRIVANDRUM

eat in the city, the Arulukam is a benchmark.

Another favourite is the **Kalavara** on Press Road near Pullmoodi Junction. Kalavara has a rooftop restaurant and serves up good vegetarian and non-vegetarian dishes at a snip. *Thalis* again are Rs21. A feast of four or five dishes between two people will set you back just Rs100. Kalavara also do a takeaway service.

The circular **Indian Coffee House** with its spiral staircase on Central Station Road is not an Indian creation but that of an eccentric Brit. Don't be put off. It doesn't stop them from putting on good breakfasts.

Athul Jyoti opposite the Secretariat on MG Road is popular for its *thalis* (Rs21) but service is sometimes a little surly and the *dosas* go cool while the waiters take their time. A better bet, next door, is the sweet shop which churns out excellent **fresh Indian sweets** (cakes). Try the cashew nut *burfi* cake and the fruit *burfi* or take home a portion of *rosmollai*. **Hotel Azad**, near Chala Bazaar is a good venue for cheap non-vegetarian meals including mutton *masala* and Kerala fish. Another commended restaurant is **Vinayak Vegetarian Restaurant** on Dharmalayam Road.

More expensive but still good value are the buffet lunches at the **Mascot Hotel** and at the South Park Hotel both at the top of MG Road. The city has many other restaurants especially by the Central Station where cheap *thali* houses are plentiful if you are hungry after stepping down from the train.

Shopping

For buying Indian handicraft, ornaments, saris, blankets etc. probably the best value for money is given at the state run **SMSM Institute** on YMCA Road behind the Secretariat. The **Kerala State Handicrafts Development Corporation** also has showrooms at the Mascot Hotel and Statue Junction.

Natesan s Antiquarts on MG Road have some fine antiques and handicrafts showing high quality craftsmanship. Be prepared for the length of time for form filling that it takes. Natesan's are one of the few shops that take credit cards outside of the major hotels. Other handicraft centres include **Kairali** opposite the Secretariat and **Khadi Gramodyog Bhavan** also on MG Road.

Book shops abound on MG Road where many Indian publications are extremely cheap. They include **Higginbothams, India Book House, Modern Book Centre, Continental Book Company** and **Pai & Company.** For British newspapers go to the **British Library** close to the Secretariat on MG Road. The papers may be a few days old but you'll be able to catch up on home. It opens from 10am till 7pm Tuesdays till Fridays.

Shirts, sandals, padlocks and the other little things you might need are cheap and plentiful in **Chala Bazaar.**

Money Changing

The Canara Bank near the Secretariat on MG Road is probably the easiest place to go to change money, travellers cheques and draw cash from your credit card. The State Bank of India generally offers the best exchange rates but the differences are marginal and most banks will offer some exchange facilities - if quite slowly.

Communicating Abroad

There are plenty of ISD/STD booths in the city. For posting parcels abroad go to the GPO. It's best to get a rickshaw there as it's on a tiny street behind the Ayurveda College on MG Road. It opens 8.30am to 8pm weekdays, 9.30am to 2.30pm and 4pm to 8pm Saturdays and 10am to 4pm

Sundays. Even on public holidays it opens in the afternoons from 2pm to 5pm.

Visa Extensions

Visa extensions are available to foreign nationals at the Office of the Commissioner of Police in Thycaud district on Residency Road. The process can take up to one week. The office opens 10am to 5pm daily save Sundays, public holidays and the second Saturday in the month.

Tourist Information

Kerala State Tourist Department (KSTD) has its main office (0471-438990) in Mascot Hotel, Mascot Square, opposite Indian Airlines. They have a reception centre at Hotel Chaitram (0471-330031) open daily from 6am to 10pm. KSTD has information counters at the airport, Park View (0471-61132), near the museum and Central Bus Station (0471-67224).

There also Tourist Information Centres at the domestic and international airports.

Hospitals

Medical College at Medical College Junction is the hospital most international visitors suffering illness or accidents are taken to. If the problem is serious the best advice is to contact your embassy/consulate immediately and request that they arrange a first-class hospital.

Travel Options

Thiruvananthapuram Airport is 6km from the city. The government has put some effort into upgrading the airport's international standing by increasing the number of available routes, including an onward flight connection to **Bangkok** in Thailand. Currently, the airport's only flights from the UK are with the weekly charter flights with package holiday companies **Manos, Somak** and **Inspirations**. The flight from Gatwick leaves on Sundays and takes 12 hours returning on Saturday nights. The cheapest, virtually flight-only tickets can be secured by booking the 'Dormitory Accommodation' option provided by both companies. The charter flights may be cheap but they are not a good choice for those uncertain of the length of their stay in India or those staying over six weeks.

Kuwait Air and **Gulf Air** also have connecting flights to **London, Paris** and **Frankfurt** generally involving a few hours waiting around in Kuwait or Abu Dhabi. **Air India** have flights via **Mumbai** (Bombay) to **London, Manchester, Frankfurt, Rome, New York** and twice-weekly direct flights to **Singapore**. Air India are a cheap option because a ticket to India is inclusive of the domestic flight but connections may mean a long wait in Mumbai.

Air Lanka have daily flights to **Colombo** airport in Sri Lanka which has regular British Airways and Air Lanka flights to the UK. **British Airways** also have regular flights to **Chennai** (Madras) in Tamil Nadu which is linked by flight and rail to **Thiruvananthapuram**. **Indian Airlines** (six days a week) and **Air Maldives** (five days a week) fly to the popular **Male** (Maldives Islands).

Air India, Gulf Air, Kuwait Air and Oman Air all have flights to the Gulf.

Domestic Flights

Indian Airlines have daily connecting flights to many of India's major cities from the domestic airport adjacent to the International Airport. Direct flights go daily to **Chennai** (Madras), **Delhi** and **Mumbai** (Bombay) and four days a week to **Bangalore**. All Air India's daily flights to Mumbai leave from the international airport. **Jet Air** are a new airline and have good, generally hassle-free daily service to Chennai (Madras). Flights to Chennai cost around. Rs2800 and flights to Mumbai approximately Rs4500.

TRIVANDRUM

Airline Offices

Most of the airlines have offices in the city. Phone lines are often continually jammed so a visit might be necessary.

Indian Airlines (0471-436870) are on Museum Road opposite Mascot Hotel. Close by, **Air India** (0471-434837) have offices in front of Kanakakkunnu Palace. **Gulf Air** (0471-68003) and **Kuwait Air** (0471-63436) are on the road to Sasthamangalam just opposite. **Air Lanka** (0471-68736), **Jet Airways** (0471-65267) and **Oman Air** (0471-62248) also have offices in the city.

Trains

Thiruvananthapuram is well connected to cities in states outside Kerala. Daily express trains go to **Jammu Kashmir** (3 days), **Delhi** (54 hours), **Mumbai** (Bombay) (45 hours), **Bangalore** (18 hours), **Chennai** (Madras) (18 hours) and **Coimbatore** (9 hours). Every Thursday an express train goes to **Calcutta** (45 hours). Direct trains also go daily to **Madurai** (8 hours, Rs52) and four times a day to **Kanyakumari** (Cape Comorin).

Within Kerala, Thiruvananthapuram has frequent services to **Kochi/Ernakulam**, costing from Rs56 second-class to Rs372 for an air-conditioned sleeper.

From **Ernakulam** there are further connections so it is possible to take the train to most parts of the state apart from the hilltop wildlife sanctuaries such as **Periyar**.

The best way to get to north Kerala is to take the express train up to **Thrissur, Kozhikode, Kannur** (Cannanore Express) or **Kasargod** (Parsasuram Express and Malabar Express).

The reservation office is on the first floor of the station building. There is a tourist counter on the far right-hand side. Trains from the city are often booked up well in advance, so book early.

If you have a problem, just politely inquire whether you are on the tourist quota but generally the station staff are very efficient and relatively quick. Remember to take your passport.

Buses

Bus services from the state capital to cities in other parts of India include daily services to **Mangalore**, twice daily to **Bangalore**, four times daily, a 17-hour bus ride to **Chennai** (Madras), six times a day to **Madurai** (7 hours) and nine times daily to Kanyakumari (2.5 hours).

Thiruvananthapuram is well connected by Kerala State Road Transport Corporation (KSRTC) buses to all parts of Kerala.

Nine 'superfast', 'super express' buses travel daily between **Kochi** (5 hours) and the capital. Buses go daily to **Thekkady** (8 hours) in Periyar Wildlife Sanctuary and to **Bekal** in the north.

Seven buses a day take the seven-hour trip to the temple city of Guruvayoor and five other buses, the 10-hour trip to **Kozhikode** (Calicut). Frequent buses go to **Kovalam** (30 mins), **Kottayam** (4 hours), **Thrissur, Varkala** (1.5 hours), **Kollam** (1.5 hours), **Neyyar Dam** (1 hour) and **Palakkad** (9 hours).

The long distance bus station is opposite the railway station. Buses also go to the main cities (including Kanyakumari) in Tamil Nadu. They are mainly run by **Thiruvalluvar** (Tamil Nadu's state bus service) whose office is at the east end of the bus station.

⊗ South from Thiruvananthapuram

Padmanabhapuram Palace and Kanyakumari

Highway 47 from Mallampuzha in north-east Kerala through Kochi (Ernakulam) and along the coast through Thiruvananthapuram to Kanyakumari (Cape Comorin) at India's southern most tip, is one of the state's most important roads. After it passes Kovalam, the highway soon enters the state of Tamil Nadu. Most of the state has evolved with different traditions to those of Kerala but that part in the south, closest to Kerala, was part of the old Kingdom of Travancore which ruled over southern Kerala. Notably Padmanabhapuram Palace was the family home of the Maharajas.

The trip south offers a fascinating vista of natural beauty, architectural wonder, philosophical contemplation and political instruction. Take out of it what you will but it's recommended for first-time visitors.

State buses, tours and taxis will take you south. There again if you want to chance your luck on the roads, try hiring a motorbike. The bus is incredibly cheap, if hard travelling. A taxi is a comfortable flexible way of travelling. It does offer the advantage of stopping off where you want and for how long you need instead of being corralled around by a tour company or rushing to catch the next bus.

The tourist taxi rate is Rs7 per kilometre so the 100km round-trip from Kovalam to Kanyakumari should cost no more than Rs750, ie. Rs250 each with three people in the car.

We aimed to set off at 8am to take advantage of the relative coolness of the day. Half an hour late we finally met up with our driver, Shareef.

Like many of the Kovalam taxi drivers, Shareef is a veteran of this trip. His knowledge gave us the bonus of a guide to the sights and sounds around us. The coastal road rarely presents a view of the sea. Instead, we were made aware of one of Kerala's special features - despite being such a verdant state it is hard to travel on any stretch of road and see not a building or a person. The highway out of Kerala is lined with shops, shacks and houses set back in the palm trees.

We stopped at a *chai* shop for breakfast, then to buy some Mango Fruity and some of those delicious red bananas. They call the state Red Kerala and red flags seem to be festooned everywhere but now we came upon four huge murals by the road side – Marx, Engels, Lenin and Stalin – not that any of them get a look in on what the Kerala Communist government does today. A lorry decorated with red banners was blaring out slogans in a square ahead as villagers went about their shopping. The red flags end at the border with Tamil Nadu.

Yes, it's a border and the taxi driver reaches over for Rs20 to pay the guard. Sometimes you pay, sometimes you don't – the rules are unfathomable – but we pass through into a land which already seems less fertile and more arid. The banana plantations and rice paddies are still there but the palm trees are less abundant, scattered by the heat. What were green foothills on our right now become the rugged brown Southern Ghats which trail off towards the Cape.

Padmanabhapuram Palace

One-and-a-half hours after leaving Kovalam we arrived in the dusty courtyard of Padmanabhapuram Palace set in the peace of the countryside. Formerly the royal residence of the 400-year-old dynasty of Travancore Maharajas, it is now a museum and scores of young women students in brightly-coloured *saris* and skirts were laughing and giggling as they waited for tickets.

The "Wooden Palace" as it is known, is the oldest palace of its size made of timber in India. It was constructed in the 1730s by **Maharaja Marthanda Varma**, said to be the founder of what is now the state of Kerala. When Marthanda Varma came to power in 1729 at the age of 23 Travancore, like the rest of Kerala, was in the grip of the Dutch East India Company who allowed the region's Maharajas to rule on sufferance. Travancore was a small bankrupt fiefdom unable to control its own army or rebellious local nobles.

With ruthless determination the new Maharaja set about establishing his supremacy. First he invited a potential rival and 42 of his noblemen to his palace. The rival was murdered, the noblemen hanged and their wives and children sent into slavery. Early on the young Maharaja signed a treaty with the Dutch who, despite the fact that they had a fortress at Anjengo near Thiruvananthapuram, conceded that henceforth their trading status was now based on the Maharaja's sufferance.

An efficient, disciplined army was trained which conquered the northern principalities up to Kochi and the Dutch were defeated in the Battle of Collachel. Some of the Dutch weaponry is on show at the Puthen Malika Palace in Trivandrum. A captured Dutch officer, Eustache De Lannoy, was enlisted on pain of death to train up the Travancore Army and build up a line of fortifications known as the Travancore Lines with which Travancore was able to keep the Dutch, the British and Moghul Emperor Tipu Sultan at bay. Contemporary portraits celebrating Lannoy's deeds are hung in the palace.

Before he died in 1758, Marthanda Varma also ordered the construction of vast irrigation programmes and the creation of new roads and canals. Charitable institutions were built and educational establishments were opened which laid the foundation for Kerala's traditionally high rate of literacy.

Under British rule Travancore was by no means the most powerful Indian state, meriting only a nineteen-gun salute but it had its own currency and stamps and kept time by the sun which meant it was 22 minutes behind the rest of India.

The tradition of ruthlessness and foresight continued through the centuries. In the nineteenth century the then Maharaja decreed a land reform which undermined the remnants of feudalism in the state. In 1936 the last Maharaja decreed that for the first time Untouchables could enter any temple in the state and in 1944, his state became the first in the whole of Asia to abolish capital punishment. At that time the state was also spending 40 per cent of its whole budget on education. Nevertheless the vicissitudes of the caste system and British rule laid the basis for the Communists to come to power in 1957. The Maharaja was allowed to hang on to most of his wealth till his death. The Kerala government now owns Padmanabhapuram.

Padmanabhapuram Palace is no Taj Mahal or Mysore Palace. It is neither grand nor opulent but functional and nevertheless beautiful in its gentility of design, a mark of a kingdom valuing strength rather than imagery. The exterior is made up of white walls holding up great beams of teak wood, supporting the red-tiled, gabled roof. Slatted and shuttered windows overlook the large courtyards. A large tank (pool) exists by the side which the family used for swimming.

It is all grander than Puthen Malika. Here teak is much more in evidence than rosewood. As in the capital's palace each ceiling has its own unique patterned wood carvings, but here the carvings are exquisite, windows are decorated with jewel coloured mica, and lions and dragons sculpted out of granite roar at the visitor.

Most famous are the well-preserved 250-year-old vivid fresco-secco murals conveying grace and religious zeal. The best murals are upstairs and we required special access to see them. The private chamber of Marthanda Varma is quite superb. A mural depicts the unity of the Dravidian goddesses with the Aryans via marriage, the theme of the Mohiniyattam dance, but for the conquering Maharaja perhaps a symbol of his imperial ambitions.

Local granite provides for the columns but the floors are laid with an environment-friendly but resistant compound made of egg-white, crushed shells, coconuts and plant juices all hardened then polished up to give a cool lustrous floor. The meditation room has two lamplights which have been alight since its construction. Two elderly women currently have the responsibility for keeping them aflame.

A guide attached himself to us as we entered. He was very informative and took us through the different chambers and courtyards, the bedrooms, bathrooms, ladies' rooms, the court, the muse room and the huge banqueting hall. That the wives slept separately was due to an unusual tradition. The Maharajas' dynasty originated from the warrior caste or *Kshatriyas* who were known as *Nairs* in Kerala. But the *Brahmin* caste, locally known as *Namboodiri*, originated from the priesthood which amassed knowledge of the scriptures and education and a degree of power.

The Maharaja's *Nair* wife was inviolate and hence to have children the Maharaja

TRIVANDRUM

used a *Namboodiri* woman as a surrogate mother, which also cemented a certain unity between the two castes in the ruling elite. With great relish we were told how the lengthy dining hall was built to seat 2,000 Brahmins who would be feasted by the Maharaja. We were shown a 38-kilo stone. Each candidate for the Maharaja's army would have to raise the stone above his head 101 times to prove his strength.

Finally the guide showed us into the portrait gallery which gives a fine picture of the lives and times of the Travancore elite. Then we thanked and paid the guide who showed us to the cafeteria, outside of which is the chopping block on which those who had offended Marthanda Varma would have their necks severed by a vicious swipe of the *kandakodali*. Nothing more vicious around now than a coconut splicer. The vendor stuck a straw in the green coconut and we drank its sweet milk.

One note, if you're also going to Kanyakumari, don't let your driver persuade you to go to the Palace after Kanyakumari. The Palace opens at 10am but closes sharply at 5pm. It is closed every Monday.

Nagercoil

Our journey south took us back onto Highway 47 towards Nagercoil. Here the landscape flattens save for a few granite buttresses rising sharply from the plain. We stopped by at a magnificent array of sky blue lions and dragons on top of a large Hindu temple. It is in this area that the houses are whitewashed in the pale blues and whites common to western Tamil Nadu. Their roofs become steeper and less ornamental.

Eventually we arrived at the small town of Nagercoil, announced by the splendid gopuram tower of **Nagaraja temple** rising above the surrounding countryside. Nagaraja is the presiding deity. The gopuram has tier upon tier of carved figures covering its four sides. Shiva and his steed, Ganesh towed by rats, Vishnu, Lakshmi, Parvathi, Hanuman, Kali, heroes, heroines, kings and queens, multi-headed figures, dancers, singers, goblins, sumptuous demons, satyrs, serpents, sprites and swans peered out onto the dusty square occupied by sweet and trinket stalls. Slumped in the midday heat were a dozen beggars (of such a range of ages that they might even have been a family concern) taking a rest from appellations to the temple visitors. It was a reminder that we had left Red Kerala and the Maharajas hadn't left much of their vaunted literary traditions here.

The entrance to the temple is once again reminiscent of the Chinese architectural styles used in Buddhism. Yet inside we also saw pillars with Jain images. The intricate wood carvings on the ceilings, walls and floors took up some time in inspection, then we were obliged to leave as this temple shuts in the afternoon.

Outside is the huge iron temple chariot six metres high and wide. The wooden wheels alone stand 2 metres high dwarfing the worshippers. Once a year it is attached to ropes and one thousand men are needed to drag it once around the temple in homage to Nagaraja.

Accommodation

Nagercoil has two hotels of note: **Hotel Ganga** (0465-32999), at Rs312 a double for air-conditioned rooms and Rs77 for a fan-only and **Parvathi International** (0465-33020) with prices at Rs300 and Rs150 respectively.

Transport

Nagercoil is an important bus station for Tamil Nadu and frequent buses go to **Thiruvananthapuram** and **Kanyakumari**. There is a also a train station 3km away from the central bus station.

Kanyakumari

At first sight Kanyakumari is a disappointment. What was all the fuss about, I wondered as we arrived at the sea front. With its rows of shops sporting faded signs and selling trinkets, beach junk, souvenirs and fruit and a Gandhi memorial reminiscent of Southport's old Floral Hall, but for the populous we might have been in a dilapidated north England seaside resort.

But there is more, much more. When we landed on the Vivekanand Rock Memorial which sprawls over the rugged island offshore, I understood why this little town attracts visitors from the length and breadth of India. It is more than a religious shrine. It is a philosophical experience.

Vivekanand Rock Memorial

After joining the disciplined queue to pay our Rs6 to board the ferry, we strolled down to the jetty. Waiting around to board the rusty old ferry were 40 or more Indians dressed in their 'Sunday Best' – *saris, shalwar khameez*, suits, *mundus* and *sarongs* like a picture postcard of the sub-continent's peoples. By the time everyone was on board the passengers must have numbered one hundred.

As I watched another old bucket cross the choppy strait from the island, it dipped and heaved so violently that from seeming to have its bow tossed skyward it would lunge into the waves and almost disappear. What a ride we were to have! It certainly beat anything at Southport fun-fair. The passengers laughed and shrieked as we were thrown up and down, water leaping out of the sea to soak us before sloshing around the deck.

Perhaps it was this short trip that shook the cobwebs from Mahatma Gandhi's and philosopher Vivekanand's mind and prepared them for their long sessions of meditation on the windswept island.

The island is the beginning or end of India depending on your perspective. Look north and before you is 2,000 miles of swampland, jungle, desert, green pastures, villages and cites all culminating in the triumphant grey and white peaks of the world's highest mountain range.

Look south and Sri Lanka is the only land mass where the evil god, Ravana, could flee. The rest is millions of square miles of the Indian ocean. Here the latter meets the Arabian Sea from the west and the Bay of Bengal from the east as if expressing in the choppy waters India's agglomeration of diverse cultures.

On a good day visitors can sit watching the sea crash onto the rocks while the fresh breeze takes one's breath away and whips up white horses from beyond the gently curved horizon. I'm not saying you'll find yourself. In fact it's a good place to lose yourself for a few hours.

Entrance into the Vivekanand Rock Memorial is Rs20 and a further few rupees to climb the steep steps to the panoramic views offered by the island's temple. Vivekanand, one of modern India's most influential swami philosophers, meditated here for several months in 1892 after the death of his guru Ramakrishna. One of his conclusions was to set sail and spread the guru's teachings world-wide and the following year he arrived in America.

TRIVANDRUM

We stayed for the sunset. We were in luck because there were few clouds to obscure the spectacular show on the horizon to the west. I could only gaze in awe as the golden orb of the sun slipped into the sea and the moon appeared out of the self-same waters in this ancient galactic changing of the guard.

Kumari Temple

Another attraction for religious pilgrims is the Kumari gopuram-bearing temple dedicated to Paraksathi, the virgin goddess. Kumari means chaste and Hindu myth has it that Parvathi came here to do penance to win the favour of her god. When rejected she swore to stay chaste for the rest of her life.

Men must remove their shirts before entering the temple and non-Hindus are not allowed into the inner sanctum. The temple is closed from noon till 5pm and after 8pm. It also attracts pilgrims to the **Kumari Ghat** where they bathe in the sea to achieve purity.

Gandhi Memorial

Near the Kumari Temple is the Gandhi Memorial Building in which Gandhi's ashes are kept. Go there on the great man's birthday, October 2, and you will witness the sun's rays falling exactly onto the spot where his ashes lie.

There's not much else worthy of particular mention in the town. The beach is rock-strewn and not very clean, being used by the fishermen as a toilet. However, food is good and cheap.

There are plenty of touts around pressing every item under the sun under your nose. One offered us a pair of Rayban sunglasses at the bargain price of Rs750. By the time our car drove off the price had fallen to Rs75 – not so much a Rayban and not so much a bargain!

Tourist Information

The Tamil Nadu Sate Government has a Tourist Office (04653-71276) on Beach Road near the State Bank of Travancore.

Accommodation

It is advisable to book accommodation beforehand if you intend to stay in the town. The hotels are often full, especially the quite good hotels on the sea-front.

Budget range

The cheapest accommodation, Rs30 per night is available at the **Youth Hostel** which is a dormitory in the **Hotel Tamil Nadu** (04653-71257). Otherwise rooms are available at Rs200 per night at **Hotel Sangam** (904653-71351) on Main Road, **Sanker's Guest House** (904653-71260) and **Vivekas Tourist Hotel** (04653-71192).

Middle range

Lakshmi Tourist Home (04653-71333) on East Car Street close to the beach is a new hotel and a good choice if you can afford the Rs175/300 charge per night. Rooms are clean, have an en-suite bathroom with modern toilets and on the first floor give a direct view of the island. The management is friendly, the food good and the hotel also offers room service, takes credit cards and changes foreign currency.

KTDC also offers rooms for Rs300 at **Kerala House** (04653-71229).

Top of the range

If you feel you need an air-conditioned room, there is a choice of only three hotels. **Manickam Tourist Home** (04653-71351) has taken advantage of its popularity and is now the most expensive hotel in town - Rs350/650 per night. Rooms and restaurant are good and some rooms have a sea view. **Hotel Tamil Nadu** (04653-71257) charges Rs275/450 and **Cape Hotel** (04653-71387), Rs275/375.

Eating Out

Restaurants are plentiful and cheaper than Thiruvananthapuram. **Manickam Tourist Home** is recommended.

Around Kanyakumari

Thanumalayan Temple is in Sucheendram, 13km from the Cape. It may cost you Rs50 to get there in a rickshaw and see the architecturally prized 18 feet tall statue of the monkey god, Hanuman and the Musical Pillars.

Non-Hindus are allowed in to join the pilgrims who particularly come for the Friday night when sunset heralds a special ceremony worth attending.

The 250-year-old **Udayagiri Fort** was part of the Travancore Lines system of fortifications built by De Lannoy in the reign of Marthanda Varma (1729-1758). It is 34km from the Cape.

Closer to Kanyakumari is another eighteenth century fortification, Vattakottal Fort. Also an hour or two's travel away are **Thirupparappu Waterfalls** (60km) Mutate Beach (32km) and Padmanabhapuram Palace.

Travel Options

Trains and Planes

Kanyakumari's nearest airport is Thiruvananthapuram. The train station is 1km away from the central bus station. Four express trains go daily to **Thiruvananthapuram** (2.5 hours) and **Kochi** (Ernakulam). The Himasagar Express leaves on Fridays for **Jammu**. The Bangalore Island Express and the Mumbai CST Express leave daily for the north passing stopping in the main Kerala cities and **Kollam** (Quilon),

Kottayam, **Thrissur** (Trichur) and **Palakkad**. A daily train goes via **Madurai** (6 hours) and **Trichy** to **Chennai** (Madras).

Buses

Kanyakumari has two bus stations, Central Bus Station and TTC Bus Station. Frequent buses go to **Thiruvananthapuram** (2.5 hours), **Madurai** (6 hours) and **Nagercoil** (45 mins). Two buses go early in the morning to **Kovalam** (3 hours). Twice daily KSRTC buses go to **Kochi/Ernakulam** (9 hours), for a fare of Rs99. Three buses a day go to **Chennai** (Madras) (16 hours). Daily bus services operate to **Bangalore** (15 hours), **Coimbatore** (11 hours), **Ooty** (14 hours) and **Kodaikanal** (10 hours).

Day Tours

KTDC operates a daily tour to **Kanyakumari** from Thiruvananthapuram which costs Rs150 and leaves the capital at 7.30am returning for 9pm. Taxis and rickshaws will also take visitors to Kanyakumari for a negotiated price.

Varkala

A long sandy beach, towering red laterite cliffs and out of them soothing mineral springs, and a good sea for swimming has made Varkala an increasingly popular resort. If you believe some guide books you'll conclude that this beach is a better option than Kovalam. It's certainly quieter – less shops, beach sellers, day-trippers etc. but overall there's not much to choose

TRIVANDRUM

between Papnasm, as Varkala's shore is called, and Lighthouse Beach. It depends what you want.

One disadvantage is that the steep walk from the beach to the restaurants on the palm tree topped cliff top takes ten minutes. So make sure you've got everything you need if you go there for the day. Two *chai* shops are all the service you'll get on the beach. The restaurants have similar menus to Kovalam but are slightly cheaper as is most of the accommodation. Bring a torch for night-time. The path along the cliffs is sometimes perilously close to the big drop - not a place to be staggering home!

Janardhana Temple

Varkala is the small village 2 km away from the beach and at its heart is the reputedly 2,000-year-old Janardhana Temple, a Vishnu shrine. The temple festivals are very colourful, with a noisy parade. Another Hindu festival to watch out for takes place in August when hundreds of Hindus perform "Vavu Bali" on the beach when the new moon appears.

Sivagiri Mutt

An Ezhava seer, Sree Narayana Guru, built Sivagiri Mutt, 3km from Janardhana Temple, as an information centre in 1904. He died here in 1928. His significance was that he preached the creed of one god, one caste, one religion. Thousands of his followers visit to pay their respects each year.

Anjengo Fort

Near to Varkala is the site of the Dutch East India's main garrison, Anjengo Fort, which in the 17th and 18th centuries protected their powerful position in the state.

Accommodation

Places on the hilltops tend to be more expensive than in the village. The last few years have seen a sharp growth in the number of visitors and hence in prices and new accommodation, particularly on the cliffs.

Budget range

In high season there are no guest houses with rooms for less than Rs200 but cheaper rooms at Rs80 to Rs200 are available in families' houses for those who ask around. The bright and quite new **Cliff House** does have some basic rooms with outside bathrooms for Rs200 but the rest of the 17 rooms cost Rs250/350 depending on whether the room is on the ground or first floor. **Mud House** just behind the Cliff Top Restaurant has basic rooms for Rs150/250 a double depending on the season.

Above a bicycle shop in the village and close to the temple the **JA Tourist Home** (0472-402453) has eight very basic but clean doubles with Indian toilets for Rs175 (Rs75 off-season) a night. The KTDC runs **Government Guest House** (402227) close to the Taj Garden Retreat. Though more than a kilometre from the beach and rather austere, it has good rooms for less than Rs100. Cheaper still, opposite the train station is the **Anandan Tourist Home** (0472-402135) which offers rooms for as little as Rs35.

Medium range

On the cliffs, **Hill Top** has ordinary rooms with baths for Rs200/300 depending on the season. **Varkala Marine Palace** (0472-403204) has air-conditioned rooms for Rs400/750, rooms without costing Rs75/400, and behind it **Motel Beach Palace** (0472-402453) has rooms for Rs350. **Akshay Beach Resort** (0472-402688) on the road to the village has rooms for Rs200/550.

Top of the Range

The recently constructed and superbly designed, luxurious hotel sitting on the cliff

Siobhan Kearney

Fred Anderson

Clockwise from top: bathtime;
Lighthouse Beach, Kovalam;
beach seller.

Fred Anderson

Phil Frampton

Minna Hildenbrandt

Top: pulling in the fishing nets, Kovalam. Above: *chai* wallah, Madurai.

Fred Anderson

Steffanie Kalt

Phil Frampton

Clockwise from top: Matsya Kanyaka, Thiruvananthapuram; chef with butterfish catch; 'Sunglass Man', Kovalam.

Steffanie Kalt

Siobhan Kearney

Top: fruit stall. Above: bullock carts in the city.

Siobhan Kearney

King Mahabali watches on: street festival.

Fred Anderson

Fred Anderson

Deborah Tilly

Clockwise from top: Napier Museum,
Thiruvananthapuram; temple elephant at
Ettumanur; advertising, Kovalam.

Steffanie Kalt

Monica Forti

Top: commuting in the Backwaters.
Right: billboard displaying Hindu gods Shiva and Parvathi.

Siobhan Kearney

Steffanie Kalt

Steffanie Kalt

Steffanie Kalt

Top: Muzhappilangad Beach. Middle: Chinese fishing nets, Kochi. Bottom: Lake Periyar.

top is the **Taj Garden Retreat** (0472-603000) owned by the Taj Leisure Group, owners of a string of five-star hotels, including the Taj Mahal Hotel, one of the landmarks of Mumbai.

Currently, hotel guests are denied direct access to the beach by the owners of the paddy fields in between the hotel and the shore. It means a long walk or a rickshaw ride to get there but there is compensation as guests can sit by the hotel's superb outdoor swimming pool. The grounds also have **tennis** and **badminton** courts, a fitness and *ayurvedic* massage centre and a **library**. With a pleasant restaurant and bar, a **beauty parlour** and **barber shop**, **fax** and **car hire** services and **safe deposit**, **credit card** and **money changing** facilities, it has pretty much everything a visitor could want

Standard double rooms from Christmas through February cost $105 a night (singles $95). Off-season prices for the eight rooms drop to $90 for a double (singles $80). There are also 18 'superior rooms' available for $110/$120 in peak season and $95/105 off-season depending on double or single occupancy. 10% luxury tax and 10% expenditure tax are additional.

Eating Out

There are plenty of restaurants on the cliffs which, as at Kovalam, serve fresh fish displayed on tables to attract potential customers. The menu is equally European but the food is slightly cheaper. Try the **Cliff Top Restaurant** which has a varied menu and serves up meals for Rs 30/85. Otherwise for those who can "splash out" dining in the stylish surroundings at Taj Garden Retreat will cost Rs 100/250 and a beer Rs 95.

Travel Options

Varkala is 54km north of **Thiruvananthapuram** and within two hours of

Kovalam (11/2 hours from Thiruvananthapuram). A taxi shouldn't cost more than Rs750 for a day trip and a rickshaw Rs600, but the railway station 3km and a Rs15 rickshaw ride from the beach has trains to Thiruvananthapuram (55 mins) regularly from 8am till 9pm, regularly to **Kollam** (45 mins) four times daily to **Kochi**, twice-daily to **Kanyakumari** and daily to **Mumbai** (Bombay), **Chennai** (Madras), **Bangalore** and **Madurai**.

Buses also go regularly to **Thiruvananthapuram** and **Kollam** but you may have to change at Paripally.

Krishnattam dancer

TRIVANDRUM

< Kottayam

TAMIL NADU

Periyar Wildlife Sanctuary

N

5
6
7
8
9
12
4
11
13
10
3
2
14
1

Mangali Devi Temple >

3km

Periyar Lake

1. Jetty
2. Aranya Nivas Hotel
3. Periyar House
4. Hotel Ambadi
5. Karthika Tourist Home
6. Woodlands T Bhavan
7. Mukumkal Tourist Home
8. Post Office
9. Bus stand
10. Lake Palace
11. Coffee Inn
12. Spice Village
13. Forest Entry
14. Wildlife Information Centre

PERIYAR

Kingfisher

MOVING ON TO **Periyar**

Periyar Wildlife Sanctuary

Thekkady, Periyar's main town, is 269 kilometres and a seven hour drive from Kovalam. Even Kochi is 200 km away so the best way to travel to one of India's largest and best-viewing wildlife sanctuaries is to go by bus or preferably taxi. There are coach tours run by various organisations but you run the risk of losing out as you get hurried from one destination to the next. A taxi will cost up to Rs4000 (Rs1350 between three people)

We set off at 9pm from Kovalam through Thiruvananthapuram (Trivandrum) on the road up to Kottayam as we wanted to get a look at Punalor on the River Kallada and further into the hills the Palaruvi Waterfalls. However, it being the dry season we were advised against it – there wasn't much water to fall.

Punalor

Entering Punalor we passed a large buffalo breeding farm and peasants gathering wood which they carried away in enormous bundles on top of their heads. They were off to make charcoal. In the fields the *dhobi wallahs* (washerwomen) had been active, neatly laying the morning's washing out on the ground to dry. Most likely some of the women had joined those busy with their ablutions in the River Kallada. A colourful, disused railway bridge spans the river, on its sturdy steel girders an announcement that it was erected in 1877.

Punalor is worth a visit if you are interested in freshwater fishing. The River Kallada on which it stands is reputed to have stocks of the giant *mahseer* fish (up to nine feet long and 100 kilos) which attract so many anglers from around the world to the Cauvery River, west of Mysore. Travancore carp and catfish are also said to be in these waters, but few locals seem to know about it. Punalor is three hours drive from Kovalam and matters weren't helped when, after turning off the Kottayam Road at Kottarakkara, the narrow road was continually overrun by cows and oxen being herded to market. Two buses a day go to Kochi via Pathanamthitta.

Forty kilometres eastwards and upwards through the Ariankavu mountain pass are **Palaruvi Waterfalls**. Here the river Kallada cascades a spectacular 300 feet in one drop which is followed by a series of smaller drops.

Pathanamthitta is an unexceptional small busy market town. Unless you want to sample small town Kerala life and get away from Western tourists there's no point in hanging around. The town is a stopping off point for pilgrims going to the shrine at

P
E
R
I
Y
A
R

Sabarimala. KSTRC **Buses** go daily to **Kochi** via **Alappuzha**. Two private buses a day go to Kochi via Kottayam and one via Vaikom.

Pathanamthitta has non-air conditioned rooms for less than Rs100 at **Anil Tourist Home** (04733-2475), on Kadammanitta Road, **Union Tourist Home** (04733-2603) on College Road, **Toby's Lodge** (04733-62521) and **Hotel Mayfair** (04733-2894) both on Main Road and **Hotel Heyday** (04733-2621) on Police Station Road.

Hotel Mayfair for Rs150 and **Hotel Heyday** for Rs160 also have air-conditioned rooms. **Hotel Dolphin Tower** (04733-3220) is the most expensive in town at Rs250 for a room with air-conditioning and Rs120 without.

Perunthenaruvi Falls

After Pathanamthitta we had to cross the wide Sambayar River at Ranni. Some crossing this. The bridge is one long cattle grid of metal rollers! Not a place to stall. Now the terrain became gently undulating with pink, orange and sky blue churches nestling in the valleys. But for the colours and the heat it might have been Thomas Hardy country. Here it seemed the only places of worship in evidence were Christian, a testament to how early Christianity took a hold and spread into Kerala's hinterland.

A detour via **Vechuchira**, 12km from **Ranni** (36km from Pathanamthitta) took us further into the hills to the scenic splendour of **Perunthenaruvi Falls**. Here the clear waters twist and gurgle before cascading angrily over granite steps beautifully sculptured by nature's hand into a ravine 30 metres deep. Large boulders and forest flank this almost undiscovered beauty spot which is a ten minute trek from Vechuchira.

Alternatively, the winding road to Chenna offers a pleasant 20 minute trek from the town through a teak plantation to the falls. Swimming is possible in the falls, cool waters but the rocks are very slippery, so we went and had a nice dip in the more tranquil pools higher up which provided a panoramic view of the surrounding countryside.

The Spice Valleys

At Kanjirapalli we turned eastwards onto the Kottayam-Thekkady road through Mundakayam, a small village of 30 with two-dozen shops, a church and a temple. We were climbing up to **Peerumedu Hill Station.**

Save for the rubber plantations in the lowlands, the valley below, like many beneath Periyar, is one big spice garden. Pepper, ginger, cinnamon, cloves, the forest dwelling cardamom spice and many others abound here. These are the spice valleys of the **Cardamom Hills** the produce of which drew ancient traders from three continents.

Peerumedu (Peermade)

Approaching Peerumedu, Kerala's celebrated **tea plantations** came into sight climbing up the hills to the north and east covering the slopes like green scales. In

PERIYAR

the distance gently rolling mountains free of flora appeared like the backs of huge mammoths stalking Lord Ayappa's lands.

No palm trees here, just deciduous rosewoods, teaks and sandalwoods. Peerumedu is 918 metres above sea level and offers ample scenic walks and trekking for those who want to escape the usual tourist routes.

The town itself is not so inviting. Deprived of the multi-use coconut tree and its fruits and with few job opportunities, save for pitiful wages in the tea plantations, the population live in grim, wooden, dust-covered shacks akin to the shanty towns of northern India. Tea sacks are used as skirts by the women and the road has been left so long unrepaired Peerumedu appears like a town the tour guides want to forget. Ironically Peerumedu still displays the relics of a summer palace of the Travancore Maharajas. **Buses** go to **Thekkady** and **Kochi**.

Accommodation is available in Peerumedu. KTDC has a motel, the **Sabala** (04869-32250) at **Kuttikanam** (KTDC motel rates apply, rooms Rs150/300). There is also a **Government Rest House** and **Hotel Himarani** (04869-32288).

Periyar Tiger Reserve

Covering 777 square miles Periyar is one of India's biggest wildlife sanctuaries. Hidden in its lush damp terrain and hilltops are an estimated 600 elephants, 450 sambar deer, 500 wild boar, 170 troops of Nilgiri langur monkeys, 21 troops of bonnet and lion-tailed macaque monkeys, 450 porcupine, 100 gaur, 50 muntjak or barking deer, 50 mouse deer, 150 giant squirrel and uncertain numbers of sloth bears, wild dogs, jackals, civets, flying squirrels, mongoose, pangolin, cobra, and otters. And, of course, 53 tigers and 15 leopards.

The Tiger Reserve was declared back in 1978, not as a large wildlife park for tiger spotters but to help reverse the catastrophic decline in India's tiger population. Hunted almost to extinction for their hides, deprived of their habitats and the creatures on which they preyed, the tiger population had fallen to just 1,800 by 1972. Since then, over the last two decades, under the government-run Project Tiger which covers 15 sanctuaries, the tiger population has trebled.

What you will actually see and hear most is not the tigers but the bountiful and beautiful birdlife – brahminy and black-winged kites, snake birds, black eagles, the kaleidoscopic colours of the short-toed eagle, quail, Sonnerat's jungle fowl, vultures, lapwing, plovers, sandpipers, blue-winged parakeets, malabar lorikeets, ceylon frog-mouths, malabar trogons, stork-billed kingfishers, chestnut-headed bee-eaters, hoopoes, crimson-throated barbets, indian golden-backed three-toed woodpeckers, golden oriole, greater racket-tailed drongo, jungle mynas, rosy pastors, golden-front-ed chloropsis, fairy bluebirds, red-whiskered bulbuls, white-breasted laughing thrushes, quaker barblers, paradise flycatchers, Nilgiri white-eyes and purple-rumped

PERIYAR

sunbirds, to name a few of the 160 or so identified species. In short, a birdwatcher's paradise.

Central to the 350 sq km designated as National Park is the beautiful *Periyar Lake*. Some say Travancore carp and *mahseer* also reside in its waters but fishing is not allowed save by the local hill tribe who have lived off the fish in the area's lakes and rivers for centuries.

The sanctuary can be divided into four categories:

1) Open grassland studded with fire-resistant vegetation and a variety of grasses including elephant grass and sachurum. 10 square kilometres of this are around Periyar Lake. It provides the grazing grounds of the herbivores from the tiny barking deer to the elephant.

2) The teak and terminalia-dominated, moist deciduous forest is also common to the area near the lake.

3) Semi-evergreen forest close to the tropical forests and wet, stream areas.

4) The *sholas* or tropical evergreen jungle of the tigers, lion-tailed macaques and king cobras. Mainly found in the valleys, this area of dense forestation and thick undergrowth covers 40% of the park.

Periyar Lake

Beautiful as the 26 sq km of Periyar Lake is, the lake is a man-made creation. It resulted from the construction of the great Idduki Dam further downstream which serves Kerala for electricity. Evidence of this is still shown by the petrifying stumps of trees rising out of the lake.

The most common and convenient way of seeing Periyar's exotic wildlife is to take a boat trip on the lake. We arrived at the boarding point in Thekkady to catch the sunset and the passengers returning from the last ferry trip of the day. The night air filled with the sound of hoopoes, mynas, drongos and treepies. Silhouettes of Nilgiri langur could be seen moving around the tree tops.

At the **Wildlife Information Centre** we picked up a useful illustrated guide book on Periyar's birdlife and studied the choice of walks and forest treks. The night was not cold but it is useful to take a sweater or light anorak as a precaution against cool nights and rain which, though it falls mainly in the monsoon, occurs all year round in this area.

We were staying nearby, so we could take the 7am ferry from the jetty in Thekkady. There we were charged Rs50 each to pass into the lake area. A heavy morning mist hung swirling over the lake, given a touch of mystery by stumps of the petrifying trees rising eerily out of the waters.

We had to hurry for we hadn't calculated for the kilometre-long walk down the dirt track and over a makeshift bridge of boulders and planks to the jetty. There, two small ferries were waiting for passengers. Later on in the day there would be four or five of the noisy chugging boats, which was a good reason to go early as the noise and immobility of the flotilla would make viewing animal life quite difficult.

Boarding the ferry cost us another Rs50 (downstairs Rs25) each. It was quite chilly so I was glad that I had remembered to bring my cagoule.

The mist began to clear and we were off. Fortunately after a short while the other ferry headed in a different direction, cutting down the noise and enabling our boat to cut the engines and stop when we came near any wildlife that might be frightened off by the noise. Stuck to

the top of the tree stumps were whitenecked storks and snake birds. wings stretched out to dry. Cormorants dived for fish and the odd blue flutter of a Kingfisher flew through the air. Egrets, heron and sandpipers stalked the marsh by the shore. A pair of binoculars would have been useful as, when we came across the park's animals, they were often too far away for all but the guide to identify.

"Bison! Bison!" the guide shouted, excitedly pointing to the top of a range of hills. Fortunately these *gaur*, often called Indian bison, were not Linford Christies as it took me some time to find them - small dots ambling along on the horizon. Easier to see were the pack of wild boar grazing and frolicking on the grass close to the water's edge and a family of otters gambolling in the shallows. A troop of Nilgiri langur came into view nestling in the trees.

Only the ferry engines. songbirds and the occasional calls of the langurs disturbed the morning's peace and, quite frankly, with the fluttering and diving birds, the glistening woodlands and the browns, greys, reds and greens of the rolling hills. The scene was so beautiful that I wouldn't have cared a monkey if we hadn't seen a tiger or an elephant.

And we didn't see a tiger - only at dusk do they occasionally lope down to the lake's perimeter. We did see a bull and cow elephant with their child foraging in the shrubs.

Now we could cut the engines and wonder at the world's greatest mammal in its natural state. No pulling logs, no temple or circus tricks, no humans aboard. It was a thrilling experience. I'm not sure I would have had the same feeling if I had come across them on a trek through the park, a little fear as well maybe but this was a moment to savour.

PERIYAR

And it was a long moment. A full-grown elephant needs ten to fifteen hours of grazing a day to keep going. So it wasn't a 'grab a quick snack for brekkie and we're off'. Instead we settled down for half an hour. It's not often one gets pleasure out of watching a breakfast being downed.

Still luckier visitors will get to see a group of elephants going for a swim, spraying the air with their trunks and climbing out of their bath only to spray themselves with a shower of dust and even roll their rear end in the dust to make sure they are dirty all over again.

Even though, unlike the larger African elephants, Indian cow elephants don't have tusks, it can be difficult to tell from a distance who's who because some Indian bull elephants, known as *makhnas*, are also tuskless. Our guide could tell - somehow. He also told us that the elephants in view were probably from a resident family, whereas there are those who migrate up to the Western Ghats and even into Tamil Nadu.

After two and a half hours we disembarked from the ferry. Most people satisfied, they made their way back up to the car park. We didn't – the sun was out bringing warmth into the morning air, the boat engines were silenced and birds set to song as the sun cleared the morning mist. Don't follow the crowd and you can sit by the lake and enjoy nature in peace.

The 4pm boat trip is more likely to catch animals coming down to the lake for a drink or supper. One warning: not everyone gives the same story of this boat trip. Two women who went in the afternoon in a fleet of ferries said that, apart from the noise of the boats, which being in a fleet couldn't stop, any animals in sight would have been scared off by the screams and shouts of the excited passengers. Stick with 7am when for everybody save the guide, it's too early to get excited.

A safer alternative is to charter a small boat between a group of people and take it onto the lake (Rs300 for six people).

The **KTDC Boat cruises** are at 7am, 9.30am, 11.30am, 2pm and 4pm. Boats can be hired via the KTDC manager at **Aranya Nivas Hotel,** Thekkady (04869-22023)

Trekking

Walks in the park are very pleasant and can be a very worthwhile way of taking in the beauty and variety of flora, fauna and landscapes.

A small group commented: "It was quite amazing. We couldn't find a guide so we took off ourselves. We saw wild boar, monkeys, bison and woodpeckers. Then we came across an elephant and we were a little scared when a pack of boar ran past it but it seemed quite tame."

Walking in the park without a guide (Rs20) is not allowed. Forget the tigers, wild elephants alone kill 200 people in India each year.

Official three hour morning walks cost next to nothing and guides can be hired from the Wildlife Centre for more extensive walks.

Watchtowers

For those who fancy a more careful inspection of life deep in the forest, there are two watchtowers available at Rs50 per day for two people from the **Forest Information Centre** (04869-220028) in Thekkady. The towers overlook waterholes and offer an excelent view of the jungle. Visiting requires preparation: you'll need food, blankets, warm clothes and candles and a guide to take you there.

Deep into the forest are two rest houses only reachable via a one and a half hour boat ride. **Forest Lodge** is in Manakaval and **Edapalayam** is 5 km from Thekkady. For bookings contact the Chief Conservator, Forest Wildlife, Thiruvananthapuram.

Visiting

Entry into the park is permitted from 6am to 6pm. Best time of the year for visiting is the dry season, September to May, when the need for water draws thirsty and then hungry animals to the lake. If you are unlucky you will at least hear the birdlife. It is, after all, a nature reserve not a safari park. But if you feel the need to get close to the animals elephant and horse rides are available nearby.

 Around Periyar

Sabarimala Temple

Lord Ayyappa is seen in the Ghats as the guardian of mountaineers and the temple at Sabarimala is the principal shrine dedicated to the Hindu warrior-god. Lord Ayyappa was the product of a fling between Mohini, the enchantress (in actuality the god Vishnu) and Shiva. Each January, Sabarimala is the destination for thousands of pilgrims to see **Makara Vilakku**, a mystic light, which is said to appear on the mountain opposite the temple. One million pilgrims now make the trip each year, making Sabarimala the second largest pilgrimage in the world.

Other religions are invited along. Indeed a Muslim priest at the entrance to the temple has the job of deciding whether visitors have purified themselves enough to enter. Sabarimala is one of the few Kerala temples a non-Hindu can visit.

Only men (and they must remain celibate) are allowed to make the trek, which they make unshaven and dressed in black. The walk through the elephant and tiger stalked Periyar was always perilous and today's pilgrims follow their ancestors' ancient ritual as they climb up from Pampa through 5km of dense forest and rugged terrain shouting, "Swami Saranam Ayyappa!" (Lord Ayyappa you are our refuge!")

The temple itself is quite modern, the entry being 18 gold steps. On their heads the pilgrims carry an *irumudi,* a bundle containing amongst other things, a coconut husk and some ghee to pour over Ayappa's head symbolising the merging of the pourer's and the god's souls. The coconut is then thrown into the fire, symbolising the empty shell of the body. Money is also thrown down to Ayappa and then used to maintain the temple and its various businesses.

A less strenuous festival, the **Vishu Vilakku** takes place in April. For festivals there are frequent buses from Kochi, Kottayam and Thiruvananthapuram to the town of Pampa. Pampa, which is on the southern perimeter of the sanctuary, can be reached by car on the way up to Thekkady from Pathanamthitta by going through Vandiperiyar or vice versa from Thekkady. The last 5km has to be done by foot. It is possible to get to Sabarimala by taking a jeep to within two hours walk away. But the whole trip will take a whole day and requires a day's provisions and provisions for an overnight stay if stranded. Sabarimala has accommodation at the temple site.

Mangala Devi Temple

A jeep or motorcycle are the only really suitable means of transport for climbing the rugged 13 km road to Mangala Devi Temple. The ancient temple was built in the Pandyan style but most of it has gone to ruins. It's worth the hour long trip for the stupendous views alone.

Idukki

Idukki, 60 km north west of Thekkady just off the road to Munnar gives its name to the great **Idduki Arch Dam** that lunges between two large granite hills to block the River Periyar on its way to the sea. Built a century ago by the British, it was the first of its kind. The British used the dam to redirect water to Tamil Nadu. Since then the dam has become a vital source of hydro-electric power for electricity starved Kerala.

Another dam has been built at *Cheruthoni* and 5km away from Cheruthoni. 1,250 metres above sea level is *Painavu* which affords tremendous views of the lowlands to the east bringing into view Kochi almost 100km away.

Idukki Wildlife Sanctuary covers 70 sq km north of the Idukki Dam and is 40 km from Thodupuzha. Elephants roam across this area. The nearest accommodation is Cheruthoni where there is a *Government Guest House* (0423-32205) and in Idukki itself which has a *YWCA* (0423-42218) and *Idukki Gate Hotel* (0423-42059) which charges Rs450 to Rs600 a night for a double.

Plantation Tours

Several hotels organise tours of the surrounding plantations. Book at *Rolex Lodge* and for Rs250 per group a guide will take visitors on a three hour trip by rickshaw to see various spice and tea plantations, waterfalls and inside an interesting tea processing plant. Expect to tip (Rs10/50) at the end.

Accommodation

Around Periyar Lake is an excellent range of accommodation catering for any budgets. It is advisable to book in advance if you want to guarantee the type of place you require. Like Kovalam, prices in this understandably popular area for tourists have risen quite steeply in the last few years but are still reasonably cheap. The two main areas for accommodation are Thekkady, by the lakeside and the town of Kumily, 4 km away.

THEKKADY Budget Range

There is no accommodation for under Rs300 in the park but just outside the entrance to the sanctuary is the excellent value **Coffee Inn** where for Rs150/250 visitors can stay in one of the inn's five "wild huts" or the two rafia tree houses. The huts are new and came about because of excess demand to stay in the one wild hut the inn used to have.

Each of the huts has its own shower and quaint furniture. They are off the road and quiet until night time when guests can sit on little terraces and listen to the sounds of the jungle - gaur barking for fear of the big cats, bats, hoopoes etc.

The huts, made with palm wood and bamboo lacing, are weatherproof. Set in a pretty garden with coffee plants and other spices they are quite charming. Rooms with shared bathrooms are also available for Rs100 in the Inn itself. The staff may occasionally seem a little po-faced but the restaurant is relatively expensive and the huts are excellent value.

Medium Range

Five minutes from the lake, KTDC's **Periyar House** (0489-22026, fax (0489-22282) has doubles for Rs500 to Rs1500 in season. Out of season (June/July) prices fall to Rs300/950. The rooms are clean and have en-suite bathrooms. The management is friendly and the restaurant serves up good food for Rs25/80. The beer parlour is a little gloomy but if you've missed out on a massage you can get one here.

Bicycles and cars are available for hire and the hotel accepts credit cards and exchanges foreign currency.

Top of the Range

Aranya Nivas (04869-22023 fax 0489-22282) is KTDC's middle range hotel in the park. Closer to the lake than Periyar House, it has all the facilities of the latter plus a pleasant swimming pool, satellite TV for insomniacs in all bedrooms and a shop. Its restaurant is good but more expensive - the evening buffet is Rs250, but the bar is one of the better ones you'll find in Kerala. The hotel has 30 double rooms costing Rs1500/2395, singles Rs1000/1150. The exception is in June/July when prices fall to Rs800/2000 (singles Rs600/1000). Luxury tax of 7.5-10% is additional.

The Lake Palace

If you want to make your visit special then stay at KTDC's opulent **Lake Palace** (04869-22023 fax 0489-22282) situated on the other side of the lake. Formerly the hunting lodge of the Maharaja, it is an excellent venue from which to watch and hear the creatures of Periyar. Both Aranya Nivas and Lake Palace throw in one free morning or evening ferry trip.

Those just arriving or returning from a day out must make sure they get to Aranya Nivas before 4pm when the last boat for the palace departs. The only option afterwards is to hire a guide and do the one hour walk – and they won't do that after dark! None of the six spacious rooms have air-conditioning. Doubles cost Rs 4000/6000 plus tax (June/July Rs2750/4000). Book early.

PERIYAR

KUMILY Budget Range

Kumily is a pleasant, rambling village. Buses and bikes are available if you don't want to do the pretty walk through the park to the lake.

Best of the cheaper guest houses is probably the friendly Mr Augustine's **Woodlands Tourist Bhavan** (04869-22027) on Thekkady Road with its garden of spice plants. Doubles cost Rs100/200 (Rs80/150 off-season). The 23 rooms are very basic, a little grim but clean. loos are Indian style. There are cooking facilities available but at a cost.

The friendly **Lake Queen Tourist Home** (04869-22086) is at the Kottayam Road and Thekkady Road junction. The restaurant is not recommended but the rooms are clean costing Rs161/268 for doubles with en-suite bathrooms (single Rs107). Power cuts can be frequent and the hotel has a very, very noisy generator.

Others in this range include the pleasant **Claus Garden**, with its reputedly excellent breakfasts, **Rolex Lodge** (04869-22081), the very grim **Karthika Tourist Home** (04869-22146) and the **Holiday Home**. Rooms at **Muckumkal Tourist Home** (04869-22086) cost Rs150/250. Its Little Chef restaurant serves good, inexpensive food and the sociable staff will serve up a hot breakfast very quickly if you're in a hurry.

Medium range

Hotel Ambadi (04869-22194) has pleasant rooms and cottages for Rs250/500 and is preferable to the rather basic **Leela Pankaj Resort** (04869-22299).

Top of the Range

Though it is outside the sanctuary, **Spice Village** (04869-22315 fax 04869-22317) makes up for it with its imaginative gardens with a multitude of spice plants common to Kerala: coffee, cocoa, pepper, cardamom, curry leaf, clove, all spice, cinnamon, tea, myrtacae – plus mango, jackfruit and rose-apple trees all very helpfully with names attached. The outdoor restaurant is excellent if expensive Rs200/300 and looks out on a dance floor, for Kathakali performances, and the swimming pool.

Recreation and education is a theme here and at 7pm each night visitors are invited to attend a lively cooking demonstration in the gardens. Outdoor activities arranged include jungle treks, and visits to tribal villages and plantations. You can hire your bike here for the trip to the lake. If it rains you can stay in to play tennis, chess or, if you miss home, Monopoly.

Accommodation is in Kerala-style cottages thatched with elephant grass. The rooms are well furnished inside and a treat to stay in. The cottages cost $90 a night (singles $80) plus luxury tax of 10%.

Eating Out

Muckumkal's Little Chef restaurant serves good cheap meals as does Periyar House. Meals at Coffee Inn are also good but more expensive. For those who want to spend on a good splurge, Spice Village puts on an excellent barbecue dinner and buffet (Rs300) as does the slightly cheaper Aranya Nivas (Rs250) by the lake.

Travel Options

Periyar can only be reached by road. Regular buses go to **Kumily** from **Kochi**, **Thiruvananthapuram**, and **Kottayam** (5 hours, Rs27).

⊗ Up to Munnar Hill Station

Nestling 1800 metres up in the hills of the Southern Ghats surrounded by acres of neat, rolling tea plantations is the hill station of Munnar. The town is 60 km north of Thekkady at the confluence of three mountain streams, Mudrapuzha, Nallathanni and Kundala. Winding lanes pass through areas beset with the fragrance of fresh tea, leading to the forests, lakes and mountains around.

To the north is **Anamudi,** at 2,695 metres south India's highest peak and ideal for mountaineers. *Anamudi* means Elephant's Head and legend has it that a god sits making sure that the mountain doesn't become any bigger and obstruct the sun from going around the Earth.

Above the tea plantations the ubiquitous *neelakurunji* plant, which blooms only once in twelve years, paints the hillsides blue. Below are the spice valleys and tropical evergreen forests. The hills are home for one of the world's rarest mountain goats, the once threatened species, Nilgiri tahr. The tropical forests are inhabited by elephants, tigers, deer and gaur bison.

Add to all these riches a cool climate with rain mainly concentrated in June and July, a good variety of hotels and some magical scenery and it is easy to understand why Munnar is such a popular venue for Indian tourists. And, given that many of the tea plantations were planted by the British who came to Munnar because of its attractive climate, it is difficult to see why so few western tourists find their way here.

Many of the tea plantation workers' homes are the wood stone and corrugated iron assemblages common to the hill stations but Munnar has a golf course and is an excellent centre from which to sally forth on a trek into the mountain wilderness or go horse riding or fishing.

Accommodation

Budget rooms are available for Rs100 or less near the bus station at **Hotel Ambat** (04865-30361) and Krishna Lodge (04865-30669) and in the town at **Guest House** (04865-30385). In old Munnar, the popular clean **SN Lodge** (04865-30212) and **Misha Tourist Home** (04865-30376) have rooms for Rs200/300 as does **Hotel Poopada** (04865-30223) outside Munnar on Manukulam Road, offering good views and a cheap, good value-for-money restaurant.

Top of the range are **Hotel View**, (04865-30567) on AM Road has a casino, a bar and a rooftop glasshouse and rooms are Rs500 a night (bookings can also be made on Kochi 360076). Similar prices are charged at **Hotel Isaac's The Residency**

(04865-30247) on Top Station Road and the splendid **Edassery Eastend** (04865-30451) cottages on Temple Road.

The attractively designed spacious **Royal Retreat** (04865-30240) is outside Munnar in the Kannan Devan Hills. Rooms are from Rs750 for a double. The restaurant is good but awkward to get to. In Munnar **Sterling Resorts** have rooms for Rs650 to Rs1250 and, out in Chithiapuram, Star Homes **Hotel Igloo** (04865-63207 fax 0484-371589) is probably the most luxurious and expensive of Munnar's hotels at Rs1500 a night. Bookings can also be made on Kochi 368490.

Travel Options for Munnar

Munnar area has no nearby rail stations. KSRTC run a daily **bus** service to and from **Kochi** (6 hours) 130 km away. There are also private buses to Kochi. Buses go to Munnar from the towns in the area and from **Kumily**.

Around Munnar

Devikulam

Sixteen kilometres from Munnar, Devikulam is another peaceful, almost romantic, hill station with velvet lawns, refreshing mountain air and the dreamy Sita Devi lake. If you're an angler, one dream you can fulfill in this lake is bagging some trout. Trout has been bred here since the days of the Raj. A **Government Guest House** (04865-64223) has rooms here.

Top Station

A 32 km one and a half hour drive eastwards from Munnar, Top Station, the highest point on the Munnar-Kodaikanal road puts you in the mountains, the stalking grounds of so many of Kerala's gods. Buses go here eight times a day and you might be the lucky one who sees the *neelakurunji* plant spray the hills violet in the one month in twelve years that it blooms. The flowers, due to bloom in 2006, are associated with Murugan, the Tamil name for Karttikeyya, Shiva's second son. A Rs400 taxi ride will get you to Top Station.

The area also has two, quite spectacular waterfalls. Between Adimali and Neriamangalm and along the Deviyar River the **Cheeyyappara Waterfalls** cascade a spectacular 1,000 feet. Nearby are the **Valara Waterfalls**.

Eravikulam National Park

North of Munnar 97 sq km have been given over to the Eravikulum National Park which is overwhelming jungle but has a rising population of the rare *Nilgiri tahr* mountain goat. 17 kilometres from **Rajamali** is the thrilling if not terrifying sheer drop from Deobolic Point sometimes called Suicide Point.

Chinnar Wildlife Sanctuary

Chinnar Wildlife Sanctuary is adjacent to the Eravikulam Sanctuary on the Tamil Nadu border. Like Eravikulam, Chinnar has mountains and jungle but it is the only part of Kerala which has a large semi-arid area.

On the edge of Chinnar is **Marayoor** town where relics from the Stone Age were dug up. The town also has an unusual playground for children - all in the one hectare beneath a huge banyan tree. Unlike in the rest of Kerala, sandalwood trees can be seen here growing naturally and visitors can see what happens to the harvested trees at the Forest Department's sandalwood factory.

Marayoor also has some basic and cheap accommodation. **Aruna Lodge** and **Uma Lodge** have rooms for Rs50 a night and the **Chandana Tourist Home** (04865-52222) charges Rs150.

Kodaikanal

Though over the border in Tamil Nadu, Kodaikanal, one of India's better known hill stations is worth a visit if you're in Munnar, Periyar or travelling to or from the temple city of Madurai. 2000 km up Kodai mountain in the Palani Hills, the station commands some of the most beautiful and panoramic views to be found anywhere in south India. The climate is temperate with cool nights, pleasantly warm days and a good refuge from the heat and humidity in the lowlands, making the hill station a popular place for Indians and foreign tourists alike. The dramatic scenery also makes the area a sought after site for Indian films and TV commercials.

Travelling up from Madurai to Kodaikanal and into Kerala or vice versa underlines the contrast between India's southern twins Tamil Nadu and Kerala. Both peoples are said to be of Dravidian origin and their languages Tamil and Malayalam have similarities but the two states, having different geography, have evolved quite differently.

The plains around Madurai are semi-arid and with the intense heat much of western Tamil Nadu suffers long droughts and water shortages. It is only relieved, to the irritation of Kerala, by drawing on Kerala's reservoirs. Vast reserves of oil, gas and coal have made Tamil Nadu an Indian industrial powerhouse while Kerala relies on its bountiful, varied crops.

In Tamil Nadu you won't see scores of children on their way to school but you will see them at another type of school - sat round a banyan tree listening to one of their elders telling them stories, many steeped in Indian myth and legend.

Soon the plain turns into the gently undulating foothills of the Palani and Kodai looms large, its slopes covered by dense forests of teak, jackfruit, *peepal* and *neem* cedar. Cars, lorries and buses must wind through this forest as the road clings to the side of the mountain providing magnificent views of the valleys below. Near the top are the **Silver Cascade Waterfalls**. Troops of curious monkeys appear at the road-side at intervals, all the way to Kodaikanal. They're quite happy to be fed from the cars.

Visitors should be prepared with a sweater or some warm clothing - it's not too cold but after 37C in the lowlands, 20C is quite a shock. But it makes sleeping easier. At night temperatures might slip to 8C and it may be necessary in your hotel to pay extra for another blanket.

The large artificial lake at the heart of the resort has facilities for rowing or paddling **boats** just beneath the Carlton Hotel. **Anglers** can get permits from the Sub-inspector of Fisheries at the junction of Observatory Road and Lake Road. On the opposite side of the lake to the Carlton Hotel one can also hire out **horses** and indulge in a gentle trot around the 5 km lake perimeter or go off on a gallop in Bryant's Park close by.

The centre of the town is a clutter of hotels, workshops, houses, shops and colourful shrubbery huddled together on the rambling roads but look up and out and the mountain setting is magnificent. Closer by, the town is edged by stone houses with neatly rolled lawns put down for the British in days of Empire.

Bryant's Park on the east side of the lake is also a creation of that era and with its hundreds of different plant species and tiered flower beds might interest those with green fingers.

Pillar Rocks

The most dramatic and most popular viewpoint near the town is seven kilometres away at Pillar Rocks. These three rocks, so called because they stand together reaching a quarter of a mile into the air, guarantee a grand vista of the surrounding hills and valleys. Easier to get to for a similar vantage point is on **Coakers Walk** which goes from Van Allen Hospital to a kilometre from the town.

Green Valley View is similar but also looks out on the Vaiga Dam. The trek to **Dolphin Rocks** is another pleasant ramble. A three kilometre climb from the lake brings trekkers to **Chettar Park** which like Top Station is home to the *neelakurunji* plant which condescends to display its pale blue flowers to the world every 12 years and attract thousands of tourists.

Solar Physical Observatory

At 2357 metres above sea level, the 90 year old Solar Physical Laboratory is built on the highest point in the area. A steep walk up Observatory Road and visitors can visit the museum which opens daily from 10am to 12am and, in season, from 7pm to 9pm.

Accommodation

Kodaikanal is another hill station where it is best to phone and book at least for one night before you go. If not you can find yourself spending an evening searching for somewhere to stay. In April the humidity and heat rises on the plains, bringing tourists up in their droves, hiking up prices twofold.

Budget range

You might request whether the hotel supplies blankets for those cool nights in a budget range hotel. Many of these are grouped round Anna Salai Road and can be pretty grotty. Best of these is probably the **Astoria** (0452-40525). The quiet, clean, but tatty **Hotel Sunrise** (0452-41358) on Post Office Road has basic double rooms offering a good view of the sunrise and occasional hot water for Rs150/250. **Greenlands Youth Hostel** (0452-41099) on St Mary's road is the cheapest you'll get. Accommodation is in dormitories.

Medium range

Hilltop Towers (0452-40413) on Club Road has rooms for Rs350/700. It's a bit of a barracks like many of the hotels up here but reasonably clean and bearable for a night. If you don't get clean sheets just request they are changed to your satisfaction. Extra blankets cost Rs20. The restaurant is cheap and does excellent masala dosa for Rs10/12.

Top of the range

The classy **Carlton Hotel** (04542-40057) on Boat Club Road looking out on the lake, has luxurious spacious rooms equipped with all a guest would need. All meals are thrown in with the room charge of Rs2800/3500 and more per night.

Eating Out

Kodaikanal has plenty of good Indian and Tibetan restaurants, food stalls, and good bakeries providing brown bread. Good cheese and home-made chocolate are also on sale. The food at the **Carlton Hotel** is good and the buffet for around Rs130 is excellent value after which one can retire to a quite well-furnished and stocked bar. If you want to stick to Kerala food try **Chefmaster** on Hospital Road.

Travel Options

There are no trains up to Kodaikanal so visitors must go by road. The **bus** from **Madurai** costs Rs17.5 for the four hour journey. There are also daily buses to **Thekkady**, 143km away, and **Kanyakumari,** 10 hours away. Hiring a taxi for a round trip via the **Backwaters, Periyar, Madurai** and **Kanyakumari** is probably the quickest and most convenient way of travelling to the hill station from Kochi or Kovalam.

PERIYAR

Lion-tailed macaque

< Alleppey Prince ■3 ■2

Vadai Canal North Bank

■9 5

Vadai Canal South Bank

●8 ■4 ●7

6●

Mullakad Road

Cullan Road

1■

Commercial Canal North Bank

< To Railway Station

●10

1. St George Lodging
2. Komala Hotel
3. Karthika TH
4. Arkadi
5. KTDC Tourist Information
6. Post Office
7. Bus stand
8. State Bank of India
9. Jetty
10. Hotel Raiban

Alappuzha (Alleppey)

N

BACKWATERS

From time to time coir factories, engineering workshops, chai shops, smithies and temples come into view. Suddenly the smell of coconuts freshly cracked open for their husks lingers in the air followed by wafts from a kitchen grilling the Kerala delicacy, karimeen fish. The sight of the foot fisherwomen is something to behold. Only their heads and their floating terracotta pots are above water as they stand patiently searching, waiting for the karimeen to see them. The karimeen then dive and bury their heads in the mud. The women feel out the fish with their toes then their heads disappear and return in a flash. Hands pop out of the water and deposit their succulent victim in the pots.

THE BACKWATERS **Venice of the East**

Stretching across 1,900 kilometres of Kerala's lowlands is a vast system of rivers, lakes, streams and canals which are known as the Backwaters. They are fed both by the sea and 41 rivers which catch the monsoon rains thundering down on the Western and Southern Ghats.

The Backwaters have been dubbed "The Venice of the East". They are that and more. For a trip along these waterways will take you both through bustling cities and rural areas as tranquil as nature in its original, vast lakes and strips of land so narrow that bus and car are banished and the boat rules.

Few international visitors come to Kerala without taking a cruise through its Backwaters. Fortunately the waterways are so extensive that they have not been turned into a tourist circus. Instead the cruises provide a vivid close up of both the exotic aquatic, bird and plant life and the day-to-day lives of the rural and coastal people whose lives the Backwaters have shaped.

Here there are wading egrets and storks searching for fish, bright blue Kingfishers and green parrots darting through the air. Snakes stalk the undergrowth as once huge crocodiles did the lakes. Sometimes the boats have to cut through giant rushes and water hyacinth so thick that the egrets use the clogging weed as a platform for fishing. Then the channel becomes so narrow that the canopies formed by the trees from either side mingle providing a little respite from the sun.

Now the stream opens out onto a large waterway busy with transporting the villagers about their business. A dug-out passes by with four young girls in neat white blouses and blue quilted tunics being rowed to school. There are two men in suits one shading his head with a black umbrella the other with his briefcase, as they joke with their ferryman, here a boat full of earthen pots following behind a flat barge of timber.

Two men punt past with a cargo of shells dredged up from the lake bed. Their shells over time have lost their protective cover. The calcium will be sent to Mumbai (Bombay) as an ingredient for toothpaste. Their boat has a curved roof of wood and plaited palms open at both ends. It is this type of vessel that is now being converted into the house-boat so popular with tourists.

Now the cruise goes down a narrow canal with houses made of brick, wood or dried palm leaves and bamboo on either bank. Women stand in the canal and pour

BACKWATERS

water from metal pots over themselves or their children. Lives here are best described as semi-aquatic. Children will learn to swim before they can barely walk. For the stream is the street in which they will play and eat, on which they will go to school and which they will use to irrigate the rice and tapioca fields.

Close by, a cotton mosquito net protects the food supply. We are three metres away. Some smile, some never look up. They have all their daily tasks to do and some have started. They are sweeping dust from the house, shooing away the cow or the hens and ducks so that tidiness can be resumed. Door-to-door salesmen are preparing their canoes. Others are taking a ferry to work or striding off to toil in the paddy fields. The boat may even stop and allow a walk around on strips of land, often only a few yards wide and lower than the canals that pass by.

From time to time coir factories, engineering workshops, *chai* shops, smithies and temples come into view. Suddenly the smell of coconuts freshly cracked open for their husks lingers in the air followed by wafts from a kitchen grilling the Kerala delicacy, *karimeen* fish. The sight of the foot fisherwomen is something to behold. Only their heads and their floating terracotta pots are above water as they stand patiently searching, waiting for the *karimeen* to see them. The *karimeen* then dive and bury their heads in the mud. The women feel out the fish with their toes, then their heads disappear and return in a flash. Hands pop out of the water and deposit their succulent victims in the pots.

Now out into a lake that so stretches to the horizon that one might mistake it for sea. Here there are *dhows* and large ferries watched from above by kites and sea eagles. Next comes a *kettuvallam* boat with its cargo of coir. The long *kettuvallam* symbolises Kerala's unity with nature. Not one nail is used in its construction, only cashews, coconuts and the jackwood tree. The jackwood tree provides the planks each of which is tied to together with coir rope from the coconut and the whole is coated with a black resin from the cashew nut. And unlike your car, the *kettuvallam* can last for half a century and more.

Lastly into town and back to the hooting horns and animated crowds. It is hard not to find some fascination in the Backwaters.

Backwater Cruises

It really is up to you and your budget how much time you have and what type of boat you travel on. The cruises can be used to take you on to your next destination and the eight hour Alappuzha to Kollam is popular. The enterprising will take a dug-out canoe of a local villager who will gladly paddle them around for Rs20/30 for a couple of hours or hire a motorised boat - though all the engined boats sacrifice aural tranquillity for speed. There are public ferries and private tours but those who crave a little luxurious peace on the placid waters can hire out a houseboat complete with bedroom, living room, chef and larder and a small lawn to eat out on.

The Snake Boat Races

Snakes and snake worship have a special place in Kerala culture. The myths of legend in the Hindu epic story, the Mahabharata, include a tale of how Lords Krishna and Arjuna burn down a great forest causing all the snakes to flee from the heat to Kerala. Spend some time in the state and you can t fail to notice one of their number slithering through the undergrowth.

Snakes even feature in the traditional jewellery, women often wearing a gold snakehood studded with emeralds and rubies. A portion of each large estate has a snake house or sarpa-karvu with a snake stone or nagakal, generally guarded by a woman. Each temple has a priestess known as a Nambiathy who is deemed to be the bride of the Nagaraja, snake king of the shrine. And snakes feature on the sterns of many of the boats cruising around the Backwaters.

Sometimes in the Backwaters you will see up to 150 men or women rhythmically paddling such a narrow boat up to 50 metres long down a canal or river. They are not on a self-powered ferry but in training for one of Kerala's great annual spectacles, the Snake Boat Races. The races, called valomkalli, take place on the Backwaters and are part of the great festivities celebrating Onam, the harvest time.

*At **Aranmula** an effigy of the local deity, Krishna, is taken on a colourful river parade with children dressed as nymphs and princesses. Onshore, huge crowds cheer while carrying their black umbrellas giving them protection alternately from the scorching sun and the monsoon rains.*

*Other snake boat races are held in Kochi, Paipad and Chambakkulam but the biggest gala is the **Nehru Trophy** race in Alappuzha on the second Saturday in August. The race is so named because former Indian Prime Minister Nehru offered to donate a prize. Cambridge educated Nehru was probably dreaming of getting up a team to race the light and dark blues of Britain's premier universities. Thousands of people pack into Alappuzha to watch the magnificently decorated long boats race on the lake to the east of the town. Behind the raised sterns designed to resemble the hood of a cobra, 100 enthusiastic rowers steered by four helmsmen or women and cheered by 25 singers of vanchipattu boat songs, power across the waters singing and shouting. Scores of boats take part in the men's and women's races.*

The snake boats were the troop transporters of the past when battles between kings were fought after the harvests on the Backwaters. Each village has its own snake boat. As they race and shout their battle cries it's easy to picture the fierce clashes of old. The best place to watch the Nehru Trophy race is the Rose Pavilion in the middle of the lake and tickets are available by the lakeside.

BACKWATERS

Organised Backwaters cruises take place from many places but the main points of departure are: Alappuzha (Alleppey) page 124, Kottayam page 127, Kochi page 145, Kollam (Quilon) page 119, Kumarakom page 129.

Others cruises are available in Alumkadavu (page 120), Chambakulam (page 127), Changanasserry (page 130) and Kovalam (page 69). Make sure you take a sun hat, sunblock and enough water.

⊗ The Backwaters Districts

The towns central to the Backwaters and most heavily dependent on the canal-like network are in the midlands coastal districts of Kollam, Alappuzha and Kottayam. These districts are named after their principal towns which are within a few hours drive or train ride away from Kochi, Kovalam and Thiruvananthapuram.

Kollam (Quilon)

Seventy kilometres from Thiruvananthapuram and on the edge of the broad **Ashtamudi Lake**, the centuries-old port of Kollam is known as the gateway to the Backwaters. At one time it equalled Muziris (Cranganore) in importance. Greek, Roman and Arab merchant vessels moored in the lake to load spices. The ninth century Chera king changed the area's name from Venad to Kollam. For a while in the twelfth century it became the Chera capital.

In the thirteenth century Marco Polo referred to the city's trade in peppers and sandalwood and its torrid heat. Today the Chinese fishing nets, massive Chinese water pots, blue and white porcelain and sampan-like boats are evidence of the influence of the port's trade with the Orient. In the eighteenth century Maharaja Marthanda Varma took his army into Kollam, successfully incorporating the area into Travancore. Then the rise of Kochi as the major port eclipsed Kollam and its pivotal roll in the spice trade.

Today Kollam is more akin to a market town, with red-tiled roofs and winding streets. The narrow lanes in the more prosperous areas are flanked by whitewashed walls and flowering trees fronting houses painted pale blues, yellows and pinks.

The Portuguese were the first European colonists to arrive here. They found the tropical climate, the proximity to the sea and the freshwater local lakes to be ideal for growing cashew nuts and so brought the cashew nut to Kerala. Kollam is the largest producer of cashew in the state and lovers of cashew nut will find plenty of shops selling fresh cashew (avoid individuals approaching you on the street. Generally they've bought old stock which tastes revolting).

The landmark building in the town is the **Church of Our Lady of Velamkani** built like a pyramid and topped by a golden Virgin. A number of eighteenth century churches are in **Tangaserri** (Thangassery), a 5km, 15 minute bus ride from the town centre and near the ruins of **Tangaserri Fort**. A kilometre on is the pleasant **Thirumullavaram Beach** where swimming is possible.

Twenty-three kilometres north of Kollam along **Highway 47** is the quiet town of **Karunagappally** where visitors can watch the incredible assembly of the long *kettuvalam* cargo boats

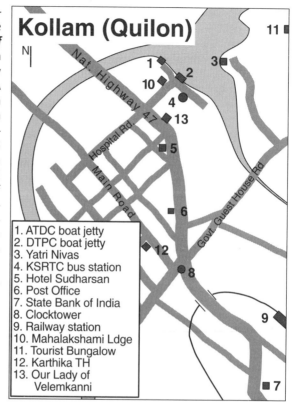

Kollam (Quilon)

1. ATDC boat jetty
2. DTPC boat jetty
3. Yatri Nivas
4. KSRTC bus station
5. Hotel Sudharsan
6. Post Office
7. State Bank of India
8. Clocktower
9. Railway station
10. Mahalakshami Ldge
11. Tourist Bungalow
12. Karthika TH
13. Our Lady of
    Velemkanni

from jackwood, coir and cashew nut. Buses stop here regularly on the way to **Alappuzha**.

Ashtamudi and Vembanad Lakes at various spots are sites for the gigantic Chinese fishing nets, most famous on Kochi harbour and these sites have the advantage of being free of the touts attracted by Kochi's tourist trade.

Otherwise Kollam is mainly used as a point of transit or as a base for visiting the Backwaters and the surrounding areas. Though for the latter, Varkala, 37km away, is probably a better bet.

KOLLAM Backwater Cruises

The **Alappuzha Tourism Development Co-operative** (ATDC) runs the eight hour Kollam to Alappuzha Backwater cruise daily at 10.30am from the jetty close to the central bus station. Reservations can be made at the **District Tourism Promotion Council** (DTPC) main Tourist Office (0474-742558) in Ashramam Guest House Complex, at the DTPC information counters at the bus and rail stations or at KTDC's

BACKWATERS

Tourist Reception Centres in Kochi (0484-353324) and Thiruvananthapuram (0471-330031). The trip costs Rs200.

The cruise stops off at **Alumkadavu** (Rs100) which is the destination for those who wish to visit the internationally renowned Indian female guru, **Amrithananthamai Devi**. DTPC also has a fleet of luxury boats and two house boats here. The two-roomed house boats cost Rs2500/3300 per day.

The other way of seeing Kollam's Backwaters is to take one of the regular local ferries from the ferry station by the Central Bus Station. Seven ferries a day do the one hour chug to **Guhanandapuram**. The first boat leaves at 7.30am and the last at 10.30pm. The two and a half hour trip to Mandronthuruthu starts at 12.30pm and 6.30pm. Ferries also take two-and-a-half hours to reach Muthiraparamb and leave at 9.30am, 4.30pm and 9.45pm. If you don't want to stay in these spots overnight, check the times of the return ferries.

Accommodation

Budget range

The **Railway Retiring Rooms** on the station's first floor are very cheap, basic but large and clean. **Hotel Railview** (0474-76918) opposite the rail station has a bar and satellite TV in the rooms which cost less than Rs100 as do the rooms at **Hotel Original** (0474-70431) and **Hotel Prasanthi** (0474-75293) in Kochupilamoodu. Very basic rooms for Rs100/150 are available at **Mahalakshmi Lodge** (0474-70431) opposite the bus station.

Hotel Karthika (0474-76240) in the town centre is a backpackers' favourite with rooms for Rs100 (air-conditioned Rs300). **Hotel Ambadi** (0474-75243) on Beach Road has rooms for Rs150/200.

Tourist Bungalow (0474-70356) is 3km from the town by the waterside and though its rooms are quite basic, the grandiloquent, spacious building and gardens make a stay a special experience. The Bungalow was the old British Residency and for less than Rs100 visitors can get a little hint of the days of the Raj.

Medium range

KTDC's **Yatri Nivas** (0474-78638), in Guest House Compound 1.5km from the bus stand, is right on the waterfront opposite the boat jetty. The hotel has large, clean double rooms for Rs150/200 (singles Rs100/150) and air-conditioned rooms for Rs400 (singles Rs350). **Hotel Sudharsan** (0474-744322) on Hospital Road with its own restaurant and bar is reasonable value though the rooms at the front are noisy. Rooms cost Rs160 and air-conditioned rooms Rs305. **Checkmate Gardens** (0474-204731) 5km away in Thirumullavaram close to Tanager Fort is the most expensive in Kollam with rooms for Rs350 (air-conditioned Rs450). The only way to spend more money on accommodation in Kollam is to spend Rs3000 a night on hiring a houseboat from the DTPC.

Eating out

Kollam, being the centre of cashew production, is the best place to buy cashew nuts and to try the various dishes which have cashew as an important ingredient. **Hotel Sudharsan** has a good vegetarian restaurant as does Mahalakshmi Lodge. **Yatri Nivas** does good snacks and has a bar.

Around Kollam

The Mother-Matha Amrithananthamai Ashram, Vallikavu

Visitors from all over the world regularly come to Matha Amrithananthamai Ashram. Their purpose is to see India's internationally renowned female guru sometimes called The Mother or Amma. Her full title is Sree Sree Matha Amrithananthamai Devi and she lives in a compound with 200 devotees at Amrithapuri where the Kollam to Alappuzha (and vice versa) boats stop for Vallikavu.

Now in her mid-forties, the Mother was only 13 when she was due to be married. Shortly after the proposed marriage fell through, the young girl proclaimed herself to have had a vision revealing herself to be a reincarnation of the Hindu god, Lord Krishna, himself an incarnation of the great god Vishnu, the Preserver.

Since then, through her teachings and charity work, she has built up a widespread following in south India and her international trips have brought her followers from many countries. Visitors are welcome to the ashram where Amma (wearing a golden robe and a crown) regularly holds forth and blesses and hugs followers and visitors alike. It is an experience many have found to be enlightening. The devotees all dress in white cotton robes, save the saffron-robed *brahmacharyn* bodyguards. Visitors are expected to dress respectfully. Food and accommodation are available for those who wish to stay.

Sasthamkotta

A one hour, 30km bus ride from Kollam, Sasthamkotta has the largest freshwater lake in Kerala. Worth a picnic or a fishing trip.

Palaruvi Waterfalls

The 100 metre high Palaruvi Waterfalls (see page 99) are 75km from Kollam in the Southern Ghats. Buses go frequently to Ariankavu. Trains go to Punalur.

Shenduruny Wildlife Sanctuary

Nine kilometres before Palaruvi and 66km from Kollam where the main road meets the road to Thiruvananthapuram is the 100 sq km Shenduruny Wildlife Sanctuary said to be resident to tigers, elephants, leopards and the lion-tailed macaque. The Tenmalai train station lies nearby and has services to Kollam.

Varkala

Varkala is an increasingly popular beach resort with a pleasant beach and, quite frankly, better hotels than in Kollam. It's 90 minutes away on the bus and a pleasant convenient place to stop for a night or more or an afternoon when travelling between Alappuzha or Kollam and Thiruvananthapuram (see page 95).

BACKWATERS

Travel Options

The nearest **airport** to Kollam is at **Thiruvananthapuram** 72km away. There are 10 daily **trains** doing the one and a half hour rail journey to **Kochi/Ernakulam** which costs Rs42 in second class and Rs185 in first. Similarly there are frequent trains to Thiruvananthapuram. Three trains a day go to **Kannur**, two per day to **Chennai** (Madras), **Kanyakumari** and **Kasargod/Mangalore**. Regular trains go to **Kottayam, Guruvayoor, Thrissur, Palakkad** and **Shornur**. Daily inter city trains also go to **Madurai, Bangalore** and **Mumbai** (Bombay).

Kollam is connected by frequent **bus** services to **Thiruvananthapuram** (1.5 hours), **Kochi/Ernakulam** (4 hours), Alappuzha (2 hours), **Punalor and Varkala** (1.5 hours). There are two buses a day to **Kanyakumari** (4 hours) and **Madurai** and daily bus services to **Madras** and **Bangalore**.

Alappuzha (Alleppey)

Alappuzha sits on the edge of the sprawling Lake Vembanad and the Kuttanad. The Kuttanad is the 75 km stretch of intricately woven networks of canals, streams and rivers that criss-cross the paddy fields and palm groves across to Kottayam. The Kuttanad was created by draining a vast lake and reclaiming the land and was the area first dubbed the Backwaters. It is now Kerala's rice bowl.

Alappuzha is a busy market town (see map on page 114). Surrounded by extensive tracts of coconut palms, Alappuzha is the centre of Kerala's coir industry. No other town in the world processes so much coir. Until the eighteenth century, the town was the former state of Travancore's main port. However Maharaja Marthanda Varma subdued Kollam which soon became the centre of the area's maritime trade.

Two major canals go through the town carrying barges full of coir. From the jetties beside these canals one can take ferry buses, motorboats or rowing boats onto the Backwaters, virtually the only reason international tourists visit this quite pleasant town. However, because it is the centre of the coir industry, it is fascinating to see how the coconut and its product, coir, dominate the town. Seemingly everybody is involved in the trade which is still organised as a cottage industry, involving families or groups of families organised as co-operatives. The coir is used to make rope, mats and baskets.

In the plantations agile tree climbers shimmy up the coconut palms, feet bound together with fibre and a machete hooked on their shoulders. The coconuts brought to ground are left in huge mounds to be hacked open. Their brilliant white flesh is scoured out for oil etc. before the husks are taken to soak in the retting pools. Retting is a natural process of softening up the husks. For four to five months the husks are left to soak in these pools in a solution created by the ebb and tide of the Backwaters. The alternate tides of fresh water from the rivers and brackish water from the nearby sea is a vital ingredient in the process, for the bacteria which soften the husks live in fresh water but breed in the sea.

When the fibres have been separated, the husks are taken to be dried and beaten by teams of squatting women. In the shacks more women prepare the fibre for the handloom weavers or manually tease and twist it into rope. The thick yarn becomes rope for the mats and high quality floor coverings which adorn houses around the world, or rope for fishermen, farmers and industry and even, in a thinner form, is used as the basis for works of art.

The Wondrous Coconut

What grows the length of Kerala and produces products that are edible, potable, durable, biodegradable, tensile and flexible? That's the coconut tree. If it's hard to visit Kerala and not see a coconut tree, it's even harder not to either step on, sit under, drink or eat this historic gift to Kerala's people.

The wood of the tree provides for boats, jetties, footbridges and houses. Its leaves are dried out and bound together or thatched for use as roofs, walls and fences. The husk of its fruit goes for making ropes, mats, baskets, wall and floor coverings, souvenirs and trinkets. The juice from the fruit provides a sweet thirst-quenching drink which can be taken naturally by the simple process of piercing a hole in the husk and the fleshy innards can be eaten directly.

Alternately, the coconut's flesh is crushed for its milk which is then used as a cooking oil or for flavouring and to soften the impact of healthy but burning chillies. In cooking, the dried and grated flesh is also used as a gravy thickener. And on Kovalam Beach you will see it sold as an oil which can be used for massage, for oiling the hair and protecting the skin from the sun.

Some historians suggest that the name Kerala does not mean 'Land of the Coconuts' but 'Land of the Chera people' but since Kera means coconut and the coconut is such a wondrous tree, why should history not throw up a clan called the coconut people?

BACKWATERS

The town of Alappuzha has few other attractions for tourists. It is mainly used as a stop-off point for the Backwater trips. Nevertheless under an hour away from the town going south on **Highway 47** towards Kollam are places worth stopping at, particularly if a visit coincides with the local festivals.

The **Sreekrishna Temple** designed in traditional Kerala style at Ambalapuzha, 14km down Highway 47 from Alappuzha, is one of the most important in the state. In the sixteenth century, the temple auditorium staged the first ever Ottam Thullal dance performance (see page 72).

Three kilometres east of Ambalapuzha at Karumadi is an eleventh century Buddhist statue known as **Karumadikuttam**, another testament to Kerala's unique religious tolerance.

Still further down the coast road near Harippad is **Mannarsala temple**, the high point of Kerala snake worship. The temple and its sacred grove surrounded by scores of sculptures of hooded cobras are dedicated to Nagaraja, the snake king. Each Kerala house is supposed to have a snake house and snakestone. Generally only the larger houses have. Those without send their snake stones or *nagakals* to the Mannarsala temple.

Thousands of Hindus attend this serpent worshipping temple's annual festival on Ayilyam day which falls in either September or October. Vishnu was carried by a serpent and the temple's idols of serpents are carried through the streets.

Still on Highway 47 and 47km south of Alappuzha is **Krishnapuram Palace,** yet another of the great Travancore Maharaja Marthanda Varma's eighteenth century constructions. The palace has a museum of antiques, sculptures and paintings but is known mostly for its marvellous 14 foot high mural, **Gajendra Moksha**, in which Vishnu sits on Garuda.

Chettikulangara Bhagavathy Temple stages its amazing colourful **Kettukazcha festival** in February/March. Effigies of horse, bulls and legendary heroes ride on chariots and scenes of mythical tales are enacted in this famous pageant.

ALAPPUZHA **Backwater Cruises**

The popular cruise south through the Backwaters to **Kollam** is a pleasant way of moving on (see page 119). In Alappuzha the cruise is operated by the **Alleppey Tourism Development Co-operative** (ATDC) (tel 0477-243462). The boat leaves daily at 10.30am and takes eight hours. Tickets cost Rs200 and are available from the **Tourist Desk Information Counter** at the main boat jetty or from various hotels including **Karthika Tourist Home** where the ATDC has its office.

Alappuzha's **District Tourism Promotion Council** (DTPC) (tel 0477-62308) operates a six hour round trip tour to Kumarakom where there is the bird sanctuary. The boat leaves daily at 10.30am from the main jetty. DTPC will conduct tours on request in vessels ranging from four-seater speedboats to the 40-seater 'luxury boat'.

Ferries are available from the ferry station close to the bus station to **Kottayam** (3 hours, Rs6), **Changanasserry** (3 hours), **Kaavalam** (1 hour) and **Nedumudy** (1 hour).

Alternatively various private boat owners are hanging around offering trips to any place the visitor wants to go including the pretty island of Pathiramanal on Vembanad Lake. Prices can be as low as Rs15 but rely on a good haggle and your judgement to get a good price.

Accommodation

Budget range

Formerly Kuttanad Tourist Home, **Arkadi** (0477 251354) has a bar/restaurant and clean but slightly dingy double rooms with attached bath for Rs100 (singles Rs60). **Karthika Tourist Home** (0477-245524) is good value at Rs100. Very cheap and basic rooms are available at **St George Lodgings** (0477-251620) on CCNB Road, South Canal.

Medium range

Just south of South Canal **Hotel Raiban** (0477-251930) has double rooms for Rs175 (air-conditioned Rs275). The best in this range is probably the large **Komala Hotel** (0477-243631) at Zilla Court Ward, five minutes ride from the bus station. Rooms cost Rs200 (air-conditioned Rs400). **Narasimhapuram Lodge** (0477-62662) has rooms for Rs200 (air-conditioned Rs300).

Top of the range

The stylish **Alleppey Prince Hotel** (0477-243752, fax 0477-243758) on AS Road is the best in Alappuzha itself. It has an inviting, attractive swimming pool and a pleasant slightly over-priced restaurant by its side.

Eating Out

KTDC's attractive **"houseboat" restaurant** besides the Tourist Information booth at the waterside puts on good, cheap food. **Komala Hotel** has one of the better restaurants for those who want Indian food. **Alleppey Prince** is more expensive but a safe option.

Cash

The **State Bank of India** on Beach Road has money changing facilities.

Travel Options

Boats and ferries are the best way to travel around the Backwaters but buses and trains are available for those in a hurry.

Trains and Planes

The nearest **airport** is **Kochi,** 64km away. **Thiruvananthapuram Airport** is 222km away. The train station, close to the sea front, is 4km from the town centre and 5km from the ferry station. Seven **trains** a day go to **Kochi**. The cheapest second-class fare is Rs20, first class fare Rs99. Trains run twice a day to **Thiruvananthapuram** and there are daily trains to **Kollam** and **Kottayam** but the ferry is a nicer way to travel. Trains also go to **Guruvayoor, Kayankulam, Trichur, Shornur** and **Palakkad**. A daily express train goes to **Chennai** (Madras) via **Palakkad**.

Buses

There are frequent bus services running to **Kochi** (1.5 hours) and to **Thiruvananthapuram** (3.5 hours) via **Kollam** (2 hours). KSRTC buses run twice daily to **Poovar** and **Vizhinjam** (Kovalam) and daily to **Pathanamthitta**. KSRTC run a daily service to **Kanyakumari** (7.5 hours) for Rs99 and a bus sets off daily for **Bangalore** (17 hours). Other buses go to **Kottayam, Thrissur, Kozhikode** (Calicut) and **Palakkad**.

BACKWATERS

Kottayam

The creamy white church spires rising above the green palms and multi-coloured bougainvillaea of Kottayam are actually set in the hills in the midst of the rubber plantations. Nevertheless, close to the **Vembanad Lake** and the **house boats** of **Kumarakom**, Kottayam is an important part of the Backwaters system. History has it that when Christianity came to Kottayam some nineteen centuries ago, the city was on the edge of the sea. Kerala's busy rivers ever shifting and depositing their heavy loads of silt changed all that.

Now the century old religious shrines nestle in the lowlands between the verdant Backwaters to the west and the rust-red Southern Ghats to the east. The Thekkumkar Maharajas ruled this area and Kottayam was their capital until the eighteenth century when the redoubtable Travancore Maharaja, Marthanda Varma, annexed their kingdom.

Kottayam has a population of 180,000 people. It is a centre for the rubber industry and of particular interest as the city is dominated, as demonstrated by their magnificent churches, by the Syrian Christian community. The Syrian Christians are so called because they trace their origins back to the arrival of the Palestinian architect and disciple, Thomas Didymus, one of the twelve disciples popularly known as Doubting Thomas.

The city being 76km east of Kochi, 174km north of Kovalam and 114km west of Thekkady, is a popular stop-off point for travellers visiting Periyar. We were journeying from Periyar by road up to Mallampuzha beneath the Western Ghats to the north. It's a long trip and there are important places to visit en route so we rested here for two nights, enabling us to visit the houseboats and bird sanctuary at Kumarakom, 12km away.

The Churches and Temples

The most important of the many churches are the two in the north of the city, 2km from the centre. **St Mary s (Valiapally)** is the larger and was built in 1515. It is famous for the Persian Cross at the side of the altar. It also has an interesting guest book with comments going back 100 years. Former Ethiopian Emperor and Lion of Judah, Haile Selassie is one of the notable signatories.

Almost next door is another **St. Mary s (Cheriyapally)** belonging to a different denomination. Inside are exquisite sixteenth century murals and paintings.

Unfortunately **Thirunakkara Shiva Temple** in the town centre is, like almost all Kerala's temples, only open to Hindus. It is built in that inimitable traditional Kerala style. If you are Hindu then inside you will see one of the region's best traditional temple theatres or Koothambalam.

Snake-boat on the Backwaters

KOTTAYAM Backwater Cruises

Boats can be chartered to go to **Alappuzha** (4 hours) or around **Kumarakom Bird Sanctuary**.

There are six ferries a day taking three hours to go to **Alappuzha**, the first at 7.15pm, the last at 5.30pm. The ferry to **Mannar** takes three hours and leaves at 2.30pm and the ferry to **Chambakulam** departs at 3.30pm and takes four hours.

Ferries leave from **Kodimatha Jetty**, 3km from the train station (itself 3km from the town centre) except in the monsoon when they leave from **Town Jetty**.

Accommodation

Though set amongst the hills, Kottayam is still hot and steamy so those who need air-conditioned rooms should book in advance. The city has a reasonable range of accommodation but it's difficult to find rooms costing less than Rs100 and those who need luxurious pampering would be better served by staying in nearby Kumarakom.

Budget range

Rooms for less than Rs150 are available at **Hotel Nithya** (0481-7849) and **Hotel Floral**

Park (0481-7108) in Gandhi Nagger, **Exon Guest House** (0481-564916), **Hotel Ambassador** (0481-560467) on KK Road, **Sakthi Tourist Home** (0481-563151) at Baker Junction. Costing Rs100/350, the clean, comfortable rooms at **Homestead Hotel** (0481-563293) on KK Road are probably the best place to head.

Medium Range

Vembanad Lake Resort (0481-564866) by the water in Kottanad has a pleasant outdoor restaurant by the waterside. As long as you have your mosquito protection on, it makes for a lovely evening eating out under the stars. The large rooms in the cottages cost Rs400 to Rs600 plus luxury tax. Beside the restaurant is a handy cruise boat for Alappuzha but it's expensive.

Prince Hotel (0481-578809) at Kanjikuzhi has double rooms for Rs250/400 and similarly priced are **Hotel Aida** (0481-568391) on MG Road and **Hotel Nisha Continental** (0481-563984) on Sastri Road. **Hotel Green Park** (0481-563331) on Kurian Uthup Road near the train station has a bar and an outdoor restaurant. Rooms are good value at Rs250 (air conditoned Rs350). **Hotel Aiswarya** (0481-61250) by Thirunakkara Temple is a little shabby. Rooms are Rs200 (air-conditioned Rs350).

BACKWATERS

Top of the Range

The air-conditioned **Anjali Hotel** (0481-53661 fax 0481-563669) on KK Road is probably the best in Kottayam itself. It has a good restaurant, a bar and **money changing facilities**. A single room costs $28 and doubles from $35 to $40 exclusive of 10% luxury tax.

Cash

Near Manorama Junction on KK Road the State Bank of India has money exchange facilities.

Communicating abroad

The town has plenty of ISD/STD booths in the centre. The main post office in the city centre, on MC Road, opens from 8am to 8pm daily from Monday to Friday.

Travel Options

As a Backwaters town, Kottayam offers the option of travel by **boat** and **ferry** but **Kollam**, **Alappuzha** and **Kochi** can all be reached direct by bus or train. The town is well situated between north and south Kerala, the Backwaters and the Western Ghats and travellers will find few towns cannot be reached by public transport direct from Kottayam. There is some distance between the various bus, train and ferry stations so it is advisable to take a rickshaw between them. The fare should be no more than Rs15.

Trains and Planes

Kottayam's nearest **airports** are **Kochi**, 76km away and **Thiruvananthapuram** 152km away. The train station is 2km from the Central Bus Station. **Trains** run to all the major Backwater towns and frequently to **Kochi/Ernakulam** (second-class fare Rs20, first-class Rs99) and Thiruvananthapuram. Twice daily trains run to **Kanyakumari** and **Mangalore** and daily to **Kannur, Shornur, Madras, Bombay** and **Bangalore**.

Bus

There are two bus stations KSRTC on TB Road in the south of the town and the private bus station close to the train station. KSRTC run frequent bus services to **Kochi/Ernakulam, Thiruvananthapuram** (Rs99) and to **Kumili** (4 hours) in Periyar. A KSRTC express bus runs daily to **Kanyakumari** (Rs99) and takes nine hours. Four buses a day also do the nine-hour, Rs90 trip to **Madurai**.

Buses run daily to Chennai (Madras) (17 hours), Mysore (13 hours) and Mangalore.

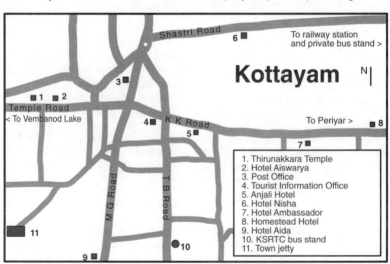

Kottayam N

To railway station and private bus stand >

Shastri Road

Temple Road
< To Vembanod Lake
To Periyar >

K K Road

M G Road

T B Road

1. Thirunakkara Temple
2. Hotel Aiswarya
3. Post Office
4. Tourist Information Office
5. Anjali Hotel
6. Hotel Nisha
7. Hotel Ambassador
8. Homestead Hotel
9. Hotel Aida
10. KSRTC bus stand
11. Town jetty

Around Kottayam

Kumarakom

Kumarakom, 12 km west of Kottayam, has a KTDC-run tourist complex sitting on the edge of **Vembanad Lake**. For those who want a relaxing break by the water it has exotic houseboats, speed boats, facilities for **water skiing** and other **aquatic sports**, and boasts a beautifully peaceful **bird sanctuary**. **Kavenatinkara** is a village known to offer good **freshwater fishing** for anglers.

Backwater Cruises

KTDC hires out their luxury houseboats complete with oarsman, chef, meals, bedrooms, living room, veranda, modern style bathroom and lawn, from their office in the tourist village (048152-258). If you can afford it, there's probably no more relaxing way of seeing the sleepy Backwaters. Double rooms on houseboats with two apartments are Rs995 to Rs1775 and a double room on a houseboat with just one apartment Rs1195 to Rs1945, all exclusive of food. Charges for cruising are Rs600 per hour.

Charges for House Boat packages for two people:
Kochi - Kumarakom - Alappuzha, 3-day trip: Rs19,500.
Kumarakom - Kayamkulam - Alumkadavu, 3-day trip: Rs19,500.
Kumarakom - Alappuzha, 24-hour trip: Rs6,500.

Cheaper tours are available from individual boat handlers who will take you into the bird sanctuary.

Kumarakom Bird Sanctuary

The Kumarakom Bird Sanctuary is a beautiful 14 acre site of an old rubber plantation on the banks of **Vembanad Lake**. The canals and streams threading through the sanctuary make a boat trip the ideal way to venture inside. Many birds from north Asia and Siberia migrate here for the winter, including the Siberian stork. The best time to visit is between November and March when one can see darters (snakebirds), cormorants, night heron, wild duck, cuckoo, golden-backed wood-peckers, crow pheasant, tree pies and white-breasted water hen.

The sanctuary is open between 10am and 6pm daily. **Buses** go regularly between **Kottayam** and **Kumarakom**.

Accommodation in Kumarakom is relatively expensive, KTDC (048152-92258) providing the cheapest rooms at Rs995 for a double on their houseboats (see above). **Taj Garden Retreat** (048152-92377), part of the five-star luxury Taj Group, is good for a pamper. Rooms cost around Rs3000 for a double.

The **Coconut Lagoon** (048192-491) owned by the Casino Group and recently built can be reached by **boat** from **Kochi, Kottayam** or **Alappuzha**. A **speedboat** can be

BACKWATERS

chartered in **Kochi** and takes 1 hour 20 minutes and a regular boat 4 hours 30 minutes. Alternatively the hotel has a boat available at set times from **Thanneermukkom**, a 50-km drive from Kochi and half-hour sail to the hotel. The hotel also provides a boat from a jetty 10km from **Kottayam** which takes half an hour. Single rooms are $80 a night for the bungalows and $90 for the Mansion. Doubles are $90 and $100 respectively. The hotel consists of a series of traditional wooden Kerala houses with modern but open air bathrooms. The swimming pool is huge with a special area for children and the hotel also has a health spa and clinic.

South from Kottayam

The undulating road south between Thiruvananthapuram and Kottayam has some interesting places which may justify a stop on the long journey. **Changanassery**, 23km from Kottayam, has the eighteenth century Thrikkodithanam Temple said to contain the original image of Vishnu worshipped by the Pandavas.

Changanassery has two hotels with double rooms costing Rs100 to Rs300 a night. They are **Hotel Vani** (0482-422403) which has a bar and roof-top restaurant and the slightly cheaper **Hotel Breeze International** (0482-422909). KSRTC run a daily express bus service to Kottayam and Kochi. Trains also go to Kochi, Kottayam and Thiruvananthapuram.

Another 15km further south is the small town of **Tiruvalla** which has a rail station which is useful given the archaeological importance of the adjacent towns. **Kaviyoor**, 5km to the east on the banks of the Manimala River has a Hanuman temple on the hill but more interesting is the 1200 year old temple cut out of the rock less than 2 km away. Only 7 metres wide, the rock temple's stone sculptures are some of the earliest examples of Stone culture. A stone *shivalinga* in a square cell forms the central shrine.

Seven kilometres away from Tiruvalla is another town, **Niranam,** whose church is said here to be the oldest in Christendom. Reputedly it was built by the disciple Saint Thomas after his landing in Kerala 20 years after the death of Jesus Christ.

The **Chennganur Temple**, 40km south of Kottayam, commemorates another Hindu legend, the sage Agastya's visit from the newly married Lord Shiva and his wife Parvathi (Bhagvathi) also known as Shakti, Shiva's life force.

So many gods wanted to attend Shiva and Parvathi's wedding in the Himalayas that they feared the sub-continent would tip over on its side. Agastya was sent to the south to ease the problem and in return was promised a visit from the married couple. During the gods' stay, Parvathi menstruated and devotees testify that the idol of Parvathi bleeds. They compete for the privilege of buying the goddess' petticoat.

Travel Options

KSRTC run a daily express bus service from Chennganur to Kottayam and Kochi. Other buses run frequently between these midland towns straddling the main Kottayam-Thiruvananthapuram road.

One of only five temple towns dedicated to Lord Krishna, Aranmula, 10km east of Chennganur is on the road to Pathanamthitta. The town stages a famous boat race on the banks of the River Pampa, at Onam, in August. In the Mahabharata legends, Krishna is incarnated as the divine charioteer, Parthasarathi taking Arjuna into battle. This is the image that is portrayed and brought to the town on five bamboo poles, the words for which gave the town the name Aranmula.

The boat festival re-enacts in songs and drama a legend involving a devout Brahmin who, having seen a vision of Krishna, decided to offer up 51 measures of rice to Aranmula temple. Rivals from another village intercepted his boat but the snake boats from the Brahmin's own village rescued him.

Aranmula also boasts two families now solely responsible for the areas production of the incredible Kannady metal mirrors. An alloy of copper, silver, bronze and lead is used to provide a glass like reflection. Once the plaything of royalty, these mirrors are available for Rs300 to Rs30,000.

Ten kilometres further up the Pampa river, during February/March the Maramon Convention near Kozhencherry uses the dried river bed to hold one of the biggest gatherings of Christians in the whole of Asia.

North from Kottayam

Ettumanur

The **Mahadeva Shiva Temple** in Ettumanur, 12km north of Kottayam on the road to **Thrissur** (Trichur) is renown for its intricate murals and carvings. However, though it is set back on the right hand side of the road going north, few locals can direct you to it. February/March is the time for the ten day annual festival when pilgrims arrive from the countryside.

The young, the old and couples with or without children sit patiently through the day in the grounds outside the 400 year old temple waiting for the festivities to begin. On specific days priests carry out elephants made from 210 pounds of gold and given to the temple by 18th century Maharaja Marthanda Varma.

It is a large temple in the traditional Kerala style with white walls supporting twin low hanging roofs. Inside the courtyard is quite a surprise. In the Christian Bible an irate Jesus is said to have cleared the money lenders out of the temple. Shiva however has conceded to let Ettumanur's tax accountants carry out their business immediately in front of the temple shrine.

Their office is a patch of ground sectioned off by rope and wooden tables. Within this sanctum half a dozen men sit in their white *mundus* counting out huge stashes of rupee coins. More coins are waiting for them in buckets or scattered so wildly across the floor that one might think that Shiva may well have tipped over one of their tables. Put Rs20 onto the piles of coins and the financiers will permit a photo to be taken.

That the temple has amassed wealth is shown by the beautiful golden idol that sits immediately before entry into the central shrine. Most of the carvings, murals and sculptures are inside and non-Hindus can see the fury of a four metre high Shiva dancing a cosmic *tandava* dance. The exterior carpentry is quite superb. The shrine's roof is covered by copper plate and the temple's friendly bull elephant is worth a word as he munches away at palm leaves preparing to perform his festive duties.

There's not much else to see in the town but Ettumanur sits at the crossroads of routes to Kalady/Thrissur, Kochi (64km) and Kottayam and buses run frequently to all these places.

Kalady Tower

Kalady

Kalady is virtually one big shrine for the great Indian religious philosopher, **Sree Sankaracharya** (Sankara) born in the town in AD788. At the time Hinduism was degenerating into ritualism. Sankara completed his studies of the voluminous Hindu Vedas and Upanishads texts by the age of sixteen. His conclusions led him to proclaim that God was absolute being, absolute bliss, and absolute knowledge.

Nothing was real, he argued, except Brahman, the universal spirit of which the human soul was part. All else was maya or illusion which, devoid of real substance, appeared and passed away. Matter did not exist.

Sankara died at the age of 32. Whether or not the pilgrims who visit the city believe that the great Advaita, pre-existentialist philosopher, existed they come in their thousands to visit the temples, shrines, *ashrams* and the tower bearing his name.

Some 80km northwards from Kottayam on the road to Thrissur and 48km from Kochi, Kalady sits on the great **Periyar River**. Indeed it was here in the river that he was said to have used his yogic powers to conjure the image of a huge crocodile about to devour him. The young boy cried out to his mother to allow him to do *sanyasa* (renunciation). Only when his mother permitted him to take on *sanyasa* did the crocodile go away. The spot is now called **Crocodile Ghat**.

The 45 metre high **Sree Adi Sankara Keertha Stamba Mandapam** is the most impressive edifice in the philosopher's name. It is situated on the main road. Visitors are welcome to climb to the top of the nine story terracotta octagonal tower which offers splendid views of the countryside and includes an 800 year-old idol of Sankara and, around the walls, a potted history of his life.

The **Sree Saradamba** and **Sree Shanakara** temples are part of the Sankara shrine, a large open complex on the banks of the Periyar. Brindavans, the altar on which Sankara's mother Aryamba was cremated is also here. The shrine is run by Sringeri Math, one of the four centres set up by Sankara in the first millennium. Like all the Sankara shrines in the town it is open to Hindus and non-Hindus. The two temples were built in 1910 by – wait for it – Jagadguru Sree Sachithananda Shiva Abhinava Narsimha Barathi Swamigal of Sringeri Sarada Pidha.

There is one 60-year-old *ashram* not in Sankara's name, the **Sree Ramakrishna Advaita Ashram**.

The Sankara Jayanti festival of celebration takes place over five days in April/May and the nine-day Navarathi festival in September/October includes the chariot festival and musical concerts.

On the picturesque banks of the Periyar 7km upstream from Kalady is another religious village, **Malayattur**. The church on the hill close by was built in AD900. There are plenty of buses from Kalady and Aluva. 22km from Kalady there is the nineteenth century **Kallil Bhagavathy** rock temple of the Jains which requires climbing 120 steps cut into the huge buttress.

Accommodation in Kalady is cheap. There are some private lodges like **Hotel Prince** and **Udaya Lodge** and a **Government Rest House**. **Sringeri Math** and the **Ramakrishna Ashram** also have very cheap guest houses.

Visitors arriving at Angamaly **rail station** can book air-conditioned rooms at the **Mundadan Tourist Home** (0484-452975) at the junction for less than Rs300. **Hotel President** (0484-452985) has air-conditioned rooms at a similar price and rooms with fan only for Rs100. **Hotel Hills Park** (0484-452126) and **Swagath Tourist Home** (0484-452443) have fan only rooms for Rs100 or less.

The nearest **airport** to Kalady is **Kochi** (48km). **Angamali** (10km) and **Aluva** (22km) are the nearest **railway stations. Buses** and taxis make the trip to **Kalady** from here. Kalady is also on the bus routes for **Thiruvananthapuram, Palghat** and **Kozhikode** (Calicut).

BACKWATERS

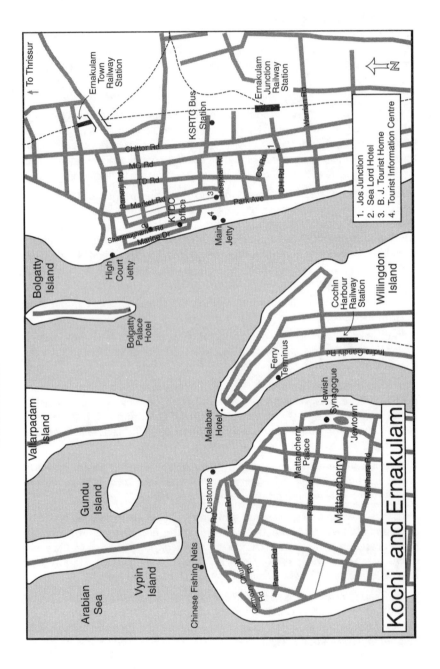

BACKWATERS

1. Jos Junction
2. Sea Lord Hotel
3. B. J. Tourist Home
4. Tourist Information Centre

Kochi and Ernakulam

⊗ Stylish Kochi (Cochin)

F or centuries Kerala's commercial capital, the busy port of Kochi, reflects the influence of the Latins and west Europeans who used Kochi to exploit the spice trade. Apart from a handful of buildings, the British left Thiruvananthapuram to develop as an Indian city. In contrast, Kochi appears positively European. Neat lines of large houses, multi-storey buildings, modern hotels, wide roads dominated by cars and trucks and busy shipping lanes predominate on the Ernakulam side of the twin towned city.

On the Kochi side the narrow terraced streets often feature small beshrubbed cottages almost akin to what one might find in those little English villages engulfed by the urban sprawls of big cities. Sadly, Kochi's principal tourist attractions are constructions commissioned and designed by Europeans. Yet the paradox is that Kochi's bustle, rumbling trucks, opportunists, hustlers and child beggars make it feel more like a big Indian city than the capital Thiruvananthapuram.

Kochi owes its existence as India's fourth largest port to two historic events. In 1341 great storms hit Kerala such that the ancient Malabar spice traders' port of Kodungallor to the north had its harbour entrance silted up. But the same catastrophic typhoons so swelled the Periyar River that it burst its banks finding a new outlet at Kochi. The result was one of the world's finest natural harbours.

In 1498 the great Portuguese mariner Vasco da Gama, searching for booty, landed at Kappad and discovered, like the Arabs, Greeks, Romans, Chinese and Marco Polo before him that Kerala had abundant and cheap spices. The spices were principally of use in Europe as preservatives and for disguising the taste of rotten meat. With shiploads of cheap pepper, cardamom, ginger, nutmeg, cinnamon, turmeric etc., the opening up of the sea route to India enabled the Portuguese merchants to undercut Venice's domination of the growing spice trade.

In the next few centuries traders, and troops to ensure the Maharaja of Kochi's co-operation, from all over Europe would find their way to Kochi. The Portuguese upset Arab domination of the sea trade. After them came fleets of Dutch, Spanish, French, Danish and English ships who moored on the waterway's shifting sands.

Kochi's name derives from a Malayalam word meaning a small place. Nevertheless when the Portuguese arrived it was the centre for the Maharajas who ruled the kingdom crossing the Kerala midlands, sandwiched between Travancore in the south and the Zamorins who ruled Malabar to the north. That Kochi resembles a European city nowadays is probably also due to the Portuguese attempts to capture the city in 1509 and 1510 which virtually flattened the old city.

Today Kochi is not a small place but a thriving city of 1.66 million people sprawling from Ernakulam on the mainland, across three islands to the peninsula on which

BACKWATERS

Kochi itself stands. It has an international airport, a full range of top class to budget accommodation and access to the popular Backwaters area.

Kochi as a staging post

Most visitors to Kerala visit Kochi as part of an itinerary which includes a boat trip on the famous **Backwaters** for which the port provides the northern most point. These are dealt with later (see page 145). But Kochi is also an excellent base for seeing much more of the fascinating state. To the east are the **wildlife sanctuaries** of Parambikulam, Eravikulam and Periyar, Thattekad Bird Sanctuary and the pretty **hill stations** of Munnar and Devikulam. To the north is the exotic Malabar coast with a host of palm-fringed empty beaches, historic sites and an almost virgin territory for international tourism.

Fort Kochi

Fort Kochi, as the district sat on the northern tip of Kochi town is called, gets its name from the old fort which overlooks the narrow outlet where the harbour opens to the sea. Kochi is the headquarters for India's Southern Naval Command and the fort is still in military use. However permission can be obtained at the fort for sight-seeing.

Chinese fishing nets

Over 1,000 years ago Chinese traders from Kublai Khan's court set foot in Kerala and left their mark on the seaport's culture. That is evident not only in the designs of the houses but also in the giant fishing contraptions employed for centuries by the fishermen at the harbour's edge on River Road opposite Vypin Island.

At first sight, the rows of *cheena vala* fishing nets appear like wooden models of monstrous spiders with a huge web attached to their legs. And the principal is pretty similar. The contraption with five or six 'legs' is carefully balanced across a fulcrum at the end of a short wooden pier reaching into the water. Two long poles act as the lever at the top of which are the pulleys, ropes with boulders attached. The weight of the boulders is used by a team of five men to lower or raise the spider and its huge net in and out of the water using elementary principals of leverage.

The fishermen take a break for ten minutes, smoking *bidis* or chewing *betel* leaf, while the fish are caught up in the spider's web. Then the gang of five haul down the ropes, raising the net with its catch. Two of the fishermen secure the rope to the ground while the other three rush forward to help one of their number who will scoop the catch out of the base of the net before the attendant crows can take their dinner. That done the monster is immersed once again beneath the waters.

We sat on the boulders watching this serene rhythmic activity of centuries which numbed time. Almost in the same moment we had a reminder of history's complexities as two mariners moored their dug-out canoe and bailed it out while behind them a small modern cruiser dominated the shipping lanes. In the hurly-burly of this hectic city even the traders and touts drawn to this tourist attraction cannot prevent this part of River Road from being a welcome haven of tranquillity.

One thing to remember - if you are taking a rickshaw or taxi make sure you ask for the fishing nets near the junction of River Road and Prince Street in Kochi. If you mention Fort Kochi you may end up like us, spending fruitless time and money as the driver tries to take you to the fort.

Saint Francis' Church

A short walk away from the nets on Church Road is Saint Francis' Church, reputedly the oldest existing European church in India. Built by the Portuguese in 1510 it was the burial place of Vasco da Gama where he rested for 14 years until the Portuguese had the explorer's remains shipped home in 1538. The Portuguese installed great *punkah* fans which are still used when power cuts close down the electric fans.

The Catholic church however couldn't hold onto the church and it became Protestant. The Dutch added a gable to the western front and then the British turned it into an Anglican church. Now it is occupied by the Church of South India. It is closed to tourists on Sundays.

Nearby on the aptly named Cemetery Road is the **Dutch Cemetery**, an interesting reminder of the important Dutch influence on this city.

Santa Cruz Cathedral

Another short walk from Saint Francis' Church along Prince Street leads to the Catholic Cathedral of Santa Cruz which has beautiful paintings on the ceilings.

Mattancherry Palace (The Dutch Palace)

On the east side of Kochi in Mattancherry district by the junction of Charalat Road and Palluruthy Road is the 440 year old Mattancherry Palace. It is sometimes called the Dutch Palace because, though built by the Portuguese in 1555 for Veera Kerala Varma, the Maharaja of Kochi, it was later renovated by the Dutch in 1663 when both the Dutch and Portuguese needed to curry favour with the Kochi kings.

The palace's quadrangular exterior lacks the quiet beauty and charm of those built later in the south by Marthanda Varma, the conquering Maharaja of Travancore, but the interior contains almost 300 square feet of magnificent seventeenth century murals, the beauty of which you will be hard pushed to find anywhere else in India. The murals depict scenes from the Indian epics, the Mahabharata and the Ramayana, including, from the latter, Rama (one of Hindu god Vishnu's incarnations) on his triumphant return to Ayodhya after his defeat of the demon king, Ravana of Lanka.

Take a look in the lady's bedchamber at the inspired picture of Krishna, the Blue God, the divine lover being caressed by his gopi lovers.

On the first floor, the Central Hall was the scene for the kings' coronation ceremonies and has a display of the Maharajas' dresswear. The palace has a central courtyard in which sits a temple dedicated to Bhagavathi (Shiva's wife, Parvathi).

The palace is open daily from 10am to 5pm but closes Fridays and national holidays. No flash photography is allowed inside.

Jewish Synagogue

Very close to Mattancherry Palace just off the congested Palluruthy Road is the small Jewish Synagogue, a lasting memorial to Kerala's ancient Jewish community. In 1561 persecution brought off disputes with Arab merchants over Kodungallur's lucrative pepper trade and forced the Jews to leave the city. In 1561 Jewtown was put up in this area and became a centre for Jewish spice merchants under the protection of the Kochi Maharaja.

The synagogue was constructed in 1568 just after Mattancherry Palace. It is the oldest synagogue in the Commonwealth. In 1662 it was destroyed in a Portuguese attack on the city, only for the Dutch to rebuild it in 1664 - testament to the religious tolerance, or guile, of the early Dutch Calvinists.

The synagogue's interior is quite beautiful. Shimmering Belgian chandeliers reflect the light from the plain white walls. On the floor are delicate hand-painted, blue willow-patterned tiles brought back from Canton in China in the eighteenth century by a rich Jewish merchant, Ezekiel Rahabi.

The synagogue holds ancient scrolls of the Old Testament, the copper plates on which the Maharajas recorded grants of privileges and a collection of gold and silver crowns sent as gifts by the Maharajas. One plate records a grant made by Maharaja Bhaskara Ravi Varman I in the eighth-century by which a small village near the former Jewish settlement in Kodungallur was handed over to a Jewish trader.

Only a handful of Kochi Jews now worship here and the decline in the Jewish community in this trading district still called Jewtown is reflected in the marriage register which records less than two dozen marriages since the British left India.

The synagogue closes for non worshippers on Saturdays and Jewish holidays. Otherwise it opens 10am till noon and 3pm to 5pm daily.

Koonan Kurishu Shrine

Also of interest to historians of religion is the Koonan Kurishu Shrine in the heart of Mattancherry district. When Vasco da Gama first arrived he was surprised to find Christians in Kerala – St Thomas (the disciple, Doubting Thomas) had successfully planted the cross in AD52. The Papacy held sway in Europe and Vasco da Gama was, it is said, a little upset that the Kerala Christians hadn't even heard of the Pope.

The Portuguese attempted to force Kerala's Christians to accept the hegemony of Rome. It resulted in a massive revolt symbolised in Mattancherry when on January 3, 1653 thousands of irate Christians tied a rope to a cross and defied the Portuguese. The oath they swore was called, "The Oath of the Coonen Cross." The Cross still stands in a small chapel. The Church didn't stand. The revolt led to the creation of the Jacobite (Syrian) Church and the Mar Thoma Church.

Kerala's Jewish Communities

Kochi Jews believe that 10,000 of their forefathers fled from Palestine in the second century and were allowed to settle at Muziris (the Roman name for Kodungallor) by a tolerant Hindu maharaja. Others have it that they came in the ninth century BC in King Solomon's ships. Still others that they were descended from the Jews taken to Babylon by King Nebuchadnezzar and there are said to be Babylonian influences in the music of the Kochi Jews.

It is likely that even before the second century the Jews were involved in trade with the ancient port of Muziris where the Periyar River met the Arabian Sea. Malabar teak has been discovered in the ruins of the ancient city of Ur. History also has it that when the Queen of Sheba entered Jerusalem she took with her "spices, gold, precious stones and the wood of the almug (sandalwood) tree from Ophir". Ophir is believed to be the city of Puhar which existed near to where Thiruvananthapuram now stands.

Hence, Muziris would have long been a potential site for Jews escaping persecution. Indeed legend has it that when Doubting Thomas landed in Muziris in AD52 he was greeted by a Jewish girl playing a flute.

The Jews became a sizeable community fitting in as traders, as had the Arabs and the early Christians. For a thousand years from the fifth to the fifteenth century, they had their own independent mini-Israeli state and a 'king' in the Muziris area which they called Shingly. The first record of a synagogue being built here was in 1344. All that remains of it is an inscribed slab in the Kochi synagogue. In the same century a Jewish poet wrote: "I travelled from Spain. I had heard of the city of Shingly. I longed to see an Israeli king. Him I saw with my own eyes."

The Jews themselves were split into three groups in a replica of the caste system. The Pardesi *or foreign/White Jews were at the top of the tree and the synagogue is called The Pardesi Synagogue. The* Myuchasim *or Black Jews were offspring of the ancient marriages of Jews to Indians and many were labourers for the spice merchants. At the bottom were the* Meshuchrarim *or Brown Jews who as slaves converted to Judaism.*

Competition between Jews and Arabs involved in the spice trade intensified leading to friction between the communities and in 1524 many Jews were massacred in a Muslim pogrom. Finally in 1561 the Kodungallur Jews were driven out of the city and fled to Kochi. Kochi's growing importance as a commercial centre enabled the new community to continue in the spice trade and prosper.

However, it was not violence which ultimately reduced the Jewish community to a handful of worshippers. The community, numbering a few thousand at its height, disintegrated through inter-marriage and, soon after Israel was established, emigration.

Willingdon Island

Between Kochi and Ernakulam is the huge man-made island of Willingdon designed by Lord Bristow and created in the inter-war years out of silt dredged to deepen the estuary. Not much to stop around for but the international airport, the main harbour and a main railway station which are located here.

Bolgatty Island

A ten minute boat ride from Ernakulam, the palm-fringed 15 acres of lush lawns and the birdlife on this peaceful island make it an almost idyllic place to find refuge from the trials of the city. It has a golf course but the main attraction for visitors is **Bolgatty Palace**. The palace was built by the Dutch in 1744. It later became the home of the British Resident of Cochin and eventually the Maharaja.

Now in the hands of KTDC as a hotel, it is being renovated after being allowed to rundown. The simple exterior with a Kerala-style roof, white walls in need of several coats of paint and suffering from some haphazard extensions, is unimposing – rather reminiscent of those fading Victorian country houses tucked away in the English countryside.

Reaching the palace at sunset is quite a romance. A tiny boat with a outboard motor is moored at the High Court Jetty and visitors are ushered on board for a princely Rs30 (the ferry is only 50 paise but goes to the other side of the island). Off we speed past moored yachts leaving behind Ernakulam's evening din. The Palace has its own little jetty and our bags get helped off the boat.

As we go down the tree-lined path to the entrance we can hear the multitude of birds twittering away their goodnights. Into the palace and up the stairs to the huge hall with glorious wood carvings. The hall leads on to a long corridor either end of which are two suites, one with three large rooms and two four-posters and the other, the smaller but more decorous Maharaja's Suite.

Everything here *is* ramshackle – the shutters, the warped doors and almost closing windows. Save for the haphazard trails of electrical wiring and plastic chairs inexplicably lined up in the corridor, it conveys a sense of history, a journey through time as one hears the British Resident and tired soldiers and footmen preparing for another sultry Indian day.

We wake up to the early morning chorus of birds and look out onto the green lawns, parched, awaiting the onset of the monsoon. Two men are line fishing on the jetty at the palace's rear. They are watched by a family taking breakfast in the Palace's pleasantly-set garden restaurant. Then a pleasant stroll or horse-ride around the island followed by a picnic sitting by the water's edge.

Vypin Island

On the north side of the narrow shipping lane and opposite Fort Kochi is the island of Vypin. At the most northerly end of the island is the small hexagonal **Pallipuram Fort**. Built in 1503, it is said to be the oldest European fort constructed in India. The Dutch captured the fort in 1661 and held onto it till the French Revolution when they sold it to the Travancore Maharaja. It is only open on Thursdays but **buses** go regularly from **Vypin**.

The attractive palm-fringed **Cherai Beach** is also at the north end of the island. It's the best beach to be found near Kochi. **Vypin Lighthouse** at **Ochanthuruth** opens daily from 3pm to 5pm and affords panoramic views of the surrounding area.

Ernakulum

Ernakulum is today the business centre of Kochi. Most of the hotels and guest houses are in this area. It is linked by ferry to Fort Kochi and the islands and by a 10km road to Fort Kochi through Willingdon Island.

If you are staying here you might want to pay a visit to **Mangrove Forest** by the waterside on Salim Ali Road just north of the High Court building. Between mid-January and early March this protected area has a stream of birds seeking refuge from the harsh north Asian winters.

Parikshith Thampuran Museum on DH Road in the grounds of Durbar Hall has a vast collection of old paintings, coins and sculptures donated by the Maharajas. It opens 10am to 1pm and 2pm till 5pm except Mondays. Admission is free.

If you've already seen Mattancherry Palace and the other Maharaja's collections then you might find the attached Kerala **Lalitha Kala Akademi of Contemporary Art** more interesting. It is open from 10pm to 5pm.

Accommodation

From cheap guest houses to the luxurious Taj Malabar and Casino Hotels on Willingdon Island, Kochi has a vast range of accommodation for visitors.

The most pleasant place to stay is in the relatively quiet area of **Fort Cochin**. However accommodation is limited.

Budget range

Brisbane Lodgings (0484-225962 fax, 484-224702) at 11401, Princess Street has small double rooms with balcony and attached bathroom for Rs125. The rooms without a balcony are bigger and cost Rs100. Mr Thommen, the manager is very friendly and helpful and the hotel is authorised to **exchange money**, has a travel agency, ISD/STD facilities and a handicrafts shop. On the same street is **Elite Hotel** (0484-225733) which is similarly priced with a popular and cheap restaurant.

Delight Tourist Resort (0484-228658) is a beautiful house and garden with friendly staff. All rooms have attached bathrooms and cost Rs100/200 for a double. Other cheap hotels include the large, quiet **Tharawad Tourist Home** (0484-226897) on Quiros Street (Rs100/150), **Grace Hotel** (0484-223584) with rooms for Rs125 (air-conditioned Rs400) and the rather grim but well-situated and spacious **PWD Rest House** (Rs100) on the waterfront.

Medium range

Hotel Seagull (0484-228128) on Calvathy Road is on the waterfront and has a bar and restaurant looking out onto the sea lanes. Rooms cost Rs200/300 (air conditioned Rs300/400) plus tax, with the higher prices for rooms with a sea view.

Ernakulam

Ernakulam is the main area of the city for accommodation. Few hotels afford a sea view but the area is conveniently close to the main stations and to the sea.

Budget range

Canon Shed Road close to the main boat jetty is the site of **Maple Tourist Home** (0484-355156) which has rooms with attached bathrooms for Rs165 (air-conditioned Rs330) and a roof garden looking out onto the harbour. Also on this road is the pleasant **Biju's Tourist Home** (0484-381881) with double rooms for Rs200 (air-conditioned Rs350) and singles for Rs110 (air-conditioned Rs280). On Shanmugham Road by the waterfront are two cheap hotels, **Hotel Hakoba** (0484-353933), rooms with attached bath Rs100 with a restaurant, a bar and a lift for the weary and **Hotel Sea Shells** (0484-353807) which has double rooms costing Rs120 (air-conditioned Rs180).

Strung out along Market Road are several of the better hotels in this range, **Modern Guest House** (0484-352130), **Coastal Lodge** (0484-373083), the reasonable **Deepak Lodge** (0484-353882) and the popular but small **Basoto Lodge** (0484-352140) round the corner in Press Club Road. All have double rooms with attached bathrooms for less than Rs120.

MG Road also has a number of cheap guest houses including the **Good Shepherd Tourist Home** (0484-352101), with double rooms for Rs170 (air conditioned Rs290) and singles for Rs 100/120. Also on MG Road is **Hotel Airlines** (0484-366633) with double rooms for Rs175 (air-conditioned Rs300) and the very cheap and basic **Apex Lodge** (0484-355355).

Cheaper still are two very basic guest houses on Banerji Road: **Madras Tourist Home** (0484-355418) has doubles for Rs70 and singles Rs38 with an attached bathroom (Rs25 for shared bathroom). Luxury tax still applies! **Hotel Megha** (0484-395305) has double rooms for Rs90 (air-conditioned Rs210/275) and singles for Rs60 (air-conditioned Rs175).

BACKWATERS

Medium range

MG Road has a good number of medium range hotels. At the cheaper end are **Queens Residency** (0484-365775 fax 0484-352157) at Shenoy Junction, with double rooms for Rs175 (air-conditioned Rs 350), and **Hotel Mercy** (0484-382480, fax 0484-351504) on Mercy Estate with double rooms for Rs250/300 (air-conditioned Rs350/500). **Dwaraka Hotel** (0484-352706) is in a similar price range.

Grand Hotel (0484-382061) has air-conditioned rooms for Rs350/700 (singles Rs300/400) and a Special Suite for Rs800. **Woodlands Hotel** (0484-351372) has a pleasant roof garden and vegetarian restaurant. Double rooms with television cost Rs350 (air-conditioned Rs650).

Chittoor Road also has several medium range hotels. **Hotel Kavitha International** (0484-350618 fax 380620) has double rooms for Rs200/300 (air-conditioned Rs350/500). **Gaanam Hotel** (0484-367123) has double rooms for Rs480/815 (air-conditioned Rs580/990). Single rates rise from Rs340 to Rs670 depending on the rooms. Room charges are inclusive of breakfast in the hotel restaurant. **Hotel Sangeetha** (0484-368487) also throws in a breakfast in its vegetarian restaurant with the room charge. Double rooms are Rs300/380 (air-conditioned Rs375/430). Single rates are Rs200/325.

On Nettipadam Road, south of Jos Junction, **Hotel Excellency** (0484-374001, fax 0484-374009) is good value for money, especially in the restaurant. Double rooms cost Rs300/375 (air-conditioned Rs550) and singles Rs250/300 (air-conditioned Rs500).

The north end of Market Road has **Blue Diamond Hotel** (0484-382115) with double rooms for Rs230/450 (singles Rs130/150). Opposite Ernakulam railway station is **The Metropolitan** (0484-352412, fax 0484-360627) which is centrally air-conditioned and has rooms for Rs750/850 (singles Rs500).

Top of the range

All the hotels listed here are centrally air-conditioned and offer a daily laundry service.

Sea Lord Hotel (0484-352682 fax 0484-370135) on Shanmugham Road close to the harbour has an excellent rooftop restaurant on the eighth floor, well above the clamour of Ernakulam's busy streets. The hotel has a lovely, clean atmosphere. Also an indoor restaurant and pleasant bar (if you want cold beer make sure you ask them to put one in the fridge or ice box for you), a currency exchange counter and a conference hall for 150 people. With 38 double rooms costing Rs600/2000 (single rate Rs500/700), it offers excellent value for money. All major **credit cards** are accepted.

Hotel Abad Plaza (0484-361636) on MG Road is another modern and clean hotel. The restaurants are excellent. With efficient staff and a fine rooftop swimming pool, it is more expensive than Sea Lord but still good value. Rooms cost from Rs1200 to Rs1750. Also on MG Road is the snazzy modern **Avenue Regent** (0484-372660) with double rooms for Rs1250/1430 (singles Rs1030/1190) and an executive suite for Rs 2350.

On the same road is **International Hotel** (0484-382091, fax 373929). Renovated two years ago, it has restaurants, a bar and a rooftop garden, money changing facilities and accepts credit cards. Rooms cost Rs800/1100 (singles Rs600/850).

The most luxurious hotel in the area is the Taj Group's **Taj Residency** (0484-371471 fax 0484-371481) which, being on Marine Drive, has a splendid view of the harbour. The Taj Group describe the hotel as "a business man's hotel" and provide the business traveller with various facilities including two conference halls, a boardroom, secretarial services, telex, fax, computer and reference library.

The 108 rooms have channelled music, Star TV and in-house movies. The indoor restaurants offer meals for Rs200/450 and a

BACKWATERS

lunchtime performance of classical Indian music and dance. Prices are very business-like. Best value are the standard rooms at $90 for doubles (singles $80). Rooms facing the sea cost an extra $15. Larger rooms cost $115 and the small suites $140 per night. Tax is an additional 20%.

Bolgatty Island

A stay in KTDC's **Bolgatty Palace** (0484-35003 fax 0471-434406) itself has not been possible recently as renovation has been due to take place but if you can persuade staff to let you stay in one of the suites, for Rs1000 it's a special treat, shambolic as they are.

Stood like insects on stilts by the water's edge, the white air-conditioned honeymoon cottages at Rs1200 make for a pleasant stay. More rooms are available in cottages for Rs625/700 (singles Rs475/525) and air-conditioned rooms Rs1200/1850 (singles Rs1000/1500). The palace has a bar and restaurant, accepts **American Express** credit cards and has a **foreign exchange** facility. Film shooting is allowed, announces the brochure to Holly/Bollywood for Rs5000 per day.

Willingdon Island

Willingdon Island has two top-of-the-range, centrally air-conditioned hotels, Casino and Taj Malabar. Both have swimming pools, a choice of restaurants, money changing and airport pick-up facilities, laundry service etc.

Adjacent to the harbour on Willingdon Island, **Casino Hotel** (0484-668421 fax 0484-668001) also arrange trips to **Periyar** and to their resort in the **Lakshadweep Islands.** Single rooms are $65 and doubles $70 a night plus taxes.

More favourably located and more expensive is Taj Residency's sister hotel, **Taj Malabar Hotel** (0484-682009) which has a tremendous location overlooking the harbour. Room charges start at Rs2600 (singles Rs2300) plus 20% tax.

Out and about in the City

The motorised rickshaws are generally the quickest and cheapest way of getting round the city. Minimum charge is Rs5 and you should be paying Rs3 per km (50% extra after 11pm). Check before you get in as the driver may not use the meter and you will have to negotiate a price. Taxi's are not metered. The official rate is Rs3.75 per km but you are advised to negotiate a price beforehand. Private local buses operate on a minimum fare of Rs1.25. Beware of pickpockets.

Eating out

Kochi has an extraordinary variety of restaurants both in type of cuisine and quality. In addition the area is swarming with ice cream parlours. There are so many restaurants it's best to try your own expedition of discovery or talk to other travellers who will advise on their favourites. Nevertheless it is a good rule of thumb that most of the major hotels serve up good food which is not overly expensive.

Fort Kochi

The outdoor **Chariot Fast Food** restaurant on Princess Street does excellent Chinese food. It may be a bit expensive for those used to living on thalis but service is quick and good coffee and tea come with a smile. Down the road is the popular budget meal **Hotel Elite** which has its own bakery producing good cakes and biscuits.

The menu is varied, the food, especially the fish, good and at Rs25/50 cheap even if the coffee and tea aren't worth drinking. Also in this price range is **Rafa** restaurant where the friendly staff serve up good chicken meals, soup and coffee.

There are other things listed on the menu which are sometimes available. Otherwise go to **Hotel Seagull** or get some good snacks off the stalls besides the Chinese fishing nets.

Ernakulam

Sea Lord Hotel's rooftop restaurant does

excellent South Indian food and fish dishes with meals for Rs50/150 and very good cocktails. *Hotel Abad Plaza* has very good Indian, Chinese and Western food for Rs100/200 in its restaurants as does *International Hotel.* For cheap *thalis* try *Athul Jyoti* on Shanmugham Road or *Woodlands Hotel* on MG Road. Close to Athul Jyoti in Shenoy Chambers is *The Oven*, a good place for Indian cakes and sweets. And if you want to escape from the bustle catch the boat to Bolgatty Island where you can eat at the slow but reasonable *Bolgatty Palace* restaurant, picnic or try out the food on offer in the small village.

Willingdon Island

Both the more expensive *Taj Malabar* and *Casino Hotels* serve up good seafood.

Entertainment

Kochi has 13 **cinemas**, including *Padmas* and *Shenoy* on MG Road in Ernakulam, *Kokers* in Fort Cochin and *Royals* in Mattancherry. It's best to check the newspapers for the mainly Hindi film showings.

Kathakali **dance shows** (see page 71) occur daily at the *Cochin Cultural Centre* (tel 0484-368153), Souhardham, on Manikath Road, from 7pm in an air-conditioned theatre. An outdoor rooftop performance is given daily at Director Devan's *See India Foundation* (tel 0484-369471) on Kalathiparambil Lane, Chittor Road South End, near the train station from 6.45pm. Get there for 6pm and you can see the brightly coloured masks being made up. Entry to both centres is Rs50. *Kerala Kathakali Centre* on River Road, near the Chinese fishing nets in Fort Cochin has a very good show for Rs50 which begins with the make up at 5pm for the full show from 6.30pm to 7.30pm.

Boat cruises

A trip by boat on the *Cochin Boat Tour* takes 3.5 hours and costs just Rs50 for a jour-

ney which takes in Mattancherry Palace, Jewish Synagogue, the fishing nets, St Francis' Church and Bolgatty Palace. It leaves twice daily at 9am and 2pm from the jetty in front of Sea Lord Hotel on Shanmugham Road, south of High Court Jetty. Sea Lord Hotel is also the starting point for the daily 5.30pm to 7pm *KTDC Sunset Tour* costing Rs30.

Backwater-village cruises

Those intent on going on the KTDC backwaters boat cruise should go to the KTDC Tourist Reception Centre on Shanmugham Road, south of the Sea Lord Jetty at 8.30am or 2.30pm. The morning cruise at least starts off slightly cooler. The trip begins and ends with a 45 minute bus ride. For Rs300 visitors are taken for 3.5 hours through narrow canals, fishing farms, villages and plantations. It is a nice sleepy way of seeing Kerala's rural life.

Tourist Desk offers a similar cruise for Rs250 from their office close to the Ernakulam Jetty at 9am and 2pm. Tickets for Backwater tours in Alappuzha (Alleppey) and Kollam (Quilon) can also be purchased at the Tourist Desk information counter.

Ferries

A trip by ferry is another way of seeing Kochi and it's surroundings. State and private ferries operate from Main Boat Jetty and High Court Jetty travelling to *Bolgatty, Mattancherry, Fort Cochin, Vypin, Ochantheruth, Vallarpadam* and *Murikkumpadam*. If these are too slow for you, you can always hire a motorboat from Main Boat Jetty for a Rs400/hour spin round the harbour.

Coach Tours

Periyar Wildlife Sanctuary

Every Saturday from the *Tourist Reception Centre* (0484-353234) at 7.30am

BACKWATERS

KTDC runs a two-day coach tour up to Periyar via the great Idduki Dam. It's a chance to see one of India's best wildlife sanctuaries (see Periyar page 101). Accommodation is booked by KTDC on request at their pleasant Periyar House. Coaches return for 8pm on Sunday.

For a somewhat different tour try the engaging Sunday outing to the scenic **Athirampalli** and **Vazhachal Waterfalls** on the Chalakuddy River 90 km from Kochi. The coach leaves the Tourist Reception Centre at 8am, returning 6pm.

Shopping

Kochi has four main markets which are interesting as spectacles in themselves but also worth a browse for bargain buys. They are on Market Road in Ernakulam and at Kaloor, Thevara and Kadavanthra. But if you want to shop in the cool, Grand Bazaar has an air-conditioned supermarket in the **Abad Plaza Complex** on MG Road. MG Road and Marine Drive are the main shopping centres.

Jewtown has a number of craft and antique shops on and around Synagogue Lane, but they can be quite overpriced and a trip to see the little spice warehouses and shops nearby would probably be more fruitful. Better value for handicrafts can be had at the **Kairili** and **Surabhi showrooms** opposite each other at Pallimuku on MG Road.

Best buys in Kochi are wood carvings, ornaments made of coconut shells, bamboo cane or *rattan* – embroidered screwpine mats – jewellery and clothes. Shops, generally closed on Sundays, open at 10am and close around 8pm.

Kurian's Eye Clinic near Guest House on Broadway and **Indian Opticals** at Pharmacy Junction, MG Road North End do replacement lenses, **contact lenses** and **spectacles**.

Cash

Canara Bank on Karrakat Rd and **ANZ Grindlays Bank** and **Andhra Bank** both on MG Road take most major credit cards and change **travellers cheques**. They are open from 10am till 2pm on weekdays and 10am till noon on Saturdays. **Thomas Cook** are on the first floor of Palai Towers. They are open from 9.30am to 6pm everyday save Sunday but exchange rates are generally better elsewhere.

Communications abroad

Fax facilities exist at the **Central Telegraph Office** from 8am to 8pm and at **Fax Call Copy Centre**, both near Bimbis at Jos Junction on DH Road, **Peter's Communications**, opposite HFDC House at Ravipuram Junction, **Replica** on DH Road and **Copy Com Service** in the SD Complex near Carona at South Junction. They also have ISD/STD facilities but there are many ISD/STD booths around the city.

Ernakulam Head Post Office is on Hospital Road and opens 9.30am to 8pm daily except Sundays when opening times are 10am to 5pm.

Visa Extensions

For Visa Extensions apply to the Office of the **Commissioner of Police** (0484-394770) on Shanmugham Road near the High Court Jetty. It opens daily from 10am till 5pm but closes every Sunday and every second Saturday in the month. An extension, if they will do it, may take more than a week.

Hospitals

Hospitals admitting accident cases (not all do and accident victims can be unceremoniously wheeled out) include **City Hospital**, MG Road, **General Hospital**, Hospital Road, **St Joseph's Hospital** and **Maharaja's Hospital** at Karuvelippady.

Travel Options

Kochi's location in the centre of Kerala affords the city a key role in the state transport network. Air, road and rail routes link

Kochi Trains around Kerala

Destination	Distance	Fare 2nd/1st Class	Time
Thiruvananthapuram	221 km	Rs 56/249	4.5 hours
Kollam	156 km	Rs 42/185	2 hours
Kottayam	60 km	Rs 20/99	1.5 hours
Thrissur	74 km	Rs 23/117	2 hours
Kozhikode	191 km	Rs 48/217	5 hours
Palakkad	150 km	Rs 48/184	2/3 hours
Kannur	281 km	Rs 66/297	6 hours

Kochi trains around India

Destination	Distance	Fare 2nd/1st Class	Time
New Delhi	2800 km	Rs290/1678	48 hours
Mumbai (Bombay)	1840 km	Rs227/1169	40 hours
Bangalore	630 km	Rs124/563	13 hours
Mangalore	421 km	Rs 90/410	10 hours
Madras	703 km	Rs130/597	13 hours
Kanyakumari	308 km	Rs 72/318	7 hours

the city direct to virtually every town in Kerala. For the Backwater towns, boat/ferry travel may be the slowest option but it's also the most interesting and relaxing. Hello Cochin is a useful booklet to pick up from city shops as it includes details on most travel times and fares.

Planes

The recently upgraded international **airport** on **Willingdon Island** was due to be fully operational by August 1997. Kochi is due to substantially expand its air operations which at the beginning of 1997 were restricted to domestic flights. Currently Alliance Air run daily flights to and from **Delhi** via **Goa**. and **Mumbai** (Bombay). They also have flights four days a week to **Bangalore** and three days a week to **Chennai** (Madras). NEPC Airlines have daily flights to Chennai and also fly to Bangalore and weekly to **Agatti** in the Lakshadweep Islands. Jet Airways run twice daily flights to Mumbai.

and Indian Airlines a weekly flight to Chennai.

Approximate prices for one way flights are Mumbai Rs4050, Chennai Rs2670, Bangalore Rs1800, Goa Rs2860, Delhi Rs8120 and Agatti Rs3290.

Indian Airlines (0484-370242) have their office on Durbar Hall Road in Ernakulam. In the same district on MG Road is the **Air India** Office (0484-353276). **Alliance Air** (0484-370242, **Jet Airways** (0484-369423) **NEPC Airlines** (0484-367720) and **Skyline NEPC** (0484-367740) also have offices in the city. The airport enquiry number when phoning in Kochi is 141. A taxi from the airport should cost less than Rs70, a rickshaw, half as much again, and a bus less than Rs2.

Trains

Kochi has three **rail stations** so it's important to be clear about which one you're visiting. **Ernakulam Junction** (phone enquiries 131) at the east end of Durbar Hall Road is

BACKWATERS

the very busy main station and most trains halt here. **Ernakulam Town** (phone enquiries 0484-353920) in the north of the city is the other inter-city rail station. The **Bangalore Express** goes from here. Bookings at the reservation counter are computerised and quite fast.

The Area manager for both stations has an office close to Ernakulam Junction. The office is very helpful if you have a problem getting high enough on the waiting list. **Cochin Harbour Station** on Willingdon Island mainly takes cargo and local trains.

Trains around Kerala.

Services run to all the main and many of the smaller towns of Kerala. At least nine trains a day travel south to **Thiruvananthapuram** (4.5 hours) with **Kollam** and **Kottayam** en-route. Trains to the northern towns of **Kozhikode** (Calicut), **Thrissur** (Trichur), **Kannur** and **Kasargod** are less frequent. On page 147 are some examples of destinations and fares you are likely to pay.

Trains around India.

Kochi is linked via express trains to a number of key cities in India. On page 147 are some examples of the times and types of fares you are likely to pay.

Buses

A bus from Kochi will take you virtually to any town or village in the state. The trick is getting to the right bus station as there are several. Booking seats is only possible for buses originating in Kochi/Ernakulam. Many buses stop at Kochi en route so it is a question of just turning up and joining the queue.

KSRTC buses go from the main **Central Bus Station** equidistant between the Ernakulam rail stations at the east end of Ammankovil Road.

Buses around Kerala

KSRTC Buses: 80 KSRTC Superfast/Super Express buses plough the road to **Thiruvanathapuram** (5.5 hours) via Alappuzha each day. One of these goes on to **Vizhinjam** (Kovalam) but it's not worth hanging around for as buses from the capital to Kovalam are frequent and cheap. Frequent buses also travel to **Kottayam** (1 hour), **Kollam** (3.5 hours), **Thrissur** (2 hours), **Palakkad** (4 hours) and **Kozhikode** (5 hours). Buses also go four times a day to **Kumili** (Periyar).

Private bus operators use four other bus stations. Ernakulam South has a midnight bus for Kumili in **Periyar**. Kaloor Bus Stand has buses for **Kottayam, Ettamanur, Punalor** and **Pathanamthitta**. High Court Junction has frequent buses to **Kodungallur** and **Guruvayoor**, a bus north to **Bekal** and buses east to **Silent Valley**, Munnar and north east to **Mananthavaadi**. Buses from Ernakulam North go north to **Kozhikode, Kannur, Bekal** and **Iritti**.

Buses around India

KSRTC Buses: 20 KSRTC buses travel the five-hour, Rs54 daily journey to **Coimbatore** (the destination for Ooty). Buses also go regularly to **Bangalore** (12/15 hours, Rs166/200) and four times a day to **Madurai** (9 hours, Rs79/90). A KSRTC bus goes twice-daily to **Kanyakumari** (9 hours, Rs99).

Private Interstate Buses mainly operate from Jos Junction on MG Road. Many buses go daily to Coimbatore. Buses also go to Madurai, **Chennai** (Madras) and **Mangalore**.

Tourist information offices

KTDC's very helpful **Tourist Reception Centre** (0484-353234) on Shanmugham Road. **Tourist Information Office** (0484-668352) is in the Old Collectorate at Fort Cochin and Government of India Tourist Office (0484-381743) is on Willingdon Island.

BACKWATERS

Around Kochi

Athirappally and Vazhachal Waterfalls

Seventy-eight kilometres from Kochi at **Athirappally**, the tributary waters to the **Chalakkudy River** rush out of the **Sholayar Mountains** of the Western Ghats and free-dive 25 metres making a spectacular waterfall popular with local tourists. Further downriver at **Vazhachal** the Chalakkudy is again forced to make another leap over rocks to find its way to the lowlands. Those attracted by the waterfalls' beauty can stay at **Richmond Hotel** in Athirappally. KTDC runs a daily coach tour from Kochi and buses go hourly from Chalakkudy town which is linked by bus and train to Thrissur (Trichur) 30km away.

Thattekad Bird Sanctuary

Thattekad Bird Sanctuary is one of the state's best. The 25 sq km of moist deciduous and evergreen forests in Idduki district are home to indigenous species such as the Malabar grey hornbill, rose-winged and blue parakeets and the rare Ceylon frog-mouth and rose-billed roller. An estimated 300 native and migratory birds rest in the forest and by the waterside.

Boat trips are organised between **Boothathankettu** and **Thattekad**. The best time for bird-watchers is between September and March and from 5am to 6pm, requiring an early drive from Kochi, 78km away on the road to Munnar, or an overnight stay at a hotel in nearby **Kothamangalam**. The keenest can book an overnight stay at the **Inspection Bungalow** (contact KTDC) in Boothathankettu.

Udayamperoor

Udayamperoor, 18km south east of Kochi on the road to Vaikom, contains the historic Roman Catholic church which gave its name to the Synod of Dyamper. Held in 1599, the Synod was called by the Portuguese to bring the Malabar Syrian Christians under the hegemony of the Vatican. The Syrian Christians split and eventually the pressure of Rome led to the Kochi-based Coonen Cross revolt of 1653.

Viakom

Situated on the road between Kochi (30km) and Kottayam (40km) and 10km from Udayamperoor, Viakom is another town associated with social turmoil. Here in 1925 protesters, with Gandhi's agreement, staged a famous sit-down demonstration or *satyagraha* against the Backward and Non-Scheduled castes, the Untouchables, being prohibited from entering the local Shiva temple.

The temple is enshrined in myth and is believed to have been built by Parasurama, the legendary god said to have created Kerala out of the sea.

Edappally

10km north east of Ernakulam on the road to Aluva (Alwaye), in the Edappally area is the site for the 1400-year old **Saint George Forane Church**. Built in AD593 on land donated by the Raja of Edappally, it is one of Kerala's oldest churches. The 'new' church beside it was built in AD1080, four centuries before European Christianity came to India. The last local Maharaja here converted to Christianity. Watch out for the annual nine-day feast in May.

Ten kilometres from Ernakulam also on the Aluva Road is the **Museum of Kerala History** which uses paintings, sculptures and video shows to illustrate the state's development since the Neolithic age. The museum opens 10am till noon and 2pm to 4pm daily except Mondays.

Tripunithura Hill Palace Museum

This old palace set on a hill 10km east of Ernakulam was set in the headquarters for the Kochi Maharajas. Now it is a state museum encompassing many of the paintings, carvings etc. amassed by the Travancore and Kochi Maharajas. One interesting exhibit is a body-shaped cage in which prisoners would be placed then hung to be pecked to death. Another is the *kingini katti*, a knife decorated with bells and used to lop off heads. Some of the carvings, like that of the Ramayana monkey-king Sugreeva, are excellent.

In the grounds is a mini-zoo with *sambar*, spotted deer and peacocks. The 50 acre compound opens daily from 9am to 5pm save Mondays.

In November/December, Tripunithura's **Sree Poornathrayeesa temple** stages an eight-day festival with *chanda meelam* music belted out by the drummers. It's worth a visit to the town on the last day when a large procession with 15 elegantly-adorned elephants marches through the streets.

The town also has the **RLV College of Art & Music** which amongst other things trains *kathakali* dancers. It is close to the temple.

Inexpensive **accommodation** is available in the town at Prasanth Tourist Home (0484-776073) and other lodges. Private buses go regularly from Ernakulam to the town which is on the road to Chottanikara. A rickshaw should only cost Rs30.

Chennamangalam

This important handloom weaving and coir processing centre was historically the seat of the Maharajas' prime ministers. Evidence that religious communities lived alongside each other for centuries can be seen by the close proximity of an 800 year-old Syrian Catholic church, an Oriental Jewish synagogue (the town was an important Jewish centre), a Krishna temple and a mosque.

Buses take an hour or so on the road north. Alight at North Parur. Then another bus or a **rickshaw** can take you the 5km to Chennamangalam. Buses are frequent. A **taxi** would cost Rs170 one way for the 42km journey from Kochi.

BACKWATERS

Aluva (Alwaye)

Unless you're caught out in transit or going to see the huge *Maha Sivarathri festival* in February there is little to entice a visit to *Aluva*. 20km north of Kochi, Aluva is Kerala's key industrial centre and the Periyar River flows through the city. Each winter the river shrinks exposing huge great sandbanks of silt collected on its journey from the mountains. The banks are the venue for the Sivarathri festivities.

Hundreds of oil lamps flicker through the night while pilgrims fast and meditate, sitting on the sandbanks. Then early next morning they rise and, shouting and chanting, leap into the river emerging to make offerings and pray in memory of those who have passed away. Besides the river is a quaint, old palace which affords a good view of the jubilant crowds.

Accommodation is available here. The *Seven Stars Periyar Hotel Complex* (0484-625024) has air-conditioned rooms for Rs325 (Rs200 without). Two budget hotels with rooms costing less than Rs130 a night are *Alankar Tourist Home* (0484-623162) and *Anamala Tourist Home* (0484-624138).

Buses go frequently to *Kochi, Thrissur* (Trichur) and *Kalady* and **trains** (Rs12/132) go frequently to *Kochi.*

BACKWATERS

A Ganesh Shrine

THE NORTH **Malabar**

The Spice Coast

Beautiful beaches, ancient towns, forts and temples, tribes with Stone Age cultures, dense forests untouched by modern man and the towering rugged mountains of the Western Ghats make north Kerala, or Malabar, as it was called under British rule, a must for travellers looking for something special.

Apart from in the main city, Kozhikode (Calicut), tourism as a trade is barely in its infancy and visitors are guaranteed all the benefits of being novelties to the friendly accommodating people of the north. Ironically, it is in Malabar that the West and the Middle East had their first contacts with south India.

Attracted by Kerala's bountiful supplies of pepper and other spices, Egyptian, Greek, Roman, Arab, Jewish and Chinese traders landed on the shores of Malabar and traded for centuries with local merchants. Some of the merchants settled, building homes, fortresses and religious shrines. India's first Roman temples, mosques, churches and synagogues were situated here when Britain was in the Dark Ages.

Later came the Chinese, Vasco da Gama from Portugal, then the Dutch, the French, the Moguls and the British. All have left some mark on Malabar's culture. The small port of Mahe (Pondicherry) in north Malabar, once a French colony, still has a separate, independent administrative status from the rest of Kerala.

The dominant indigenous rulers had been the Zamorins who ruled from Kozhikode (Calicut). They fought frequent battles with the maharajas of Kochi taking the old Kochi state capital of Thrissur. The Portuguese arrived with a Bible and rosary in one hand and a cutlass in the other leading to a lengthy series of violent clashes with the Zamorin forces in the sixteenth and seventeenth centuries until being driven from the Malabar coast by the Dutch in 1664. Thence followed the English (and the French who established a foothold in Mahe only to lose the territory to the English in the 1760s).

Haider Ali, who was the first to use rocketry in warfare, was the erstwhile ruler of Mysore in the mid-eighteenth century. His mission was to drive foreign troops from Indian soil and he fought many battles against the British and French. At one time he drove the British back to the walls of Madras and almost out of south India. He took Malabar before he retired after a defeat in 1781.

Haider Ali died in 1782. The same year his son Tipu Sultan took control of the Mysore army and routed the English army led by Colonel Braithwaite. Tipu Sultan overran Malabar, taking control of the northern spice trade, eliminating Zamorin rule

MALABAR

and much of the old feudal system of power. The dominance of Islam in the north is mainly accredited to his rule. The Malabar people who converted to Islam at this time are still known as *Moplahs*. Many women in the north had previously practiced polyandry, the sexual opposite of Muslim bigamy, and Tipu Sultan abolished 'the women's right to choose'.

That Tipu Sultan could not extend his rule south into Travancore was largely down to the transformation of Travancore into an effective fighting unit by Maharaja Marthanda Varma and Tipu's inability to arrive at a strategy for defeating the courageous snakeboat troops of the Backwaters.

In 1783 and again in 1792 the British forced the Sultan out of Malabar. Finally in 1799 the British defeated and killed him. The Zamorins were effectively pensioned off and Malabar placed under the control of the Madras state governors. In 1956, Malabar was incorporated into the new state of Kerala.

The region's great forts testify to the battle ground that Malabar became. In the far north is the majestic Bekal Fort built by a local Raja then occupied in the eighteenth century by Tipu Sultan's troops. Beneath the Ghats in Palakkad is the Tipu's inland fort built by Haider Ali. Kannur has the enchanting Portuguese built Saint Angelo Fort and **Thalassery** has an English built fort.

Malabar's population is predominantly Muslim. Hinduism is more in evidence in the south of the region where **Thrissur** (Trichur) and **Guruvayoor** are important Hindu temple cities. Despite Malabar's mercantile history, the area is devoid of any major industrial centres. For when the river silted up the port at Kodungallor in 1341, its role as the principal maritime city shifted to Kollam and later Kochi.

Malabar is extremely fertile and still a major source of spices, fruits, vegetables and timber. Topographically the area can be divided into two, the coastal strip and its hinterland tapering off towards the north and the mountains with their densely-forested slopes on the eastern border with Tamil Nadu and Karnataka.

The coastline is bedecked by hundreds of tiny fishing villages and blessed with some of the most attractive of Kerala's sandy, palm-tree fringed beaches, many within 2km of the coastal highway. The more humid hinterland is dotted with small market towns amongst the fields.

Malampuzha in Palakkad is an inland tourist resort generally only visited by Indians. The town sits beneath the towering Western Ghats. Great rivers flow down from the mountains and have been harnessed to provide Kerala with hydro-electric power. In the wildlife sanctuaries beneath the Ghats, new plant species are still being discovered. Tribes live in the forest, some only discovered by the authorities in the 1970s. In their facial and physical features are the signs of Kerala's Aboriginal and African ancestry. Tragically many have been disoriented, if not set back, by contact with modern civilisation.

The Kerala government has plans to develop the tourist industry but these are still plans and a lot has to be done. In the meantime the area remains largely a virgin territory for international visitors and cheap.

Kodungallor (Crangannore)

Sat on the banks of the Periyar estuary, 40km from Kochi, Kodungallor is in the far south of Malabar. Formerly the ancient port known to the Greeks and Romans as Muziris, the British gave it the name Crangannore. Recently state authorities reverted the official name back to its Malayalam title Kodungalloor.

Muziris was a trading centre with the Arab ports when Alexander the Great of Greece sent his ships to trade for 'the passion of the Greeks' – pepper. The Kodungallor temple required devotees to bring pepper as offerings for the gods and it seems this provided for a flourishing local market.

The Romans also sent their ships in search of pepper. Their presence in Muziris was such that at the beginning of the first century AD a temple dedicated to Emperor Augustus was constructed in the town. The Roman scholar Pliny the Elder complained that the elite's greed for pepper was draining the government of funds, and Roman coins have been found in the town.

Soon after came Thomas Didymus, one of Jesus' twelve disciples, fleeing with his followers from Roman persecution. Saint Thomas is said to have landed here in AD52 and built the first Christian church in India. Saint Thomas converted several members of the high Nairs and Namboodiris' noble castes and Christianity flourished throughout Kerala.

It is uncertain when the first Jews arrived but the story of Saint Thomas disembarking to be greeted by a Jewish flute player may be true. The Babylonians are said to have traded here and the Israelites, also fleeing persecution, who purportedly arrived in 587BC. What is certain is that the Jewish community became so important that they even had their own semi-independent state in Kodungallor known as Shingly.

Arabs competed with Jews for the Malabar spice trade long before the arrival of Islam. But when Islam arrived it came through Kodungallor. In AD629 two Muslim Imams settled with their families in the town establishing *Cheraman Juma Musjid*, India's first mosque. Cheraman was the Kerala king who converted to Islam and emigrated to Mecca. Interestingly, like the early Christian churches, the mosque's low sloping roofs and veranda more resembles a Hindu temple than the opulent spires and minarets so common in Kerala today.

The mosque, rebuilt in the 16th century still stands one and a half kilometres from Kodungallor town. Hindus and Christians also attend the mosque on auspicious occasions to bring oil for the celebrated lamp in its central shrine. However tolerance does not extend to allowing women to enter. All women are barred. Male visitors can get shown round by speaking to the imam in the house opposite.

The battle for the spice trade between the Arab and Jewish merchants led to increasing animosity between Muslim and Jew. Pogroms in which many Jews were killed and the silting up of the city's port after the great storms of 1341 eventually forced the Jews to abandon Shingly and move to Kochi where they were offered the

MALABAR

Maharaja's protection.

There is little left in this town, but the mosque and an old Portuguese fort, to suggest that it was once an important international trading centre and first point of contact for visiting civilisations. However accommodation is reasonable and it's only a boat-ride from the relaxing Cherai Beach. Two 'superfast' buses run daily from Kochi (50km) to Kodungallor and similarly from Thrissur in the north.

Accommodation

Cheap lodges are available otherwise **Hotel Prasathi** (048880-2939) has rooms for Rs75 to Rs180. **Hotel Kairali** (048880-2631), **Hotel Indrappastham** (048880-2678) and **Polakulath Tourist Home** (048880-2602) all have rooms for Rs100 to Rs260.

Thrissur (Trichur)

The small relaxed city of Thrissur is said to be the cultural capital of Kerala. As such it is surprising how little it features on the itineraries of international visitors to the state. It is 80km from Kochi and on the main routes north and east to Mysore. It has a rich history, fine churches and temples and good accommodation and is within 40km of some of India's best beaches. One of the reasons is precisely that the Kerala government have concentrated on marketing the south. The beaches are still free of hotels and Thrissur's principal role as a cultural centre has the drawback that non-Hindus are barred from the great temples in the town. Nevertheless the city has other interesting features.

Thrissur is an abbreviation of "Tiru-Shiva-Perur" meaning "the town with Lord Shiva's name". Sat on a hillock in the centre of the city is the spacious, and excellently maintained, centuries-old temple dedicated to Shiva. Even if it can only be viewed from the outside the splendid **Vadakkunath Kshetram** temple is worth a look.

Despite its size, the tradi-

Map legend:
1. Vadukkanath Temple
2. Lourdes Cathedral
3. Pathan's Palace
4. Hotel Elite
5. Sree Buddha TH
6. Hotel Luciya
7. Railway Station
8. Kerala Bharan
9. Juma Masjid
10. Sakthan Thampuran bus stand
11. KSRTC bus stand

Thrissur

tional Kerala-style, low-hanging roofs and the dominant use of wood give it a serene non-assuming appearance most fitting for one of the world's few major non-prose-lytising religions. In contrast inside, for the devotees, there are excellent murals and paintings depicting scenes from the Mahabharata epic and a wonderfully carved theatre hall.

In the main shrine Lord Shiva is represented by a *mahalingam* phallic symbol but it is hidden from view by a three-metre high mound surrounding it, made up of cen-turies-old dried *ghee*. Cow's *ghee*, used as cooking oil, is the traditional offering to the *mahalingam* and some of the ghee near the base is said to be 1,000 years old.

A glance at a map of the town or an aerial view reveals how Thrissur's layout was boldly designed. The hillock on which the temple stands is the base and is surrounded by a circular road. From here four roads radiate out, each connected by a series of concentric roads.

Other interesting temples at the bottom of the hillock include the pink and white Vadakkunath Kshetram to goddess Parvathi and the Krishna temple of **Thiruvambadi** in the town centre.

The Pooram 'Elephant' Festivals

April/May sees the annual Hindu Pooram *festival celebrations in and around temples across Kerala. Huge great processions are staged in which beautifully caparisoned elephants take pride of place. Probably the biggest and most colourful of these is the Thrissur festival around the Vaddakunath temple.*

Tens of thousands of onlookers flock to the city sitting on the hillock occupied by the temple and anywhere else they can, awaiting the after-noon's festivities. Then a line of two-dozen elephants appear each with their heads decorated with glittering gold leaf and their backs carrying three Brahmin (priest caste) mahouts.

The central elephant carries a large image of Shiva, the temple deity. Slowly they march to the bottom of the hill where they turn to face another line of elephants. An orchestra of flute (kuzhal) players, bell-metal trumpet (kompu) players, brass cymbal (elatalam) clashers and 100 chenda *drummers blares out, exciting the crowd.*

This part of the Pooram festivities was introduced by a former Kochi Maharaja and now a competition takes place as the crowds sit unfazed right in front up to the feet of the 4.5 ton animal. The orchestra increases the speed and intensity of traditional Kerala chenda meelam *music and the* mahouts *do an arm dance with fluffy white yak-hair fly whisks. Suddenly each rider unfurls a pink and gold parasol with which*

they will compete with the other side in a dazzling dextrous display.
Standing upright on the elephant the mahouts compete in exchanging
their parasols at speed. The crowds roar and the party's on. Time and
time again the whole process is repeated, the crowd roaring and
lurching in unison. Darkness falls and one of India s biggest and
noisiest firework displays explodes across the skies.

Close to Thrissur, **Arattapuzha** *village has an equally colourful festival,*
the images of the deities of 41 temples being carried in a procession.
And if you can't make these incredible demonstrations of man and
elephant in the spring, a special elephant march is held with 30 to 40
elephants in Thrissur on January 9 of each year.

If you have missed out on Thrissur and Arattapuzha then there's always
the Irinjalakuda elephant festival with its modest but equally
caparisoned and decorated 13 elephants on the march at the same time
of the year. The ten day festival is organised by the **Koodal Manikyam**
temple, the only temple in India to be dedicated to Rama's brother,
Bharatha (Rama, an incarnation of Lord Vishnu, is celebrated in the
Ramayana epic).

Visitors are allowed to enter the temple and see its splendid kuttam
balam theatre if they wear a dhoti. The temple is a kilometre from the
Irinjalakuda bus stand which is a stop for many buses from Thrissur,
23km away. Accommodation is available in the town.

The pink spires of Our Lady of Lourdes Cathedral make for another imposing religious shrine in the city close by the Shiva temple. Wonderfully bright and airy, the cathedral also has a pretty underground shrine.

Thrissur has a large **zoo** and an **art museum** set in 13.5 acres, two kilometres from the city centre on Town Hall Road. The zoo has lions, tigers, sloth, bear and the rare lion-tailed macaque. The famous snake park with its king cobra, varied pythons, vipers and rat snakes is worth a peek. The museum has a good collection of stone sculptures and traditional oil lamps. The *Archaeological Museum*, also on Town Hall Road, has some good reproductions of the murals at the Dutch Palace and sculptures in stone. The museums and zoo open from 10am till 5pm daily except for Mondays.

Near Nehru Park there is an aquarium open from 3pm to 8pm daily. The shops in the city are good for gold jewellery, sarees and traditional Kerala handicrafts such as the brass lamps. In Irinjalakuda close to the Bharatha temple, **Natan Kairali** is a cultural centre dedicated to Kerala's lesser known dance and theatre. *Koodiyattam, nangiar koothu* (where one woman dances) and puppetry are taught here.

Accommodation

Budget range

Because of the number of visiting pilgrims, Thrissur has plenty of cheap lodges with rooms for Rs120 or less. These include, on Railway Station Road: **Chandy's Tourist Home** (0487-421167), **Aradhana Tourist Home** (0487-424938) and **Hotel Dwaraka** (0487-422165). On MG Road there is the **National Tourist Home** (0487-424543) and **Hotel Peninsula** (0487-335537) and on Chembottil Lane, **Sree Buddha Tourist Home** (0487-427689) and **Premier Lodgings** (0487-421913). **Jaya Lodge** (0487-423258) on Kuruppam Road and **Kerala Bhavan** (0487-421010) on Post Office Road also have cheap rooms.

Medium range

Yatri Nivas (0487-332333) on Stadium Road has air-conditioned rooms for Rs250 (Rs100 without) a bar and restaurant. It may be large and pretty basic but **Pathan's Lodgings** (0487-425620) near the entrance to the **Hotel Elite** has rooms for Rs175 and is very handy for the excellent restaurant of the same name in the hall below.

Allukkas Tourist Home (0487-424067) on Railway Station Road has rooms for Rs100 to Rs250.

Top of the range

The best in town is probably the recently renovated and, with its white colonnades giving it the appearance of an old colonial residence, very attractive **Hotel Luciya Palace** (0487-424731, fax 0487-427290) on Marar Road near the train station and the main temple hillock. Charges for the double rooms range from Rs275 (Rs210 single) for a non air conditioned room to Rs1000 for the air-conditioned deluxe suite. Luxury tax of 7.5-10% is added. The 37 rooms have room service, cable TV and telephones. The hotel also has a good restaurant, a nice bar beside the lawn, fax facilities and accepts credit cards.

On Kuruppam Road, again close to the temple hillock in the centre, **Hotel Elite International** (0487-421033, fax 0487-399057) is two-star status and has the same prices and facilities (eg. bar, credit cards etc.) as Luciya Palace. With its upper floor balconies offering a superb view of the city and its special kiddies' park it does have some charm but the 78 rooms are not as well kept as the Luciya.

Casino Hotel (0487-424699) on TB Road looks rather dreary but may be up for refurbishment. Room prices here are similar to the two hotels above.

Eating Out

The clean and very busy vegetarian Pathan's Palace close to the **Hotel Elite International** is the local's favourite and with meals for Rs12/30 excellent value for money. **Kerala Bhavan** on Railway Station Road has cheap *thalis*. **Hotel Luciya Palace** also has a good, if more expensive restaurant pleasant for eating on the lawn at night.

Around Thrissur

Good roads connect Thrissur with the lake at **Peechy Dam** which is beautifully set 23km away in the foothills of the Western Ghats. The dam adjoins a wildlife sanctuary. Take a boat out and you may even see elephants coming down for a drink in the winter months. Accommodation is available here.

Close to Thrissur is the village of **Machat** into which thousands of Hindu devotees stream for the annual five day **Mamankam Festival** of the Devi temple. The special feature of the 600 year old Mamankam festival is the absence of elephants from the procession. Instead hundreds of devotees carry elaborately-painted, giant dummy horses.

Part of this colourful post-harvest festival is the carrying of the *Elayath*, the living representative of the Devi, on the shoulders by *eduppanmar*, members of a group of families from the local village. In four days the *Elayath* must visit and bless the houses of all the devotees who are spread over half a dozen

MALABAR

villages. Consequently it is usual to see the *eduppanmar* running with her from house to house and village to village.

Travel Options

Train and Plane

The nearest airport is 80km away in **Kochi**, a 1.5 hour train ride away. **Thiruvananthapuram** is 322km and a seven hour rail journey away. The railway station is south west of the town centre. Frequent trains go to Kochi/Ernakulam (second-class fare Rs23, first-class Rs117), Thiruvananthapuram, **Kollam, Kottayam, Kozhikode** (3 hours), **Shornur** and **Palakkad**. Four trains a day go to **Guruvayoor**, three a day to **Kanyakumari** and there are twice-daily trains to **Kannur, Alappuzha, Mangalore, Chennai** (Madras) and **Mumbai** (Bombay). Trains go daily to **Delhi** and **Bangalore**. Every Friday the Himasager Express leaves for Kashmir.

Buses

Thrissur has three bus stations. The KSRTC bus station is close to the train station. Private buses go mainly from Sakthan Tampuran Bus Stand, one kilometre south of the centre, but also from Priyadarshini Bus Stand on the north side of the centre. KSRTC run frequent bus services to and from **Guruvayoor** (1 hour), **Kozhikode, Kannur** (5 hours), **Palakkad, Kochi** (2 hours), **Kottayam** (3 hours), **Alappuzha** (3.5 hours) and **Thiruvananthapuram** (7 hours). Buses go to all the local towns.

Twice a day KSRTC buses go to **Mangalore** (8 hours) and daily to **Vizhinjam** (Kovalam). Six buses a day go to **Bangalore** (13 hours) and three run daily to **Mysore**. The best way to get to **Cheruthuruthi** is to go to Priyadarshini Bus Stand where buses leave every 15 minutes.

Cheruthuruthi

A 32km, one hour ride from Thrissur is Cheruthuruthi on the banks of Kerala's longest river, the Bharathapuzha, is the home of the famous **Kerala Kalamandalam Music and Dance Academy** specialising in *kathakali*. Founded in 1927 by the famous Kerala poet Vallathol, the centre is the training ground for many of Kerala's *kathakali* dancers. Its graduates are respected in international theatre around the globe.

Here the artists gain diplomas after studying all the complex facial, neck, arm, hand, leg and foot movements and their combinations dictated by this classical dance form. Every other related aspect is covered – make-up, *chenda* music, *koodiyattam* acting, *maddalam* etc.

For Rs750 per term, three- to twelve-month courses are available for non-Indian nationals. Visitors are welcome to watch the classes which only take place on weekdays. Free performances are given in the academy's superb theatre (a replica of the wooden sloping roofs of the traditional Koothambalam temple theatres) on January 26, March 13, August 15, September 18 and November 9.

Nearby there is a **Kathakali Museum** and a museum dedicated to the poet Shri Vallathol Narayana Menon, the centre's founder. Students have to find accommodation elsewhere but there is a **Government Guest House** in Cheruthuruthi. **Buses** go every 15 minutes between **Thrissur** and **Cheruthuruthi**.

Accommodation and Travel

Shornur just 3km away has cheap guest houses for less than Rs60 a night. Shornur is also the nearest train station and is on the main line for trains from **Kochi** (3 hours and Rs29/104 for a second-class ticket), **Thiruvananthapuram** (8 hours), **Kollam, Palakkad, Kannur, Bangalore, Chennai** (Madras) and **Mysore**. It also has regular bus services to **Thrissur**. The academy shuts for April and May. For further information contact: The Secretary, Kerala Kalamandalam, Cheruthuruthi PO, Thrissur, Kerala.

Guruvayoor Temple City

Just off the coastal Highway 17 and 29km from Thrissur is Guruvayoor, one of India's most important and sacred destinations for Hindu pilgrims. Thousands of pilgrims enter the small town. The site of the pretty **Rudratirtha Tank** beside the Sree Krishna temple is said to be sacred.

Rudratirtha was once a beautiful lake. Here Shiva and Parvathi welcomed Lord Parasurama, legendary creator of Kerala, who brought with him Guru, the preceptor of the gods, and Vayu, the god of winds. Guru and Vayu were searching for a holy spot for the idol of Krishna, recently departed from Dwaraka on earth to his heavenly abode. They were satisfied with the site – hence the city bore the name of Guru and Vayu.

Inside the temple, again barred to non-Hindus, are exquisitely carved pillars, stone sculptures, a 33 metre high gold-plated *dhwajastambam* or flag-post and from 3am to 10pm a continuous stream of rituals. One interesting offering to the deity is the *thulabharam* in which the devotee sits on one side of massive balancing scales. The other side is loaded up with bananas, coconuts, sugar, jaggery or whatever the devotee chooses. The devotee's equivalent in weight is then donated to the temple. It is not clear whether the devotees fast or feast beforehand.

A glimpse of the temple is possible from the outside but the events in front of the temple are also interesting, hundreds of people sat around waiting for their time to enter the temple, and the temple's 43 elephants coming and going. It's also an important bazaar with lots of little shops selling jewellery, ironware, *saris*, cassettes etc.

Krishna temple's ten-day elephant festival takes place at the time of *Ulsavam* (February/March). Festivities open on the first day with an elephant race. For the next week elephants daily lead the processions. The ninth day is *Palivetta*, when Krishna on an elephant hunts down human frailties represented in the form of men dressed as animals. The festival is completed by Krishna's image being immersed in water and locals jumping in to partake of the good fortune that bathing with their god will bring.

Guruvayoor has lots of other temples: **Mammiyur's Shiva temple**, said to be even older than the main temple, **Parthasarathi Krishna temple** and **Tamarayur Vishnu temple** to name a few. An engaging small town, it has a fascinating offshoot at **Punnathur Kotta** where the main temple's elephants are kept. Inside is a 400 year old Zamorin prince's palace which, though it has sadly been left to deteriorate, has some beautifully carved doors, ceilings and a dance hall which one day an enterprising official will make into a tourist attraction in itself. The compound is open daily for visitors between 8am and 6pm.

MALABAR

Punnathur Kotta Elephant Fort

Four kilometres along winding roads from Guruvayoor, after several stops to ask the way, we reached the site of an old Zamorin fort. The fort is now a huge open-air compound with 36 female and seven male elephants belonging to Guruvayoor's Sri Krishna temple. We were met by a friendly mahout offering to show us around. His lithe sun-baked body carried no fat, only the muscles required to control his powerful five-ton elephant.

One elephant was being led off for a bath in the waters of the large tank formerly used by the Zamorin's now dilapidated former palace. The elephants take their bath daily. Three times a week the mahouts in charge of their elephant give him or her a two to three hour massage, soothing the muscles which must carry its huge frame.

Small elephants will have two mahouts to take care of them. The biggest elephants, like 50-year-old Padmanaban, grow to three metres and require three mahouts. The mahout will train then look after the elephant till it dies. Lakshmi, the oldest, was already 87 years old, far older than the average 70-year life of an Indian elephant. She had been retired from temple duty for seven years and, having problems with eating, was restricted to a rice diet.

The other elephants stood around with their powerful back legs tied by long chains to the ground allowing them a certain freedom of movement. Each had their own patch of ground and a corrugated iron shelter beneath which they could hide their sensitive skin from the blistering sun while they munched on their mounds of palm tree leaves.

Watching them serenely at work on their food, one can marvel at how the wily intelligence of the elephant has turned its muscular trunk into an arm, using the sensitive tip of the nostril as a very dextrous hand. This great, seemingly cumbersome, animal can use its trunk not only to smell, sense, carry food and water to its mouth and spray and powder itself but also to carry a tree and, when trained, unlock and lock doors, even untie ropes.

Thirteen of the female elephants were absent. They were marched off early in the morning to perform at another temple. They had a busy schedule as they are hired out by the Sri Krishna temple for other festivals in the area. Several of the tuskered males had their front and back legs tied. Two mahouts were gesticulating at a large male which was making out to charge one of them. They were attempting to calm him. Our guide explained that this elephant was in the dangerous masht period suffered by all males for three or four months of the year.

The masht period is provoked by secretions from near the elephant's ears causing the bulls to become angry and sometimes wildly aggressive. It's dangerous work for the fastidious mahouts. They must spot the onset of this period and take immediate action chaining the animal and withdrawing him from festival duty. In the last eight years four of the temples' mahouts had been killed

Indeed the next day a newspaper reported that an elephant had run wild at a temple festival in the area killing one of his mahouts and an onlooker. It was easy to see why the temple preferred females. Another incident illustrated the close bonds formed by the mahouts in their perilous livelihood.

A mahout became angry with his disobedient elephant during a nearby festival. In frustration the mahout started shouting at his charge and landed a kick on the cow elephant's leg. A policemen intervened. A rowdy argument ensued, the result of which the mahout was arrested and carted off to the local police station. In protest his fellow mahouts followed riding their elephants to the police station which they surrounded for two hours. With the local police unable to leave or enter the station and the elephants knocking down the station walls, the bewildered, incarcerated mahout was eventually released.

MALABAR

Around Guruvayoor

Chavakkad is another typically attractive, palm-fringed, sandy Kerala beach. The mausoleum of Haidross Kuttee, the right-hand man of Haider Ali of Mysore, is here, a relic of the eighteenth century Mogul invasion. Just a kilometre away in Palayur is the site of an ancient church said to have been built by St. Thomas the Apostle.

Staying in Guruvayoor provides an excellent opportunity to explore the beautiful coastline. Further north, along the coastal Highway 17, are four excellent golden beaches less than two kilometres from the road. Vadanappilly and Triprayar Beaches are close to Kavakkad, 10km north of Guruvayoor. Puthu Ponnani and Andathodu Beaches are just south of Ponnani and 20km from Guruvayoor.

Accommodation

During the various festivals in the town many hotels may be full so it is advisable to phone and book accommodation in advance. There are plenty of cheap guest houses offering basic rooms for Rs100 or less in Guruvayoor.

They are mainly grouped in West Nada in which are **Pachens Tourist Home** (0487-556279), **Archana Lodge** (0487-556643), **Murali Lodge** (0487-556363) and **Indian Tourist Home** (0487-556455).

Hotel Vanamala Kusumam (0487-556702, fax 0487-555504) on South Nada, 200 metres from the temple and 500 metres from the rail station, is bright and clean and probably one of the best available in the town.

There is a **vegetarian restaurant** and **credit cards** are accepted. Rooms have satellite TV, telephones and room service. Air-conditioned rooms cost Rs350 (Rs250 without) plus tax, but for those who wish to splash out there's an air-conditioned suite available for Rs850).

KTDC run **Hotel Nandanam** (0487-556266) and its **vegetarian restaurant** on East Nada near Garuda Statue. Rooms are Rs200/400 (singles Rs150/250) plus tax. Other similarly-priced hotels on East Nada are **Hotel Elite** (0487-556215), **Hotel Vyshakh International** (0487-556188) and **Poornima Tourist Home** (0487-556691).

Travel Options

Kochi airport is 100km away and Thiruvananthapuram is 330km away. Five **trains** a day go to Kochi (2 hours and Rs27/62 in 2nd class), four go to **Thrissur** and two to **Thiruvananthapuram** (7 hours) and **Nagercoil**.

Buses run frequently to **Kozhikode** (3 hours). Several buses a day also go to **Kochi** (3 hours), **Kottayam, Palakkad** and **Coimbatore** (4 hours). Buses go to **Madurai** (8 hours) and **Mysore** (8 hours). Buses go frequently to **Thrissur, Kozhikode** and other major northern towns.

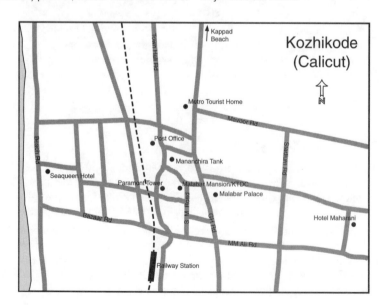

Kozhikode (Calicut)

The northern city of Calicut or Kozhikode, as it is now known, was originally brought to the notice of the west by Marco Polo who observed the excellent quality of the textiles in the city's markets. The term calico still refers to a type of cotton cloth today. He observed that the Chinese would send ships manned by up to 300 sailors bringing in silk, gold and silver and returning with 6,000 baskets of pepper, textiles and medicinal herbs.

In the latter half of this millennium Kozhikode has been the Kerala city most associated with the old spice trade by the rest of the world. In the fifteenth century the Chinese were the principal traders with Malabar, maintaining a fleet in Kozhikode port and a fort in the city. At Kappad there is still a *cinnaceri* - the word for a Chinese settlement.

For long the headquarters for the powerful Zamorins who ruled this area, the port later witnessed major battles with the Portuguese invaders, the British and Tipu Sultan's troops, all sent to control the spice trade.

After Vasco da Gama had landed at Kappad just north of the city he demanded that the Zamorin permit him to set up a factory and trading post in Kozhikode. A factory was built but its 50 Portuguese workers were killed following a Portuguese attack on an Arab ship in the harbour.

Thence followed a series of vicious battles and in 1509 and 1510 the Portuguese virtually destroyed the city, eventually subduing the Zamorin forces. Later Dutch, French then Tipu Sultan's forces dominated the city until the British secured the power. The centre for the spice trade shifted south first to Kollam then to Kochi and Kozhikode's regional importance declined.

Sadly today Kozhikode is a shadow of its majestic past. The port is now a centre for the exporting of timber and the palaces and forts have gone. All that is left of the great Zamorin palace and fort that stretched one mile in circumference, dominating the city, is the large Mannanchira tank in the centre. Nevertheless, it is a busy, friendly city with an airport and good accommodation. With some interesting historical monuments, good beaches and wildlife sanctuaries in easy reach, Kozhikode is a useful staging post for visiting Malabar.

The **Pazhassiraja Museum** is a small museum 5km from the city. It was named after the Raja who fought off the British for five years when they tried to overrun the Western Ghats. The museum has antique bronzes, old coins, copies of mural paintings, temple models and megalithic monuments from dolmonoid cysts and umbrella stone. It opens daily from 10am until 5pm but is closed on a Monday. Adjacent is the **Art Gallery and Krishna Menon Museum** with the same opening times as the Pazhassiraja. It displays paintings by Raja Ravi Varma and Raja Raja Varma.

MALABAR

Two kilometres from the rail station there is a **CVN Kalari centre** which specialises in training combatants for *kalarippayattu*, Kerala's ancient martial arts. Demonstrations are given on request for visitors between 6am and 9am and 5pm and 7pm.

Mananchira and **Mananchira Maidan** in the centre, a kilometre from the bus and train centres, are now a park and tank. The tank has a musical fountain. The Kuttichira area has the old **Muccunti Mosque** built under the Zamorins. Like India's first-ever mosque in Kodungallor it displays traditional Kerala architecture. The attractive **Tali Temple** in the south of the city was built in the fourteenth century by the Zamorin, Swamy Thirumalpad.

Kozhikode also has an aquarium, a planetarium and the beautifully designed **Central Library**. The silk quarter close to where the Chinese Fort was situated reflects the past Oriental influence on the city.

The city borders the sea and there is a sandy strip of quiet beach but like most big ports the sea is not clean. The same can be said of the beach at Byepore, 10km from Kozhikode. Byepore is one of Kerala's biggest ports and a shipbuilding centre. In Byepore, the yards still build *urus* or large country and sea-going boats and, despite business collapsing during the Gulf War, *dhows*.

Accommodation

Budget range
Lakshmi Bhavan Tourist Home (0495-63927) on GH Road, close to Malabar Palace Hotel and **Hotel Amrutha** (0495-65944), near Moffusil Bus Stand, have double rooms for under Rs100. On Mavoor Road, **Hotel Sajina** (0495-76146) also has rooms for less than Rs100 and a restaurant, as does **Metro Tourist Home** (0495-50020) which also has air-conditioned rooms for Rs250 at the junction with Bankhall Rd. Further from the centre on Taluk Road, the **Hotel Maharani** (0495-76161) has a garden and bar and rooms for Rs100 (air-conditioned Rs300).

Medium range
KTDC's **Malabar Mansion** (0495-722391) on SM Street at Mananchira Square may have a rather grim exterior but the rooms are large and clean with room service, modern toilets, telephones and an attached bar and cheap restaurant (meals Rs20/30) run by a friendly efficient management. For the price, singles Rs175 plus tax (Rs450 for an air-conditioned suite), doubles Rs225 and Rs500 respectively, it's reasonable value.

Slightly more expensive is the friendly **Sea Queen Hotel** (0495-366604, fax 365854) overlooking the sea on Beach Road where the carpeted single rooms start at Rs 235 and doubles at Rs295. The hotel's large rooms are not as good as the bright entrance would suggest but the 'Double Room Deluxe' is good value for Rs650. The bar's grim but there's a good non-air conditioned restaurant (meals Rs50/100) where one can also drink, and the hotel accepts credit cards and travellers' cheques.

Other similarly priced hotels are: **Paramount Tower** (0495-62731) and **Kalpaka Tourist Home** (0495-60221) on Town Hall Road, **Alakapuri Guest House** (0495-65351) on MMA Road, **Hotel Hyson** (0495-766726) on Mavoor Road and **Sasthapuri Tourist Home** (0495-60381) on Jail Road.

Top of the range
Manuelson's fabulous four-star **Malabar Palace** (0495-721511 fax 721794) on GH

Road has 52 centrally air-conditioned rooms, money changing facilities, a bar and 24-hour coffee shop and an excellent restaurant. Double rooms cost Rs1195 (singles Rs975) and Rs1450 (singles Rs1195) for the executive floor.

Eating Out

A meal at **Malabar Palace** will set you back Rs150 to Rs600 but the food is the best in the city. **Paramount Tower** has a rooftop restaurant for those who wish to escape the noise of the city. Getting around is less hassle in the northern towns because the rickshaw drivers use their meters, so explore the city. While you're in the city pop down SM Road where Kozhikode's renown fresh *halvah* and hot banana chips are on sale. The *halvah* is said to be the best in India.

Tourist information

The Kerala Department of Tourism has a tourist information centre open from 10am to 5pm (closed Sundays) in the railway station. KTDC has its **Tourist Reception Centre** at Malabar Mansions on SM Street. The main **post office** is at Mananchira. **State Bank of India** branches on Bank Road and Palayam Road have banking facilities for foreign nationals.

Travel Options

Planes and Trains

Kozhikode Airport is 23km south-east of the city on the road to Kottakal. **Indian Airlines** on Bank Road (0495-766243) operate daily flights to **Mumbai** (Bombay), **Chennai** (Madras) and **Bangalore**, five days a week to **Madurai** and three days a week to **Goa**. **Jet Airways** (0495-356518) also run daily flights to **Mumbai**. Between them Indian Airlines and **Air India** (0495-766669) have flights to the Gulf states of **Abu Dhabi**, **Dubai**, **Sharjah**, **Muscat** and **Kuwait**.

Kozhikode is well connected with major cities in Kerala and has daily trains to **Delhi**

and **Mumbai** (Bombay) and twice-daily trains to **Chennai** (Madras). The train station is in the south of the city near Ansari Park. Trains go frequently to **Kochi** (5 hours and a 2nd class fare of Rs48/137), **Mangalore** and **Kannur**. Three trains a day make the nine hour trip to **Thiruvananthapuram**, and two go daily to **Palakkad**.

Buses

The KSRTC Bus Station and the New Bus Stand are on Mavoor Road and the Old Bus Stand is at the junction of GH Road and MM Ali Road. Buses run frequently to **Kochi** (5 hours), **Thiruvananthapuram** (9 hours), **Kottayam** (6 hours) and **Bangalore** (10 hours and Rs 166/200). Six buses a day go to **Mysore** (6 hours) and daily to **Chennai** (Madras). Around Malabar there are frequent services to **Kannur** (2 hours), **Thrissur** (3 hours), **Guruvayoor**, **Sulthan Batheri**, **Kasargod**, **Bekal**, **Mannarkkad**, **Mananthavaadi** and **Palakkad**.

Mosque in Vizhinjam.

MALABAR

Around Kozhikode

Kappad Beach

Fourteen kilometers north of Kozhikode just off Highway 17, is Kappad Beach, an excellent place to stay if one wants to avoid the noise and bustle of the city. Calm waves lap the rock-studded, sandy beach which appears to extend for ever. Kappad has one hotel, two *chai* shops close by and little else. During the day a few fishermen from Kappakadavu village tend to their boats, otherwise the beach is almost deserted.

Dusk brings scores of young men and women from the city crammed into rickshaws or sauntering in on their motorbikes. Many take to the rocky promontory jutting out from the shore where there is a small temple said to be 800 years old. They are a friendly crowd and it all makes for a beautiful sunset.

Morning arrives and the beach, with a sea that is safe for **swimming**, is virtually yours again. If you find Kovalam or Varkala too busy or want a base for seeing north Kerala, Kappad is a splendid alternative.

Kappad Beach is also famous as the spot where Vasco da Gama made his historic landing on Indian soil. Where the narrow coastal road hits the beach there is a monument marking the arrival of his three ships. Apart from that and lazing on the beach, near the village, there is the old *cinnaceri*, Chinese settlement, to search out.

Accommodation and travel

The scarcity of accommodation which keeps the beach so peaceful can also be a problem. Rooms are available for less than Rs100 with local families. There was a budget hotel but recently it closed down. But for those prepared to spend Rs700 a night the modern and clean **Kappad Beach Resort** (049668-3760, fax 0497-233218) gives very good value for money. The hotel has 16 rooms in four bright cottages, each with a balcony furnished with a cane swing chair and overlooking the beach.

The **rooftop restaurant** is quite charming and, though service is typically slow and beer is Rs70 a bottle, the meals are good and cost just Rs60/100. Rooms cost Rs700 a night plus tax or Rs900 with air-conditioning. The resort also has a good *ayurvedic* massage centre.

Plenty of **buses** go along Highway 17 from **Kozhikode**, alternatively a rickshaw should be no more than Rs80 and a taxi Rs100.

Thikkodi Lighthouse

Thikkodi is another 15km northwards along Highway 17. Thikkodi Lighthouse looks on Velliyamkallu, a rock that has destroyed many a ship. Indeed the remains of the scuttled ship which prompted the black-and-white hooped lighthouse to be built

MALABAR

can still be seen. Migrating birds use Velliyamkallu as a stop-off point on their journeys north and south.

Kottakal

Kottakal is the home of the **Aryavaidya Sala**, a 95 year old internationally known centre for India's popular *ayurvedic* treatments. *Ayurvedic* medicine, while being holistic, bases itself on herbal treatments and the centre has one of the biggest herb gardens in the world, guaranteeing a myriad of delightful scents for the visitor.

The Sala is said to have a treatment that will restore a person's youth. Just in case you're already packing your bags, it involves seclusion in complete darkness for one year.

Treatment is available at the centre for foreign nationals. But courses which last for at least seven days require a minimum of ten days prior notice. Accommodation is available.

*Eight kilometres from nearby Tirur up the great Bharathapuzha River is Thirunavor which has little but a music festival to remind visitors of its extraordinary heritage, the **Mamankam Festival**. For centuries the surrounding countryside was ruled by the Cheraman Perumals, a ruling elite originating in Tamil Nadu. The Perumals held the huge Mamankam Festival every twelve years. A new maharaja would be chosen at this festival. After a great feast in his honour, the outgoing Maharaja would bring the festival to its height by dismembering his own body with his sword - a system which could have saved a few countries a lot of problems. The last festival was held in 1755.*

Kottakal is a good place for picking up rosewood furniture. The town is 48km from Kozhikode, 188km from Kochi and is on the road up to Ooty (140km) in the hills. It has some budget **accommodation**: *Sajidha Tourist Home* (04934-2519), on Mallappurram Road, *Priya Tourist Home* (04394-2412), on Main Road, and *Pullickal Lodge* (04394-2492) opposite the bus stand. All have basic rooms for less than Rs100. More upmarket at Rs200/300 are *Reem International* (04394-2302) and *AM Tourist Home* (04394-2231) on Main Road.

Buses travelling between *Kochi* and *Kozhikode* stop here frequently but the nearest mainline **train station** is in *Kozhikode*.

Peruvannamuzhi Dam

For a peaceful day out boating and visiting uninhabited islands beneath the mountains rising to the east, Peruvannamuzhi Dam is a one hour, 60km bus ride away. The dam has a **bird sanctuary** and a **crocodile sanctuary**.

MALABAR

On the road North to Kannur (Cannanore)

It's a two-hour, 93km journey north by road to reach Kannur (Cannanore) from Kozhikode. The roads are now flanked by women veiled or in their black *burkhas*. The town is adorned with mosques. Temples are still in evidence but this is Moplah country. Much has been said to the detriment of this area but its people are friendly and the atmosphere relaxed. The sun still beats down on the palm trees daily and there are still all those beautiful clean beaches within a few kilometres of the coastal highway and towns.

One of the most intriguing spots on the way is not a mosque but an old Hindu temple near Vadakara on the coast.

Lokanarkavu Temple

Reaching the 1500-year-old Lokanarkavu Hindu temple complex from Kozhikode, one hour away, sounds easy – and it is up to Vadakara (Badagara) for it doesn't require leaving Highway 17. Lokanarkavu is the most confusing 5km away from Vadakara that could be imagined but the temple is reasonably well known and we got there in the end. Why did we come? We had been promised a mini-Khajuraho, a cluster of temples with erotic carvings in north central India, and of similar delight.

Our car passed down a long mudtrack road besides which were the usual rural shambles of shops and houses. We stopped to pick up some buttons, 50 paise to have them sewn on a dress. For the seventh time we were told the way, this time by the gesticulations of a grey-haired man who, with his saffron robes, might have just come away from the pilgrim centre.

Dust billowed up around the car as we drove past a handful of shops selling fruit and souvenirs and three old temples appeared before us, We had arrived. It was clear to the bare-chested men sat on the wall close to the temple gate why we had come to this out of the way ancient shrine. "Wait! Wait! Guide will come." After five minutes of stares and smiles a squat, bearded man in blue khaki, barefoot with a white scarf draped around his neck, hurried over to us.

"I can only give you some time. I am very busy." He then spoke so quickly in his Ind-glish that it was impossible to understand his description of the first Shiva temple. So it was a relief when he turned, said "I'm busy, very sorry" and walked away. An old, bandy legged man with a white, but thick mane of hair then pulled on my arm motioning that he would take us round. "Could we go into the temple?" He wiggled his head. At first I thought he meant no, as one does in south India. I asked again. His head wiggled again. "You must take off your shirt and *chappals*." Fine, I thought. "You must put on a *dhoti*."

But no *dhoti* was available that day. Strange, but this is one of Kerala's oldest Hindu temples and non-Hindu men and women are permitted to enter. Must be village rules.

The temple was neither magnificent nor imposing but had a beautiful serenity with its stone sculptures and wood carvings, There are three temples. The oldest temple, and first, is dedicated to the Goddess Durga, the second to Shiva and the third to Vishnu. Beside the Durga temple is a huge tree which has been turned into a shrine for the elephant-headed God Ganesha.

Three rock-cut caves and two tanks also sit in the large complex. In the midday heat one can imagine the slow, imperceptible passage of time through a thousand years of worshipping in the temple, of marriage and birth offerings, of morning baths in the tank and sunsets sat in meditation.

The temples are still in use but battered by dust and kept up with difficulty by the clearly impoverished country people. The middle temple was the one we had really come to see. Were there really erotic temple carvings supposedly reminiscent of Khajuraho which had escaped the notice of the voyeuristic west? There were certainly no big hordes of titillated tourists here.

Well it's not Khajuraho, but the carvings on the doorway of the middle temple are as good and as erotic as anything one can see in Khajuraho. In some ways they are better – above our heads were not dust-worn stone sculptures but beautifully oil-painted wood carvings, perfectly preserved after one thousand years.

Getting to Lokanarkavu by bus is simple. **Buses** go regularly to **Vadakara** from **Kozhikode** and as regularly from Vadakara to **Lokanarkavu**.

Mahe (Pondicherry)

Sixty kilometres from Kozhikode, Highway 17 dips gently into a small river valley with fishing boats moored in the harbour where a river flowing down from Wynad forest meets the sea. We didn't see the sign but we had temporarily left Kerala. The small town of Mahe is part of the Union Territory of Pondicherry in *Tamil Nadu*. As such it is sometimes referred to as Pondicherry which can cause confusion.

The French arrived in Mahe in the seventeenth century to gain a base for their spice trade activities. Mahe, covering just nine square kilometres, is a very small part of the state of Pondicherry (480 sq km) called a 'Union Territory' because it covers the four separate former French colonies including Karraval and Yanan on Tamil Nadu's east coast. Now a small fishing village, the narrow winding main streets with small shops stacked together almost as terraces are a little reminiscent of an old French village. The French were driven out by the British in the 1760s and save for the beautiful church of Saint Theresa there is little else to proclaim their former presence.

The main advantage of Mahe being part of Pondicherry is cheap alcohol. Available at half the price charged in Kovalam, the beer and spirits attract drinkers from far afield. There are no beer festivals but there is a cosy fishing harbour for putting the old feet up and watching the tide roll in.

Accommodation and travel

All the accommodation here is rather basic. The cheapest at Rs25 is the **Government Tourist Home** by the river and near Tagore Park. If it's full then there

MALABAR

are rooms for Rs110/270 at **Hotel Arena** (0497-332421) by the river on Maidan Road and **Sara Resort** (0497-332503) on Station Road. **Buses** go frequently to **Kozhikode** and **Thalassery** (Tellicherry) which, 8km away, has much better accommodation. A daily bus arrives from **Thiruvananthapuram** (16 hours) via the main towns in the south and other buses stop en route between **Thalassery** and **Kozhikode**. The nearest mainline **rail station** is at **Thalassery**, a rickshaw ride away.

Thalassery (Tellicherry)

Within 20 minutes of leaving Mahe and getting back onto this recently modernised section of Highway 17, the pleasant town of Thalassery (Tellicherry) comes into view. This is the town where in 1683 the British East India Company first established a trading post. Twenty years later they built the sizeable **St Michael's Fort** that sits on the hill overlooking the harbour. The fort is almost completely intact with a lighthouse and battlements that offer a good view of the town.

The fort is used by the Thalassery Public Works Department and unfortunately much of the interior is used to store old equipment but some of the contraptions are so ancient they themselves are worth a look. The Department's staff are friendly and will probably offer to take you round the fort and its two underground caves.

Slightly lower down the hill is a neat tidy church and cemetery built in 1889 by the German scholar Doctor Herman Gundert. Thalaserry is also the main nursery for Kerala's famous **circus acrobats**.

Just north of the town the riverside is extremely picturesque. The town itself boasts little else. Nevertheless the nearby beach and the availability of excellent value for money accommodation makes Thalassery another excellent place to stay for seeing the north. 35km to the east is Aralam Wildlife Sanctuary which covers 55 sq km and is home to elephants, sloth and mouse bears and deer. It is near the town of Iritti on the northern road to Mysore. Buses travel from Ernakulam North and Kozhikode to Iritti. Guest houses are available in the town.

Muzhappilangad Beach

Five kilometres north of the town centre, Muzhappilangad Beach is undoubtedly one of the finest in Kerala. Its 20 metre wide strip of white sand arcs for 4km around the bay. Palm trees sweep to the north end while the south has a jagged line of rocks jutting out of the calm, turquoise sea. The last rock islet is sufficiently large to accommodate a sandy cove. The sea is tranquil enough for a safe swim but it's best to take a boat out if you want to sunbathe on your very own desert island.

Behind the shore is a small fishing village with less than 1,000 friendly unobtrusive people. There is a *chai* shop just off the road leading to the beach. Except for Sundays, the only day when the beach sees any visitors, there are normally only fishermen and their families. There is apparently some accommodation being built here.

The alternatives are to take a room with a family or take a **bus** (Rs3) or **rickshaw** (Rs25) and stay in *Thalassery*.

Buses head north every ten minutes along Highway 17 toward *Muzhappilangad* from the Thalassery bus stand. Alight at the stop for Muzhappilangad and it's still a 2km walk to the beach but there are normally one or two drivers sleeping in their rickshaws at the fruit and drink shop by the main road.

Accommodation

Logan's Road running through the centre of the town is the central axis for the hotels and guest houses. The road has guest houses with basic rooms for less than Rs100 including **Residency Hotel** (0497-24409), **Minerva Tourist Home** (0497-21731) and **Brothers Tourist Home** (0497-21558). The same road has the more expensive **Paris Lodging House** (0497-231666), with rooms for Rs165, (air-conditioned Rs 225) and close by in Narangapuram, **Hotel Pranam** (0497-220634) rooms Rs130 (air-conditioned Rs 300).

The best accommodation in the town is by far at the bright and relatively new **Paris Presidency Hotel** (0497-232666 fax 0497-233666) similarly on Logan's Road. The train and bus stations and the shopping centre are close by. The four storey hotel has a lift leading up to attractive, clean, large, well furnished rooms. The staff are friendly and the elegant air conditioned restaurant serves superb food for Rs40/50.

When clean towels, soap, 'electronic' telephones, satellite TV and room service are thrown in, Rs240 (singles Rs210) for a double room (air conditioned Rs330) and Rs420 for the air-conditioned deluxe suite, this is probably amongst the best value for money accommodation in Kerala.

Thalassery is 68km from Kozhikode and 25km south of Kannur (Cannanore). All are on the coastal Highway 17 and frequent **buses** run between them. Frequent services are also operated to *Mananthavaadi* in the Western Ghats. Occasional train services link Thalassery with *Kochi* (second-class fare Rs62/178), *Thiruvananthapuram* and *Mangalore* in Karnataka state to the north.

Kannur (Cannanore)

One of the surprisingly neglected historic cites of Malabar, if only for reason of visiting the gargantuan, imposing historic St Angelo Fort, is Kannur. Now a busy market and textile town, Kannur was once the seat of the North Kolathiri Rajas who grew rich on the trade which passed through its port and withstood the demands of the Zamorins who threatened them from the south.

At one time Kannur was only second to Kodungalloor in importance for Kerala's maritime spice trade. Marco Polo described the port as a great emporia of the spice trade. Then in 1498 the Portuguese arrived in the ships of Vasco da Gama. Kannur is the site where his fleet first touched land but da Gama decided to land further south at Kappad.

In 1500 the Portuguese troops set about making Kannur their main military base, building St Angelo Fort which overlooks the port's attractive natural harbour. They held the fort till the Dutch took it from them in 1663 signalling a change in influence for the local Rajas. In 1790 the British established their prominent interest in the area by taking the fort. They weren't to leave the town for another 157 years.

Kannur is 90km north of Kozhikode and 32km north of Thalassery. From the rooftop restaurant of the Kamala International Hotel one is offered a tremendous vista of the surrounding countryside. Here there are still the plantations of coffee, rubber, cashew nut and banana that supplied the town for its spice trade. North, south and east palm trees mat together to form a dark-green carpet washed by the blue sea to the west. The town itself is almost reduced to the size of a hamlet as the palms hide thousands of houses and huts beneath their canopy.

St Angelo Fort

Walking at midday along the grassy battlements of the triangular St Angelo Fort, the many buildings are so intact with cannon, cliffs, sun and shimmering sea stuck in their century old stances that vivid pictures are easily invoked of the plights of those assigned to march it's parade ground. Scorching heat, cawing crows, the rush of the waves crashing on the cliffs, hour in, hour out, till the peace of nightfall illuminated by hundreds of little fires and a wondrous starlit sky.

Much has been left to the imagination by the authorities here. There is not a solitary explanation of the historic importance of the fort anywhere in or around the grounds. The only sign as one enters the 492 year-old edifice is to explain to visitors that they face heavy fines for removing or damaging any part of the fort.

The fort was completed in 1505 to the pleasure of the Portuguese Viceroy, Almedia. They held it during 158 years of not quite unending confrontation with the rajas and peoples of Malabar. The Dutch occupation of the fort began in 1663 and lasted till 1772 when they sold it to Ali Raja of Kannur. His tenure of the fort was to be the shortest in it's history. The British turfed him out in 1790 and then stayed until it was time to leave India.

The British rebuilt the fort. Of this there is evidence in the various soldier's quarters which are superbly intact as are the dozen or so powerful cannon turned to threaten any ships entering the harbour. Evident are the huge walls, a large moat, two massive fresh water wells and vast buildings for the arsenal and food rations that made the fort siege-worthy

That the authorities appear to have neglected the site – weeds overrunning walls and steps – cannot totally disappoint. Its stories are abandoned to your imagination. What the stone slab standing on the northern wall with a skull and bones inscribed on it represents, one can only guess. Maybe pirates got a decent naval burial then? The fort is open till 6pm and, contrary to some guide books, not occupied by the army but run by the Archaeological Department.

Accommodation

Budget range

The best bet is to stay in Thalassery but those stuck in Kannur needing basic accommodation can get rooms for Rs150 or under at KTDC's *Yatri Nivas* (0497-500717), near the police club, *United Tourist Home* (0497-60078) by the bus station and *Abhilash Tourist Home* (0497-602343) on Station Road. *TKT Tourist Home* (0497-502968) on MA Road (doubles Rs100, singles Rs60) is typical Kannur budget accommodation with basic double rooms on the second floor. The rooms are a little grim but equipped with a modern toilet, a fan and a mirror and some have a balcony.

Similarly priced are *Plaza Tourist Home* (0497-60031) by the train station, *Safire Tourist Home* (0497-60021) on Bank Road, *PSV Tourist Home* (0497-63371) and *Kavitha Tourist Home* (0497-60091) on SN Park Road and *Meridian Palace* (0497-501676) on Bellard Road. KTDC also has a *Motel Aaram* (0497-760220) in Kallissery. Fan-only rooms cost Rs150 (air-conditioned Rs300).

Medium range

Slightly more expensive than the budget hotels are *Omars Inn* (0497-63313) on Station Road and *Hotel Savoy* (0497-60074) on Beach Road. Omars is opposite the train station and has a restaurant, some rooms are air conditioned (Rs300) and all rooms have a telephone. Fan-only double rooms cost Rs175. The Savoy is Rs35/75 cheaper.

The most expensive hotel in Kannur is the *Kamala International* (0497-670001, fax 501819) on SM Road in the heart of the town. The 36 room hotel was undergoing refurbishment in spring 1997 - and there was a lot to do – but the roof garden offers excellent views and an escape from India's never-silent traffic. At Rs450 (Rs350 a single), the fanonly double rooms are good value. Room charges then rise to Rs1000 but their Rs1000

a night 'deluxe suite' is not so deluxe. The food in the slightly shabby restaurant is very good and the menu wide ranging enough for you to read it twice over again before your chosen dish has arrived. Rooms have **fridges**, TV and 24-hour room service. **Credit cards** are taken but sorry, it's unlicensed. This is the north. Beer is still easily purchased but its use not so widespread.

Around Kannur

Situated on the banks of the Valapattanam River in *Parassinakadavu* 18km from Kannur is *Parassinakadavu Madapura Sree Muthapan Temple*, the only temple in Kerala which performs the Theyyam folk dance for visitors. Non-Hindus are allowed inside the temple to watch when Theyyam is performed during the daily poojas, 5am to 8am and 6.30pm to 8.30 pm.

In the *vellattam* performance, toddy - the alcoholic drink made from coconut milk - and fish are offered up to a powerful god known as Muthappan. The priest, magnificently dressed, is accompanied by *chenda* music and eventually launches forward to bless each member of the congregation.

Frequent **buses** go between *Parassini-kadavu* and *Kannur* but a **taxi** is the surest bet.

Nearby is *Parassinakadavu Snake Park*, the only one of its kind in Kerala. It has three snake pits and glasshouses with king cobra and many rare species. Humorous hourly demonstrations are given by keepers who play with the dangerous reptiles. The park opens daily from 9am till 5.30pm.

Ezhimala, 50km north of Kannur on Highway 17 is unusual for a coastal town on this route. It is almost 300 metres above sea level. Nearby on the hillside are an old mosque, sculptured pillars, an old burial chamber and a cave. **Buses** regularly stop in the town on their way between *Kasargod* and *Kannur*.

MALABAR

Travel

The nearest **airport** is at **Kozhikode**, Kochi is 317km away and Thiruvananthapuram 538km away. **Trains** run south to **Thalassery, Kozhikode** (2 hours and Rs66/189 2nd-class fare), **Kochi** (7 hours), **Thrissur** (4.5 hours), **Kottayam**, and **Thiruvananthapuram** (13 hours). Trains go north to **Kasargod** and **Mangalore**.

Buses run frequently to **Thalassery**, Kozhikode (2.5 hours), **Kochi** (8 hours), **Mananthavaadi** (3.5 hours) and **Mangalore** (5.5 hours). Buses go twice daily to **Thiruvananthapuram.** Six buses a day also go to Bangalore (9 hours).

The District Tourism Promotion Council (DTPC) has an office near the Civil Station (0497-67336).

Bekal Fort and Beach

Bekal is a small town 1 km from two of Kerala's most attractive large beaches. We are now in the far north of Malabar, 100km and a two hour drive north from Kannur and a 638km train ride away from Thiruvananthapuram. Karnataka state takes over the territory 50km further north and east. The state government has plans to develop this area for tourism but as yet Bekal and its surrounds are totally undeveloped for tourism, a bonus for adventurers.

Bekal Fort

A dusty road away from Bekal town towards the beach leads to the enigmatic, vast, ancient fort of Bekal. The fort stands on top of a hillock, the rocks at the bottom of which used to be swept by the sea on three sides. Now silt, dumped by the sea and the busy Chandragiri River to the north, has pushed most of the fort a little away from the sea.

With a three kilometre circumference of thick granite walls set on laterite, the fort is one of Kerala's most majestic, commanding views of the sea ways and the coastline. For an even grander view one can climb the towering rampart on the south side of the fort up which cannon were hauled to be fired at approaching enemy vessels. Few of the buildings remain intact except underground but the elaborate entrance and gates are fascinating.

Most of the week, the fortress is almost empty, more people are usually sat line fishing on the rocks beneath where the fort looks down directly onto the sea. Weekends are a different story when local youth come out to play. As with St Angelo Fort, the authorities have left no explanation as to the historic importance of the fort, nor its origins. This is even more of a shame because Bekal Fort is accepted as an Indian construction as opposed to Kerala's other major military constructions.

The fort's history seems unclear. The likelihood is that elements of the fort were built and rebuilt to suit the needs of different eras. Some authorities believe it dates back to AD300/600 and was built by the Kadampa dynasty which ruled the western part of Mysore district. Later the Kolathiri Rajas controlled the fort. One report says the fort was built in 1502 by Ekkary Sivappu Nayak of Bednone under the Vijayanagar empire which finally crumbled in 1646.

It is known that Tipu Sultan troops occupied the fort for some time in the late eighteenth century. An old mosque said to have been built by his regime stands close by. After defeating Sultan, the British hold on the fort was not relinquished until India's independence in 1947. The fort is open between 8am and 6pm.

Bekal Beach

To the north and south of Bekal Fort are two excellent long, palm-fringed, largely empty beaches. The beach to the south has access via a small fishing village. On the north side of the beach are the welcoming mariners' boathouses and workshops, all made from thatched palm tree leaves. Walk south and it's you, the beach and the ocean for as far as one can see.

The beach north of Bekal Fort is just as attractive, arching gently round the bay. It can be reached via a one kilometre dirt track. It's clean and quiet, save for occasional fishermen and their boats. The undertow can be dangerous.

Northern Kathakali

Bekal's **Mookambika Kathakali Vidyalaya** is one of only two Kerala schools teaching the *kalladikodan* style of *kathakali* dancing. *Kalladikodan* is *kathakali* in its original form. It was popular in the far north for over 200 years. Its artists would be fed, clothed and housed by local landlords and fans of *kathakali*. Sadly its exponents are virtually on their last legs. Septuagenarian, Kannan Pattali has been practising and performing the *kalladikodan* style since he was nine years old.

Now Pattali runs the Mookambika school. No longer being supported by the schools, the *kathakali* dancers have to do other jobs, studying *kathakali* only part time. Kerala Kalamandalam only teaches the central and southern styles of *kathakali*. So dance enthusiasts may want to take a bus or taxi and pay Mookambika a visit to see this unique historic dance form.

Accommodation

For a special experience it's worth a stay in the **Government Guest House** (near the seaward facing wall of Bekal Fort). During the day one can saunter round the fort or down to the beaches. In the evening after the fort's gates close at 6pm one has the fort and its sunset to oneself save the old chap who runs the guest house. To oneself is hardly an exaggeration as the guest house only has two rooms, so it needs to be booked in advance (contact **Kasargod District Collector** 0499-520666) unless visitors want to take a chance and if unlucky find a place in Bekal town or Kasargod.

The guest house rooms are basic, with Indian toilets, but are reasonably spacious for only Rs50. The friendly old caretaker can make you *chai* and sells cold drinks but otherwise visitors have to buy food in or eat out before the fort shuts its gates at night. Luckily there is a *chai* shop serving food for Rs10/20 roughly 2km away.

For staying in Bekal itself, the only alternative is the basic **Eeyem Lodge** (0499-680343) in **Palakunnu** village, three kilometres north of the fort. The lodge has a friendly management but some of the rooms are pretty shabby. Nevertheless with fan, mirror, 'modern' toilet and table, if you pick the right room you've got good value at Rs55/70 a night (singles Rs45). The lodge is a 10 minute walk from the beach and, next door is a *chai* shop and **restaurant** offering meals for Rs10/20. The train station is five kilometres away to the south.

Those who want more comfortable accommodation have to go to Kasargod 16km further north along Highway 17. Buses are frequent but few main line trains stop in Bekal so those travelling by **train** need to alight at *Kasargod* and take a bus or Rs70/85 rickshaw/taxi ride.

Kasargod

Kasargod on the Chandragiri River is the most northern town of any note in Kerala. A busy market town, it is the administrative centre for Kasargod District which reaches north and east to the borders with Karnataka and includes Bekal to the south. There is little of note in the town but it is a main line railway station and on Highway 17, thus linked to Goa, Mangalore, Kochi and Thiruvananthapuram.

Just south-east of the city is the large square *Chandragiri Fort*, one of a string of fortresses built in the 1600s by Sivappu Nayak of Bednone. That this is Muslim country is easy to see. The small town of Manjeswaram a few kilometres away from the Karnataka border boasts 15 mosques.

For a cheap stay, it may be better to go to Bekal - providing rooms are available. Kasargod is a noisy town and **accommodation** not particularly good. Near the bus station are a few cheap guest houses including *Enay Tourist Home* (0499-521164), *Ceeyel Tourist Home* (0499-530177) on MG Road, and *Aliya Lodge* (0499-522897), all with basic rooms for Rs60/70 a night. The 'deluxe' rooms cost Rs100 and worth it to get the minimum of comfort.

Hotel City Tower (0499-530562) on MG Road and also close to the bus station is the only non-budget hotel in the town. Rooms cost Rs320/450 (singles Rs200). It has reasonable air conditioned and fan-only rooms all accessed by the lift or stairs. The restaurant is reasonable and the meals, at Rs35/60, inexpensive. Though the hotel has its own generator, when we were there it took some time to work so a trip in the lift can be pretty precarious.

Little English is understood by the staff so be prepared for the full Indian experience: wrong food, wrong drinks, four calls for morning tea, editions of *Indian Express*, then napkins sent as loo paper, three staff to settle your bill etc. – an Indian version of Fawlty Towers. Good fun – if you're not in a hurry.

Travel Options

The nearest **airport** to Kasargod is 54km to the north at *Mangalore*. Kochi airport is 432km away and Thiruvananthapuram is 654km away. **Kasargod railway station** is well served by trains travelling between *Mangalore* in Karnataka and *Kozhikode*. Getting to Kasargod from the south requires changing trains at Kozhikode or Kannur. Frequent bus services stop off en-route between Kochi, Kozhikode and Mangalore.

🕸 The Forests and Mountains of Malabar

Inland Malabar contains some of Kerala's most scenic and remote districts. Wynad and its forests contain rare species, near Stone Age tribes and beautiful lakes. Palakkad is similar and above them both tower the Western Ghats or Sahya mountains (the local name for the Malabar stretch of one of India's major mountain ranges). Now we are heading south-west from Bekal, Kannur and Mahe, first reaching Wynad, the inland region at the foot of the Western Ghats.

The Wynad Region

Reaching Wynad, the 'Kashmir of Southern India' requires a twisting, winding trip up hill and down dale with two dozen or more hairpin bends. The landscape is spattered with hills and valleys and the scenery is dominated by the mist-clad mountains to the east. Close by are variously, the light, almost grey barks of rubber trees fixed with tiny cups to drain off their sap, plantations of coffee, tea, cardamom and pepper, rice paddies, steep valleys with dense green foliage and rust-coloured knolls. Wynad's rivers and streams show off spectacular waterfalls furnished by the monsoons which have made the area one of Kerala's most lush and damp. Indeed the hill area near Kalpetta known as Lakkadi has recorded the second highest level of rainfall in the world. Yet not much further eastwards in Tamil Nadu are areas which have seen no rain for years.

Mananthavaadi

Around 90km south east of Kannur at 500 metres above sea level lies the town of Mananthavaadi. Accommodation in the town is basic, but cheap, for those who use it as a base for exploring the beautiful forests that surround it and the ever-present looming mountains to the east.

In the town is the tomb of the indomitable Pazhassi Raja who used guerrilla tactics in the mountains and forests to fight off Lord Wellesley's advancing British troops for five years. Lord Wellesley (the famous Duke of Wellington) had to content himself with beating Napoleon at Waterloo. There is also a park nearby in memory of Pazhassi Raja.

Mananthavaadi is on one of the main routes to Mysore and regular buses go to and from Kannur, Thalassery and Kozhikode. There are also buses twice daily to both Mysore and Ooty (Udagamandalam) in Karnataka and daily to Kochi 335km away. The nearest train station and airport are at Kozhikode.

MALABAR

Hu-man or Hu-woman rights?

"Police Atrocity" declared the headline in The Hindu daily newspaper. Seven young men had been arrested following an anti-alcohol demonstration in Thirunelli, close to Mananthavaadi. The men, aged 20 to 22, were then locked up in the local police cells. The "atrocity" the newspaper commented on led the men to take legal action against the police and take their protest to the National Human Rights Commission. The young men claimed that the police had stripped them naked and placed them in a cell with seven girls for two days and two nights.

The Commission suspended the police involved and ordered them to pay the boys compensation of Rs10,000 each out of their police salaries. The seven girls, it seems, received no compensation.

Accommodation

Mananthavaadi has a few budget hotels all costing less than Rs100 per night including *Elite Tourist Home* (04962-40236), *Deluxe Tourist Home* (04962-40307) and, cheapest of all, *Dreamland Lodge* (04962-40276).

Around Mananthavaadi

Kuruva Island is 16km from Mananthavaadi on the Kabbani River which flows north eastwards into Karnataka meeting up with the famous Cauvery River. Kuruva is one of several small islands in the river which have spurned fascinating ecosystems of rare plants and birds. Bird watchers may also be attracted by *Pakshipathalam* which has a bird watching tower to view the rare species common to this area, a ten kilometre trek from Thirunelli.

Twenty kilometres east of Mananthavaadi is the *Begur Wildlife Sanctuary* near the border with Karnataka. But a more developed sanctuary is over the border, the 640 sq km *Nagarhole National Park* whose Forestry Department conducts wildlife tours. *Jungle Lodges* are available and can be booked by phoning Bangalore (080) 5586163. The Kabini River runs through the park providing beautiful settings. Bamboo basket-boats are available for a row on the river. The best time to visit is between June and October. There are no buses which cover the 38km Mananthavaadi to Nagarhole road which means a taxi or jeep ride to get there or entering the park by bus from Mysore or Hunsur in Karnataka

Thirunelli has an important Vishnu temple sometimes called the "Kasi of the South". The town is 32km from Mananthavaadi and nearby is *Papanasini*, a mountain stream not to be missed because legend has it that visitors are granted eternal bliss.

MALABAR

The Tribal Peoples of Wynad

Twenty-five per cent of the population of Wynad is said to consist of tribal people or adivasi. *The tribal people are so called because they lived in small settlements largely isolated from Indian civilisation. As recently as 1970 a 'Stone Age' tribe was discovered in the Nilambur valley. The* Cholaniken *were still living in caves in similar fashion to that indicated by some of Kerala's archaeological digs.*

In some of these tribes can be seen traces of Kerala's Austric/Negrito past with facial features similar to Africans and Australian Aborigines. Indeed Wynad is also sometimes known as 'Africa in Kerala' but that may as much be down to the terrible poverty.

Most of the tribes live in thatched huts and 90% live below the poverty line. When the government introduced the 1969 Land Reform Act which gave each family a plot of land, the tribal people benefited least. Not only have many never received their land but thousands have had land taken away from them by land encroachments. The Paniya *people have lived near Mananthavaadi for 6,000 years. Paniya means one who doesn't work. They do work - in the paddy fields - but 70 per cent are still landless, 95 per cent illiterate and the prey of religious groups reputedly offering them sums of money to sign up to the various mosques, temples and churches.*

Nearby, eight kilometres east of Mananthavaadi, is Valliyurkavu Bhagavathi temple. *The temple is devoted to the Goddess Durga and every year in February/March tribal people attend a special two-week festival. It was in this temple that the* Paniya *people used to be sold as slaves.*

Kalpetta

Kalpetta, is the administrative centre of Wynad. 30km south of Mananthavaadi and 65km north-east from Kozhikode, it is well situated as base camp for trips around Wynad. A plus is that the town has a variety of accommodation for visitors. Near the main bus station are two budget hotels charging Rs75 a night, *Arun Tourist Home* (04936-2039) and *Megha Tourist Home* (04936-2584). *Hotel Rocky Rosya* (04936-2001) on Emily Road and *Hotel Haritha Giri* (04936-2673) on Guest House Road are more upmarket, charging between Rs250 and Rs400 for fan-only and air-conditioned rooms.

Frequent **buses** ferry passengers to and from *Kozhikode* via Vayitirri. At least six buses a day go to *Mananthavaadi* on their way to *Mysore* and *Bangalore*.

MALABAR

Around Kalpetta

South-west of Kalpetta along the Kozhikode road is **Pookot Lake** which, unlike Periyar, is quite natural. The surrounding evergreen forest, a children's park and available boats make the lake a pleasant attraction. A **fresh-water aquarium** helps visitors to identify the varied fish that occupy local waters. Beside the lake is a District Tourist Information Centre (04936-2134).

The lake is three kilometres south of **Vayittiri**. Nearby is **Tusharagiri** and its **waterfalls**. A trek from Tusharagiri can be arranged starting at the waterfalls and climbing up through dense evergreen forests populated with exotic bird and animal life. Start in the morning and you'll reach Vayittiri by evening. Another excellent trek can be arranged to Chembra Peak, 14km south west of Kalpetta. Chembra at an altitude of 2100 metres is Wynad's highest peak.

The Hindu Jain religion was popular in this area and evidence of this is the **Anathanathaswami Temple** in Puliyarmala, 6km from Kalpetta.

Sulthan Bathery

Sulthan Bathery takes its name from the fort that mogul Tipu Sultan is said to have built here in the late 18th century. There is no evidence as to the whereabouts of the fort. Equally a conundrum is the spelling of the town's name. Sultan Battery, Sulthan's Battery, Sutan's Battery, Sulthambettery, Sulthanbatteri and Sulthanbatheri are just some of the variations one might come across. The town was previously known as Ganapathivattom and it seems something went astray in the name change. My friend called it "assault and battery".

Sulthan Bathery, surrounded by tea, coffee, spice and cocoa plantations, is another town from which forays can be launched into the surrounding hills and valleys or as a stop off point when travelling to or from Mysore/Ooty.

Accommodation and travel

The town is 24km from Kalpetta, 48km from Mananthavaadi, 98km from Kozhikode and 326km from Kochi. Buses go regularly to Kalpetta and at least twice daily to Ooty. Sulthan Bathery is a stop-off point for five KSRTC bus services running daily between Kozhikode, Kochi, Mysore and Bangalore.

Budget accommodation is available at the **Government Guest House** (04968-20225) and the **PWD Rest House** (04968-20225). Otherwise the KTDC has the small **Motel Aaram** (04968-22150) on Cheemal Road. KTDC motel rates apply (fan-only rooms for Rs150, single Rs100, and air-conditioned rooms for Rs300, single Rs250). **The Resort** (04968-20582) hotel also has fan-only and air-conditioned rooms for Rs185/350.

Around Sulthan Bathery

One of the Pazhassi Raja's 200 year old forts still stands at **Panamaram**, 29km from Sulthan Bathery. Sixteen kilometres from Sulthan Bathery is the town of

MALABAR

Ambalavayal. From here a five kilometre morning trek will take visitors to the famous *Eddakal Caves* which feature many New Stone Age paintings and writings on their walls. The caves close at 5pm.

Sixteen kilometres east of Sulthan Bathery, close to the Karnataka border on the south side of the Mysore road is **Muthanga Wild Life Sanctuary.** Muthanga is sometimes referred to as the Wynad Wild Life Sanctuary. It is part of a National Park including Mudumalai in Tamil Nadu and Bandipur in Karnataka and only Periyar covers a greater territory in Kerala.

The area boasts an important **elephant training camp**. Wild elephants can cause serious danger to villagers and their crops. The job of the incredibly courageous mahouts is to capture them. Often riding elephants themselves, they catch their victims using lassoes, then spend months training them to become working elephants in temples or in industry.

The flora and fauna are similar to Periyar but the best animal sightings are during the monsoon months up to October. **Accommodation** is available for less than Rs200 a night by contacting the Chief Wildlife Warden (080-3341993) in Bangalore.

Palakkad District (Palghat)

Palakkad is half steamy, inland lowlands, the other half is divided between dense jungle and rugged mountainside. Here are the still to be uncovered mysteries of Silent Valley, tribal people, and wild life sanctuaries alongside huge dams and plentiful temples. Known as the granary of Kerala, Palakkad furnishes the cereals for Kerala's *rotis, naans* and loaves, the waters for its taps and the electricity for its offices. Orchards of oranges, plantations of tea, coffee, banana, teak and cardamom are plentiful.

A region of fascinating contrasts, Palakkad is split through the middle by Highway 47 which springs up in Thrissur, passes through the district's main towns of Palakkad and Malampuzha before going on to Madras on India's east coast, a journey of 620km.

Palakkad

The 80km drive from Thrissur up to Palakkad is on probably the best stretch of road in Kerala. It has to be, what with so many juggernauts heading north-east to the industrious Tamil Nadu towns such as Coimbatore (known as the 'Manchester of South India' not for its football team but its factories) and Madras. The journey can be broken at Peechy Dam (see page 159) which is just south of the Highway as it enters into Palakkad itself.

Smack in the middle of Palakkad town is a huge well-preserved monument to the old town's former importance, Tipu's Fort. The fort was built in 1766 by Tipu Sultan's predecessor, the great Haider Ali of Mysore. After his death Tipu had to fight several times to regain the fort before the British turfed him out in 1790 and took it over for their own use.

MALABAR

Ancient temples abound in the town but unless the visitor wants to use it as a base camp for scouting the district, he or she might well trundle on up to the more relaxed Malampuzha. Palakkad is certainly better situated than Malampuzha for trips to the north of the district which includes Silent Valley and the south which includes the excellent Parambikulam Wild Life Sanctuary.

Palakkad has a **Tourist Information Counter** near Children's Park. The main **post office** is at Sultanpet and opens Monday to Saturday from 8am to 6pm and tourists who wish to exchange money can do so on English Church Road at Hotel Indraprastha.

Accommodation

For those stuck on the way up to Palakkad on Highway 47, KTDC has a *Motel Aaram* (04922-220240) in *Alathur*, the town on the River Gayathri. KTDC motel rates apply (rooms Rs150/300). Palakkad town has a good range of accommodation.

Budget range

Budget accommodation is mainly centred on GB Road where *Kalpaka Hotel* (0491-24632), *Ashok Tourist Home* (0491-536661), *New Fashion Lodge* (0491-827546) and *Aristo Lodge* (0491-827326) have basic rooms for under Rs100. On the same road *Hotel Devaprabha* (0491-823383) is slightly more expensive.

Medium range

KPM Tourist Home (0491-824601) on Press Club Road and *Surya Tourist Home* (0491-538338) in the Surya Complex have rooms for Rs250/350.

Top of the range

Fort Palace (0491-534621) at West Fort, *Hotel Rajadhani* (0491-28949) on Shornur Road and the slightly more expensive *Hotel Indraprastha* (0491-534641) on English Church Road have rooms for Rs400/700.

Travel Options

The nearest **airport** is 55km away in *Coimbatore*, Tamil Nadu. Kochi is 160 km away and Thiruvananthapuram, 382km. Palakkad Junction, 5km from Palakkad town, is the main **rail station**. **Trains** arrive from and travel to *Delhi*, *Bangalore*, *Kanyakumari* and Trichy daily. Twice-daily trains travel to and from *Alappuzha* and *Mumbai* (Bombay). Trains run frequently to *Kozhikode* (3.5 hours and Rs41/119 for 2nd-class fare). Trains are thrice-daily to *Chennai* (Madras) and four times a day to and from *Thiruvananthapuram* (8.5 hours), *Coimbatore* and *Mangalore*.

Palakkad is well served for inter-city **buses** with three bus stations which shouldn't be confused: the KSRTC (Kerala State) bus station, the Municipal Bus Station and the Town Station. The KSRTC Bus Station has many buses going to *Thiruvanathapuram* (8 hours), *Kochi* (4 hours), *Thrissur* and *Coimbatore* (one hour). A daily bus service runs to *Chennai* (Madras) and twice a day buses also plough the five hour journey to *Ooty* (Udagamandalam).

The Municipal Bus Station has plenty of buses to and from *Kozhikode* and is the alighting point for *Silent Valley* (Mannarkat town) and *Parambikulam Wild Life Sanctuary* (Pollachi town and change for Parambikulam). Buses travel frequently to *Mannarkat* and hourly to *Pollachi*.

The Town Bus Station has buses to *Thrissur*, *Guruvayoor* and *Malampuzha*.

Around Palakkad

Parambikulam Wildlife Sanctuary

Forty-nine kilometres south-east of Palakkad, *Parambikulam Wild Life Sanctuary* is one of Kerala's best. Elephants, tigers, gaur, panthers, wild boar, Nilgiri langur, lion-tailed macaque, *samber* and *chital* roam across its 285 square kilometres. King cobra and Indian rock python slither through the lush, tropical and moist deciduous forests. In particular the park has Kerala's largest population of *gaur*, the biggest species of ox on Earth. The sanctuary is centred on three reservoirs, Parambikulam, Peruvaripallam and Thunakadavu. These reservoirs have **boating facilities**. Please note, they are also known for their large population of crocodiles.

Near to the park office at Thunakadavu stands *Cannimare Teak Tree* – Asia's tallest. The sanctuary has two watchtowers - at Annapadi, eight kilometres from Thunakadavu and Zungam, five kilmoetres from Thunakadavu. Mountaineers will be pleased to know this area is said to have good **climbing** and **trekking** routes which can be accessed by permission of the Warden at the park office.

The sanctuary is open to cars and coaches from 7am to 6.30pm when the gates are firmly closed. **Accommodation** is available at *Thunakadavu* in the Forest Department's *Inspection Bungalow* (Rs300/600) and *Tree Top Hut* (Rs250) by contacting the Range Officer. The best months to visit are in the dry season between February and April.

Taking a car or jeep is the most convenient way of getting to Parambikulam, Otherwise the bus journey from Palakkad involves a one hour trip to *Pollachi* where **buses** leave twice daily (10am and 5pm) for Parambikulam and return at 7am and 1pm.

Silent Valley Wildlife Sanctuary

Nature lovers seeking new adventures might well head towards the mysteries of the dense tropical jungle of Silent Valley Wild Life Sanctuary 79km north east of Palakkad. The sanctuary's 90 sq km contain one of India's last significant stretches of true tropical jungle. Elephants and tigers roam and the thick undergrowth has promoted rare species of plant life and raised the probability that other species remain to be discovered.

The valley is one of those formed by tributaries to the River Bhavani flowing into Tamil Nadu. Just to the north, *Attapadi* is a vast valley formed by another tributary. This valley is mainly occupied by tribal people.

The main town is *Agali* and **accommodation** is available here at the PWD Rest House. The other Attapadi town of *Anakkatti* is linked by road and regular **buses** to *Mannarkkad* (38km) and *Palakkad*. Mannarkkad (Mannarghat) also has a PWD Rest House (contact the Palakkad District Collector) and trucks and jeeps for hire to get to Silent Valley. The best time to visit is between September and March.

Silent Valley can also be reached from **Coimbatore** and its **airport** 40km away in Tamil Nadu. Arriving from **Thiruvananthapuram** by public transport requires a **bus** or **train** to **Palakkad** and an onward journey by bus to Mannarkkad or on further to Anakkatti. The alternative is to change at **Kochi** where a private bus service runs daily from High Court Junction bus stand.

Nelliampathi Hill Station

Nelliampathi is a popular hill station with excellent trekking trails. It is a three hour, 75km trip away from Palakkad and, at 1600 metres above sea level, is surrounded by panoramic views of hills draped by plantations of tea, coffee, orange and cardamom. On Nellikotta and the other peaks grow huge great teak trees valued for their wood.

Malampuzha

Twelve kilometres east of Palakkad is Malampuzha. We are still in the steamy, low-lying hinterland surrounded by plantations of bananas and coconut. But the great crags and buttresses of the Western Ghats tower above us to the east offering glorious dawn and dusk vistas as the sun's rays illuminate and then shadow the hills. Possibly, just possibly, the mountains offer a part of Kerala that isn't colonised by people, for the mountains appear sheer and too magnificent to be siezed by any but the gods of Hindu myth said to reign thereon. Of course a great many of these hills are in Tamil Nadu but there is no iron curtain. Trekkers and mountaineers are free to wander these mountains and set up new routes with would-be local sherpas.

Malampuzha is an engagingly pleasant town which has fashioned itself as a tourist attraction. Its lake, parks and floral gardens are popular with Indian visitors. Few Western visitors stop off here unless they're travelling from Coimbatore 42km away or Ooty hill station. Reportedly the lake, which has **boating** facilities (even water scooters), is popular with a handful of international **anglers.**

The lake above and just to the east of the town was formed by a huge hydro-electric dam across the Ponnani River. Just beneath the dam is a smaller lake with boating facilities watched over by an extraordinarily explicit, full frontal bronze statue of the folklore fertility goddess,*Yakshi.* Behind her stretch the town's 'Rock Garden' suitable for a stroll but most popular for the nearby aerial ropeway which carries the adventurous across the gardens – as they cling on.

The north side of the lower lake is edged by two beautiful floral gardens bursting with fountains, hundreds of varieties of roses, every shade of bougainvillaea, reds, scarlet, pinks, cerise, yellow and white, *gandaraja* trees and *ariliarili.* Close to the lake and surrounded by a small moat is an intricately designed 'Japanese' garden reached by an oriental wooden footbridge. Smiles everywhere, the floral gardens have made Indian visitors happy since their creation 40 years ago.

The conduit for irrepressible joy is the adjacent children's park where, despite orders to the contrary, India's grown men and women don't let the children have the swings and slides to themselves. Seeing men queuing up on the slide waiting their turn and

MALABAR

elders dallying hearts-a-free on the roundabouts is a jolt to Western sensibilities but the evident joy is a lesson in letting the child come out of us occasionally.

Immediately opposite the entrance to the gardens is a small aquarium with some of the saltwater and freshwater fish common to Kerala - golden cypren, Travancore carp, karimeen etc. and a zoo. Back in the town there is a fair (fantasy park) with a snake park nearby.

Accommodation

There are a few cheap lodges in the town but best value is probably **Hotel Dam Palace** (0491-815237) on Malampuzha Road. Rooms cost Rs125/450. There are 12 charming, if a little shabby, cottages some of which are air-conditioned. Room service is available and the friendly management aren't licensed to sell beer but will fetch it in for guests. The restaurant is reasonably priced. **Anglers** will also get well advised on where and when to fish in the lake.

KTDC's **Garden House** (0491-815217) is perched on top of a hill offering excellent views particularly at night when one can take drinks from the bar on to the rooftop and gaze over the lunar-illuminated mountains. The flip side is that while the management are friendly, the place is in need of renovation and with few guests in during the week, the menu a little limited – one dish. Rooms vary in quality costing Rs250/500 a night plus tax. **Credit cards** are accepted and the hotel arranges boating trips on request.

A whole colony of minute red ants crept into my holdall just before we left the hotel. When we arrived at Kappad, six hours late, our driver opened the boot and gleefully commented, "yerumba, yerumba". The little beasties were making an attempt to colonise my other bag. My first job on entering my hotel room was to clear the invaders out which took 45 merciless minutes. What they thought of their new beach home I couldn't say but they were none too keen to give up their squat on my property. Indeed, the next day some who'd managed to dig into the holdall's lining were forcibly ejected at Kasargod, 370km from home. So biologists puzzled by the rapid spread of this species will understand – they are ingenuous travellers.

Top of the range of accommodations in the town is **Gorvadhana Holiday Village** (0491-815262) on Rock Garden Road which has 10 rooms in five attractive, well-furnished, air-conditioned cottages for Rs600/850 plus tax. The complex was built in 1996 and is well designed with a lawn for guests to take meals, a children's play area and a conference centre seating 1000 people.

Travel Options

Buses travel frequently between **Malampuzha** and **Palakkad** where visitors can catch a wide range of trains and buses travelling around Kerala and Tamil Nadu. The nearest **airport** is **Coimbatore** 45km away in Tamil Nadu.

MALABAR

Leaving Kerala

After a trek behind the veil masking Kerala's hidden world the best option is to return to Kovalam and laze awhile on the beach. We rested up by the sea and took delight in filling our heads with memories and our bags with last minute shopping.

I phoned to confirm my flight home, just making the three day deadline prior to which one must confirm flights. Steffanie took a Rs3.50 bus-ride into town and bought a Rs41 train ticket to Madurai in Tamil Nadu. She was taking the eight-hour trip to visit the centuries-old Sree Meenakshi Temple with its wondrous *gopuram* and magnificent Hall of 1,000 Pillars. Next stop would be Khajuraho's vast multitudes of temple sculptures glorifying the sexual pleasures of the Hindu gods.

For me hedonism would be packed away until the next trip. I spent the last two days searching for a young hotel manager. I'd lent him Rs5000 which he said he would repay. He'd disappeared off the beach but eventually he repaid some of it. He'd filched a fortnight's income off me. I'd lost an hour's pay.

I'd been tricked. But Kerala is no trick of the eye, or of any sensation. I'll be back. If you go, so will you.

Your say

When you've visited Kerala, you'll have you're own impressions, likes and dislikes. Your comments will be invaluable to us especially if you have new discoveries, different insights and humourous tales to tell. Share them with us and we'll share them with others who might be thinking of travelling to Kerala.

If you would like more copies of this book for you or your friends, send a cheque or postal order for £9.95 per book with your address to MHi Publications, PO Box 17284, London SW16 5ZP.

About the Author

Phillip Roy Frampton visits Kerala regularly and believes it is one of the best tourist destinations in the world. He has travelled to four continents as a researcher and journalist. He smokes, drinks and enjoys nature, sport, cafe life and travelling. He claims to speak 21 languages but only ten words in each.

He doesn't enjoy the run-of-the-mill, burger joints (except in expensive places like Paris where it means one can sit down for a cheap meal), pretentiousness, being ill, being broke, time-wasting, rudeness and intolerance. He lives in Manchester – address available with bio-data and horoscope.

Index

I N D E X

INDEX